MEDITERRANEAN
STREET FOOD

MEDITERRANEAN STREET FOOD

Stories, Soups, Snacks, Sandwiches, Barbecues, Sweets, and More, from Europe, North Africa, and the Middle East

ANISSA HELOU

Photographs by the author

HarperCollins*Publishers*

Page v: A family eating harira in Jame' el Fna, Marrakesh

HarperCollins books may be purchased for educational, business, or sales promotional use. For information, please write: Special Markets Department, HarperCollins Publishers Inc., 10 East 53rd Street, New York, NY 10022.

FIRST EDITION

Photographs © 2002 by Anissa Helou
Designed by Joel Avirom and Jason Snyder
Design assistant: Meghan Day Healey

Printed on acid-free paper

Library of Congress Cataloging-in-Publication Data

Helou, Anissa.

Mediterranean street food: stories, soups, snacks, sandwiches, barbecues, sweets, and more, from Europe, North Africa, and the Middle East/Anissa Helou.—1st ed.

p.   cm.

ISBN 0-06-019596-7

1. Cookery, Mediterranean. I. Title.

TX725.M35 H45   2002

641.59'11822—dc21

2001051451

02 03 04 05 06 /RRD 10 9 8 7 6 5 4 3 2 1

For Mona and Suzanne

CONTENTS

ACKNOWLEDGMENTS   XI

INTRODUCTION   XV

SOUPS   5

SNACKS, SALADS, AND DIPS   17

PIZZAS, BREADS, AND SAVORY PASTRIES   75

SANDWICHES   125

BARBECUES   157

ONE-POT MEALS   171

SWEETS AND DESSERTS   213

DRINKS   247

SELECTED BIBLIOGRAPHY   258

INDEX   261

A Kurdish lady selling her produce
in Konya's central market, Turkey

ACKNOWLEDGMENTS

WITH EVERY BOOK I write, I get to add new names to my list of helpers, mostly friends, who were kind enough to assist me in one way or another with my research, recipe testing, or writing. Here I would like to express my gratitude to all of the following:

In England: Peregrine and Patricia Pollen, my adoptive family in England, for lending me their camera before I bought mine and letting me test recipes in their kitchen; Rena Salaman, whose book *Greek Food* was a marvelous guide to Greek cuisine, both in Greece and outside—Rena also kindly allowed me to adapt some of her recipes; Richard Hosking, for helping me test and perfect several of the baking recipes while Dan Lepard was always ready, at the other end of the telephone, to advise on all things to do with baking; Sami Tamimi, for giving me all the Israeli recipes together with information on how they are made and sold in Israel, also for helping me test these and others; Arabella Boxer, for advice on Crete and testing recipes; and Maria Jose Sevila for advice on Spanish street food; Jill Norman, for reminding me that paella is part of street food in southern France; Jossy Dimbleby for introductions in Damascus, Dr. Phillip Mansell for introductions in Istanbul, and Christine Garabedian for introductions in Tunis; Deborah Curtis, for discussing some aspects of the introduction with me; Becket Bedford, for brilliant legal advice; Paul Gatt, for photographic advice; Alan Davidson, Helen Saberi, Elisabeth Luard, Theodore Kyriakou, Jeremy Lee, Simi Bedford, Zelfa Hourani, Peter Fuhrman, and everyone at Sandoe's, my favorite bookshop in London. And Caroline Davidson, my friend and agent, who as usual gave me indispensable editorial advice.

In Italy: Ilaria Borletti, for being, as ever, a marvelous friend and giving me the opportunity to explore Sicily by having me to stay in one of the most magical properties there and arranging for me to meet various people; Suni Agnelli, for lending me her car to drive around the island and for letting me stay in her flat in New York; Principessa Stefania Raffadali, for taking time out of her busy schedule to take me around Palermo, Erice, and Trapani in search of street food; Marchesa Anna Tasca Lanza, for having me to stay in Regaleali and showing me how to make sfincione, arancini, and Sicilian ice cream; Max Rabino and his parents, for kindly putting me up in Genoa and arranging for their housekeeper and excellent cook, Nadia Battini, to show me how to prepare various Genoese recipes. Max was also a terrific guide around Genoa, as was Giulio Frezza, who introduced me to some great friggitorie.

In France: Anne-Marie and Guy de Rougemont, for being such great friends, always receiving me warmly in their beautiful home in Camargue, and for helping me find whatever food I happen to be looking for; Jacqueline de Guithaut, for finding me recipes; Laurence Dumaine, for introductions in Marseilles; Philip and Mary Hyman, for testing some recipes in their fantastically well equipped kitchen; and Roger Mistraki.

In Tunisia: Khalid Djallouli, for arranging my trip there and showing me around; Rania and Ibrahim Saley and their cook, Fatiha, for taking the time to talk to me about Tunisian food, and Hussein, my driver there.

In Greece: Diane Kochilas, for all her help in Athens; Marina and Alicia Coriolano, whom I met up with after many years and who were wonderful guides in Athens, showing me places I may not have found on my own; Christoforos Veneris, Aristides Pasparakis, and Babis Mastoridis, for their help in Crete.

In Morocco: Mortada Chami, owner of the fabulous Stylia restaurant in Marrakesh, who as usual received me most generously and had his cooks prepare special street and other dishes for me; Lawrence and Peter Brady and Aziz el Kir, of Maison Mnabha, and their cook Khadija, also Aziz's family; Abdelslam Arabe and his family; Mustapha Blaoui; Ncuyr Hajj Mustapha bin al-Haj Omar; and Jose Alvarez, who happened to be in Marrakesh at the same time as I and bravely accompanied me on some of my street tastings.

In Turkey: Nevin Halici, whose *Turkish Cookbook* was, like Rena's in Greece, my perfect guide both in Turkey and outside. Nevin was a most generous hostess both in Konya and Istanbul; in Konya, she took me everywhere, and when she could not be with me in Istanbul and Izmir, she drew up a list of all the places where I would find typical street food. She also let me adapt some of her recipes and checked them for mistakes—any mistakes that remain are mine. Ahmet Ergun and his family, for very kindly receiving me in their lovely home in Meram; Vedat Basaran, for a lavish meal at Fethiye; Ferda Erding, for coming to Izmir with me; and Andrew Finkel.

In Lebanon: My mother, Laurice Helou, for being as usual a tremendous support and helping me test many of the baking and other recipes; Reda Mamari, for helping me with my trip to Cairo, and Jeanine, Toni, and Elias Mamari, his parents and brother; Jacqueline and Marco Ayoub, for introductions in Cairo; Raji kibbe at el-Soussi in Beirut, who very generously prepared for Jacqueline and me a luscious spread of his various street specialties; George Dhoche, Nayla Audi, Kamal Mouzawak, Rabih Kairouz, Janane Mallat, and Mounir, my taxi driver, even if he nearly made me miss my plane.

In Syria: Moayad Marwah, David Baldwin of the British Council, and the Reverend Stephen Griffith.

In Egypt: Nina and Hassan Behnam, for being wonderfully hospitable and also for lending me Rami from their office to take me around old Cairo; Cesare Rushdy at the Four Seasons Hotel; and Atallah Kuttab.

In Spain: Alicia Rios and Don Munson.

In the United States: Susan Friedland, for being so enthusiastic about the idea of Mediterranean street food, for commissioning the book and editing it so brilliantly, and also for giving me the opportunity to take the photographs myself and letting me test recipes in her kitchen; Lucy Albanese, Roni Axelrod, David Koral, Roberto de Vicq de Cumptich, Monica Meline, Vanessa Stich, and everyone else at HarperCollins who worked on the book; Joel Avirom and Jason Snyder for such a beautiful design; Julie Logue-Riordan, for being such a perfect recipe tester and improving several of the baking recipes in her extremely well equipped American kitchen; Charles Perry, Nancy Harmon Jenkins, Paula Wolfert, and Roberta Klugman.

Finally, I would like to thank all those nameless people on the streets who graciously let me interfere with their work while I was photographing them and asking endless questions. I would also like to apologize to those who have helped me but whom I have forgotten to mention.

INTRODUCTION

WHEN I WAS A child in Beirut's belle époque, during the late 1950s and early '60s, when Lebanon was the Switzerland of the Middle East, my mother never allowed me to eat on the street. My uncles would take me and my sisters for long walks along the Corniche, the seaside promenade, which in those happy days was lined with street vendors selling all kinds of tempting goodies: sesame galettes that looked like handbags, grilled corn, mountains of seeds and nuts spooned into cones made out of old newspapers, luscious sweets and candies, ice cream, and refreshing drinks. I walked past the vendors, longingly watching their carts and the people gathered around them, wishing I could join in. Every time I would repeat, "Why does everybody in Lebanon eat on the street but not us?" And my uncles would reply, "Girls from good families don't, but you can buy whatever you want and take it back home to eat there." Sadly, they never understood that it was not the same.

Eventually I grew up and my mother and uncles no longer had any control over what I ate or didn't eat on the street. And because of the "forbidden fruit" quality that street food represented to me as a child, I became totally fascinated by it. When I started going out on my own, I would drag my friends on the way back home, late in the evening, to a vendor to have a bowl of hot, milky salep (a sweet, thick milk drink made with a small amount of powdered dried orchis tuber). In the morning I would often stop at a bakery to have manaqish (thyme bread), and if I was out of the house for lunch, I would buy a falafel sandwich or a spinach triangle. And whenever I traveled, food markets were always one of my prime destinations.

Then I left Beirut to live in London, and my life changed in more than one way. When I went out for an evening stroll, it was not to watch the sun set over the Mediterranean but to walk along crowded streets or, more agreeably in the summer, in green parks. Often there would be no sun and no street vendors, except for smelly hot dog and hamburger carts or grilled chestnut vendors who charged exorbitant prices for their measly portions. And instead of shopping in open-air food markets or buying from fruit and vegetable carts that stopped below my win-

Buying acorns in Marrakesh

dow, I went to supermarkets, where the produce came from greenhouses, was out of season, and more often than not, smelled of nothing. If I went to a greengrocer, I was not allowed to choose my own produce. It is not surprising, therefore, that I missed the jumbled profusion of our seasonal harvest and my mother haggling over prices while exchanging niceties with the vendors about their families. It was not surprising, either, that I started cooking my mother's recipes so far from home.

Paris, where I went after London, was another story. Even if the city is not by the sea, it is the capital of a Mediterranean country with a culture and a way of life, at least in the south, that are closer to mine. It is also closer to other Mediterranean countries. From there I regularly traveled to one or another of these, and each reminded me of home. As for eating in the street, I was back in business. Whether it was time for breakfast, lunch, or dinner, there was always an ambulant vendor, a hole in the wall, or a café opening onto the street providing fun and tasty specialties to eat. And for the times in between, there were all kinds of different snacks and drinks to calm one's hunger pangs or quench one's thirst: hard-boiled eggs or acorns in Morocco; baked sweet potatoes or sweet couscous in Egypt; sesame galettes in Greece, Turkey, Syria, Lebanon, Israel, and Egypt; and chestnuts, corn on the cob, nuts and seeds, and freshly squeezed fruit and vegetable juices, not to mention ice cream, pretty much everywhere.

An amazing variety, indeed, for a region like the Mediterranean, which today can be considered a small, internal sea, a kind of saltwater lake between Europe and Africa, stretching to the Near East. However, in ancient times (and in regard to food, we must take into account very old traditions), the Mare Nostrum of the Romans was the entire world. It was divided into different regions, three of which are particularly relevant here: the western, which includes Spain, France, and Italy; the Levantine, or eastern, encompassing the Balkans, Greece, Turkey, Syria, Lebanon, and Israel; and the southern, with Egypt, Libya, Tunisia, Algeria, and Morocco lining its shore. Likewise, you can divide Mediterranean street food into three separate categories with similarities within each.

Admittedly, you will not find much proper street food in the western region. France, Spain, and Italy have such long traditions of formal restaurants, comedores, and trattorie that people cannot be satisfied with just ambulant vendors hawking their fare from street to street. Also, the lack of street food probably goes back to the time before trains and cars, when travelers stopped

A fūl and ta'miyah cart standing empty during the day in Ramadan; just behind is a pile of loose rubbish, a common site in Cairo.

overnight at inns that provided meals, unlike the khans of the eastern and southern regions, where travelers could stop to sleep but not to eat and had to rely on street vendors for their meals. Another reason for this difference could be the nomadic tradition, which did not exist in the western Mediterranean. Still, you will always have a choice of cafés, tapas bars, friggitorie (fry shops), or panini bars in which to stop for a quick bite (only Sicily, probably because of centuries-old Oriental influences, is different, closer to its eastern and southern neighbors across the water). Then from Greece east- and southward, you start finding street food, although the scene in Greece is still pretty close to that in the western Mediterranean: more tavernas than ambulant hawkers. It is when you get to Turkey and move southward that you start seeing food cooked and sold on the street. In fact, Turkey and Morocco have the most exciting street food in the Mediterranean, possibly because they are more jealously protective of their traditions.

Life in the medinas (old cities) of Marrakesh and Fez, for instance, has not changed much since ancient times. People may have televisions and other modern conveniences inside their medieval houses, and some of these houses may have been converted into quaint maisons d'hôte (the Moroccan equivalent of bed & breakfast), but the street vendors are still there, cooking over charcoal fires with utensils that have been passed down from their fathers and grandfathers—it is mostly men, not women, who cook on the street. Whole lambs are still baked in earth ovens, precariously built above ground in the daily souks (markets) because they are used once a week (the daily souks are itinerant souks that take place only once a week), and more lastingly sunk into the ground in the medina because they are used every day.

Lambs are also herded live in the souks for people to buy and take home to fatten and then slaughter for celebratory meals. For everyday meals, though, people buy chickens or pigeons, also live, not only in Morocco but in Syria and Egypt too. The vendor kills the bird on the spot and places it against an antiquated contraption that vibrates against the skin to pluck the feathers. He then rinses the stripped bird in a bucket of water that looks as if it is swarming with germs, having been left unchanged all day. Hygiene, or the lack of it, is part of the adventure.

Eating on the street implies certain risks, and therefore not all experiences have a romantic aura. In Egypt, you must be particularly careful, even if the locals are usually extremely welcoming. On my last visit to Cairo, I happened to pass a fine-looking koshari cart in Khan el-Khalili (the old bazaar) and immediately stopped to take pictures. The vendor shooed me away and we started arguing about why he would not let me take photographs. I did not insist and walked away. When I returned the next day, however, I found him a changed man, very friendly. To my horror, he offered me a bowl of koshari (a mixture of pasta, rice, and lentils), which I simply could not refuse—throughout the Arab world it is very bad form to turn down anything that is offered to you. I had to eat it using one of the tin spoons he kept in water to clean them after each customer. My only remedy was to ask him to add a lot of shatta (chili sauce), wondering if chili did actually counteract germs.

A safer way to sell tea in Sariyer, Turkey

Live chickens for sale in Damascus, Syria

Perhaps it did or perhaps my prejudices were misplaced, but I never suffered any ill effects. Still, the next time I walk around the streets of Cairo, I will carry my own cutlery.

The apparent (and often it is only apparent) lack of hygiene should not deter you from eating on the street, either in Egypt or anywhere else. It is a great way to get to know both the food and the people of the country you are visiting (obviously, a rudimentary or, even better, decent knowledge of the local language is an advantage). The food is often prepared and cooked right in front of you, and just by watching, you can learn about ingredients and techniques, not to mention what the food should look and taste like. You also get to make friends with the locals. Throughout the region street vendors, with only a few exceptions, are a convivial lot, as are their customers. Eating on the street is ideal for those traveling alone. Another advantage it has is its informality. You can have a simple snack or a full meal, and you can start in one place and move

Waiting for the muezzin to announce the sunset in Al Hussein, Cairo, Egypt

on to another and yet another for different specialties. It's far more amusing than being stuck in a restaurant with a set menu and seating arrangement.

An added advantage to eating on the street is that the food changes according to season or to the religious calendar. Depending on the time of year, you will be able to sample dishes that you might not find at another time. The atmosphere in the street changes as well. For instance, during the month of Ramadan, when all good Muslims fast from sunrise to sundown, there will not be much to eat during the day. Plenty to buy and take home to prepare for iftar (or fütür, the first meal after breaking the fast) but hardly anything to eat on the spot. Even restaurants are closed during the day. Come evening and the scene changes dramatically. Just before the sun sets, ambulant hawkers emerge, some with typical food and others with Ramadan specialties in readiness for the nightly feasting, while cafés and restaurants start setting their tables with the initial "breakfast" essentials: a drink, a salad, a dip or two, and bread.

The sight of people, including young children, sitting patiently in front of their food, waiting for the evening prayer to announce the setting of the sun and therefore the break of the fast, is remarkable. The calm and patience they all show after a long day's fast, when not even a drop of water is allowed through their lips, never ceases to amaze me. Another extraordinary spectacle is the special "free meal"—tables sponsored by local merchants, mosques, or rich individuals, which are laid for the destitute. Even on these *ma'edat al-rahman* (tables of the compassionate, as they are known in Egypt), the poor people don't rush to the bread waiting for them.

Bread, of course, is the real staff of life, and nowhere more so than on Mediterranean streets. From plain loaves to pizza, crêpes, or savory pastries the choice is everywhere considerable. In Morocco it is still the custom to make the bread dough at home and take it to be baked in the local bakery. If you walk through the medina around lunchtime, you will see young boys and girls carrying unbaked loaves on wooden trays and weaving their way through the crowd to the oven nearest their home. In the souks in Syria, people buy their pita bread ready-made, but you will see them spreading the hot loaves right on the pavement or folding them over ropes to cool before stacking it again. In Egypt the bread is carried in lovely wooden cages that the vendors balance high on their heads to carry through the narrow, congested streets of old Cairo.

Most of these breads are used to make sandwiches, street food par excellence. One of the most amusing sandwich sellers I have ever come across was a fellow in Merjah Square, Damascus, Syria. His colored wooden cart carried a glass cabinet artfully decorated with different herbs and vegetables, all very fresh, which meant he replenished them daily. Amid all this freshness sat a boiled sheep's head, grinning even though it was about to be hacked to pieces. Surprisingly, the meat was cold, and after the vendor arranged it on a double layer of pita bread, he garnished it with chopped herbs, sliced tomatoes, and pickles and sprinkled the whole with lemon juice infused with garlic—a very good garnish with leftover lamb meat for those who are squeamish about boiled heads.

When I think of bread on the street in Europe, the first image that comes to mind is the classical sight of the French carrying their baguette home at mealtime, familiar to all those who have spent time in France or have at least seen movies about France's *vie en rose*. In Italy, every time I look through the window of a panini (sandwiches) bar and see the piles of different sand-

Pulling out a mechoui from the oven in a daily souk near Marrakesh

wiches, each covered with a folded napkin to keep the bread from drying, I am reminded of the old ladies in Italian films, always featured sitting by their doorways, each with a scarf over her head. And the picture would not be complete without another of my favorite sandwiches—well, not quite, more of a garnished bread than a sandwich—which is the Spanish pincho (meaning "pricked," to describe canapés made with thin slices of French bread topped with a wide variety of garnishes and stabbed with toothpicks). Throughout Spain platters of pinchos are lined along the bar, and you help yourself to as many as you like. When the time comes to settle the bill, the waiter counts the small sticks on your plate to add up your total.

Bread alone would be dull without the other great mainstay on eastern and southern Mediterranean streets: grilled meat, fish, or chicken. You will never need to ask where the nearest barbecue stall is. Just follow your nose, and as soon as you start smelling grilled meat or seeing clouds of smoke, you will know you are approaching one. Mind you, if you walk through a small Christian Lebanese town or village at lunchtime on Sunday, you will smell grilled meat

Selling prickly pears in Marrakesh

everywhere. This is barbecue day, when most families bring their charcoal brazier out onto the balcony or terrace to grill their meat or chicken—and they are always ready to invite you in for a taste. In the days before refrigeration, animals were butchered only on Sunday and the meat was cooked and consumed on that day at large, festive gatherings of family and friends.

Two foods that seem to be scarce on the streets are one-pot meals and soups. After all, they are easy, comforting, and quick, both to prepare and to consume. Yet you really see them only in Greece and Morocco. In Greece they are served in the café/restaurants in the markets; in Morocco they are served on the streets. In Spain one-pot meals are offered in small portions as tapas in the bars. In France and Italy you won't find much in the way of one-pot meals or soups, although spaghetti was a street dish long ago, eaten with the fingers. According to Italian historians, the three-pronged fork was devised at the court of the Bourbons in Naples so that spaghetti could be eaten elegantly.

Finally, when it comes to sweets, you will again find a divide between the different regions. Eastern and southern Mediterranean people are renowned for having a sweet tooth. A typical Lebanese breakfast, for instance, is a sweet sandwich made by filling a "handbag" sesame galette with hot semolina and cheese pie (künafa). The fat part of the galette is slit open and the inside moistened with sugar syrup. Then a large slice of pie is crammed into the opening and more syrup is poured over the pie. Totally irresistible, even if it clocks in at a thousand calories a bite. It is no wonder that, with breakfasts like these, the Arab world thinks plump is beautiful—it has to be. Fortunately, or not, there is no such indulgence in the western Mediterranean. Even though people celebrate various saints' days with special sweets and desserts, theirs are never as sinful.

And there is nothing sinful about Mediterranean street drinks. In fact, they couldn't be more healthy. Whether you sit on a café terrace to sip an iced citron pressé (freshly squeezed lemonade) or stop at a dilapidated stall for a glass of sugarcane juice or sit on a bench by the Bosphorus and have a vendor pour you a steaming cup of tea, you will always feel reinvigorated afterward. Or even compelled to take a photograph. I remember one time, when I was in Damascus, I was walking up souk Hamidiyeh early one evening and saw a man selling tea off his bicycle. He had fitted a small gas burner behind the seat, on which a kettle was boiling away, and he had attached a tray with the tea-making and serving equipment to the handlebar. Ingenious, though dangerous.

Bicycles seem to be a favorite means of transport for street vendors. From pails of milk to trays of fresh fruit and vegetables, all are resourcefully fitted onto them.

Depending on the season, a vendor will hand you a bag of figs or a slice of watermelon, which in Israel may be served with feta cheese. Or he may peel you a prickly pear—in Morocco you buy them in little mounds of three or four, with an extra one thrown in if you become a regular, while in Sicily they are sold by the unit. By the way, peeling prickly pears is no longer a risky occupation. The thorns are burned off with blowtorches before the fruit is picked and taken to market. However, I still remember how fascinating it was, in the old days, to watch a vendor set about this treacherous task: how he positioned his fingers on the skin in between the thorns and the way he changed from one position to another between cutting off the ends, making the slit down the middle, and finally peeling off the skin on either side of the fruit.

Sadly, many things have changed on the streets since I strolled along the Beirut Corniche as a child, longingly eyeing all that I was not allowed to have. The Corniche itself, after a long and bloody civil war, is no longer the golden meeting place it used to be, and as a result there are not so many vendors. I am now back in London and once again living in a Nordic climate. But one change has turned out for the better: my mother is no longer so rigid about the etiquette of eating on the street. Recently we were in Aleppo together, and even though she would not buy anything for herself to eat on the street, she did furtively snatch a bite of my omelet sandwich.

Anissa Helou, London

MEDITERRANEAN STREET FOOD

ABOUT THE RECIPES

I have divided the following recipes by type of food instead of by order of eating. This way you can enjoy them as if you were on the sunny streets of the Mediterranean, without being restricted by the notion of a conventional menu. However, if you would like to organize them into three-course menus, the recipes in chapters 1–4 can all be served as starters, those in chapters 5 and 6 as main courses, and those in chapter 7 as desserts. I do hope that the selection I have included here will provide you with an exciting introduction to the street food of a fascinating region, where the sun shines almost all year round, where the people have a bright disposition, and where the food is not only delightful but also healthy.

A NOTE ABOUT INGREDIENTS

Freshness and seasonality are paramount to the cooking of the Mediterranean, and I always make a point of using organic ingredients. I suggest you do the same. The flavor is infinitely better and will make a real difference to the various dishes you will be cooking from this book. The only time I prefer canned to fresh is in the case of tomatoes. It is not often that you can get tasty fresh tomatoes in northern countries. So I always use canned tomatoes. As for seasonings, I use only sea salt: fleur de sel for salads and uncooked dishes and sel de Guérande for cooking. I use fine raw cane sugar instead of refined sugar, and I generally buy my spices on my travels, again because they are fresher. I do not specify any of the above in the recipes, as you may have difficulty finding organic ingredients, fresh spices, or fine raw cane sugar. However, if you can, try to follow my example or at least buy the best and freshest ingredients available. You will be rewarded time and time again by producing excellent dishes that will impress your family and friends.

The following shops have a mail-order facility and will send you whatever exotic ingredient you require.

Oriental Pastry and Grocery Co.
172 Atlantic Avenue
Brooklyn, NY 11201
Tel: (718) 875-7687; Fax: (718) 875-0776

Kalustyan's
123 Lexington Avenue
(bet. East 28th and East 29th Streets)
New York, NY 10016
Tel: (212) 685-3451 ; Fax: (212) 683-8458
www.kalustyans.com

Sahadi's
187 Atlantic Avenue
Brooklyn, NY 11201
Tel.: (718) 624-4550 ; Fax: (718) 643-4415
www.sahadis.com

*B*ut in the medinas there are restaurants where the rich fellah [peasant], who has come to buy spices and textiles, will find touajen [stews] simmering in copper casseroles, couscous piled into snowy masses on huge platters, chickens colored golden by saffron, pieces of fried shad, thin pancakes and almond pastries dripping with honey. From the street he will see all this food cooking in an arsenal of shining pots placed on large ranges covered with zelliges [colored mosaics]. Sitting at a table and served as he chooses, his palate will be dazzled by the skilful cuisine of this town.

Toward Bab Sensla there are simpler shops where in the spring he will find the greasy pan in which tiny fish are frying surrounded by plates of mallow and fennel garnished with preserved lemons and olives and hard boiled eggs sprinkled with cumin. The sellers of iced leben [yogurt] and fruit juices have their drinks in earthenware jars. The harira will boil all day in casseroles that look like vats and will be served in the traditional way to the laborer who has come alone to the town after he has finished work. All this rustic food is presented in displays which overflow onto the street and which are protected from the swarms of flies by a dozing child mechanically swinging the tail of a horse.

The seller of brochettes sits in front of his embers, looking like a buddha behind a chest of perfumes. The smell of the grilled meat will seduce you and sharpen your appetite. You will buy half a bread in which you will bury the grilled meats. What a feast! When night falls the half-naked doughnut seller will be kneading the dough that should have risen by dawn. The glimmer of the gas lamp will give his gestures a fantastic dimension which is multiplied by their moving shadows. The pastry cooks, near Qaraouine, will offer colored cakes in decorated platters, some will be covered with honey and others sprinkled with sugar.

You will taste these soups, dishes, brochettes and pastries and if the oil and the butter are good you will find them as fine as those prepared in homes. The unexpectedness of these meals on the trot will seduce you as much by the atmosphere of the place as by their taste. And they will cost you only a few dirhams.

Zette Ginaudeau-Franc,
Les Secrets des Cuisines en Terre Marocaine, 1991

Soups

Chickpea and Lamb Soup ✦ *Harira*

Chickpea Soup ✦ *Lablabi*

Fava Bean Soup ✦ *Beyssara*

Tripe Soup ✦ *Iskembe Çorbasi*

Snail Soup ✦ *Babouch (Ghlala)*

A large potful of patsas (tripe soup) simmering
in a café in Chania's central market, Crete

Chickpea and Lamb Soup

HARIRA

THERE ARE SEVERAL PLACES in the world where street food is particularly enticing—among them Singapore, Istanbul, and Marrakesh. The last is one of my favorites, especially at Jame' el Fna, a huge square at the entrance of the medina that every day undergoes a magical change. During the day the place is nearly empty, except for a few juice and nut sellers and Berber ladies wanting to decorate your hands with intricate patterns in henna (a natural dye). However, as the day draws to an end, a horde of people descends on the square. They have come for the evening's entertainment: ambulant cooks who every night set up their trestle tables, benches, and makeshift kitchens in a huge rectangular formation and street entertainers who amuse the crowds with snake charming, storytelling, dancing, magic healing, and other diversions. The cooks are grouped by specialty: the soup stalls at one end, the snail ones at another, and the barbecue and various other food stalls in between.

The soup corner is instantly recognizable by the small plates of dates neatly arranged on the tables. They accompany harira, Morocco's national soup and the first nourishment Moroccans take when they break their fast during Ramadan. Throughout that time, the dates are replaced by chbakkiyah (a sweet pastry). The sweetness of the date or chbakkiyah accompaniment provides a good foil to the slightly tart soup.

SERVES 6

⅓ cup dried chickpeas, soaked overnight in plenty of water with
    ½ teaspoon baking soda

7 ounces lean lamb, diced into small cubes (about 1 cup)

1 medium onion, thinly sliced

⅓ cup chopped flat-leaf parsley

pinch saffron threads

¼ teaspoon ground ginger

¾ teaspoon finely ground black pepper

1 14-ounce can peeled tomatoes, coarsely chopped

2 tablespoons unsalted butter

¼ cup broken vermicelli

⅓ cup chopped cilantro

¾ tablespoon tomato paste

juice of 1 lemon, or more to taste

3–4 tablespoons unbleached all-purpose flour

salt

1 Drain and rinse the chickpeas. Spread them on a clean cloth. Cover them with another cloth and, with a rolling pin, crush them lightly to split them in half and loosen their skins. Put them in a bowl of water and stir with your hands until the skins float to the surface. Skim off the skins, add more water, and repeat the process a few times until you have discarded all the skins.

2 Put the drained chickpeas in a large saucepan. Add the lamb, onion, parsley, spices, tomatoes with their juice, and 2 quarts water. Bring to a boil over medium-high heat. Drop in the butter, cover, and let boil for 1 hour.

3 Stir in the vermicelli, cilantro, tomato paste, and lemon juice and reduce the heat to low.

4 Mix the flour with ⅔ cup water and dribble the mixture into the soup, stirring constantly to prevent lumps from forming. The soup should thicken to a velvety consistency. Add salt to taste and simmer for a couple more minutes, or until the vermicelli is cooked. Taste and adjust the seasoning if necessary. Serve very hot.

Chickpea Soup

LABLABI

THIS WARMING SOUP, POURED over bread and garnished with a knob of harissa and a pinch of cumin, is a winter specialty in Tunisia. Another winter soup you see in the medina is hergma, which is made with sheep's trotters, calves' feet, or lamb's head. The seasoning for hergma is more or less the same as for lablabi but without the garlic, and the broth is thickened with egg at the end of cooking. In Morocco *hergma* refers to a quite different dish, which also is sold on the street (page 200).

SERVES 6

1½ cups dried chickpeas, soaked overnight in plenty of water with
     1 teaspoon baking soda

¼ cup extra-virgin olive oil

juice of 1 lemon

1 tablespoon harissa (page 67)

5 cloves garlic, crushed

1 tablespoon ground cumin

salt

TO FINISH:

2–4 slices day-old bread, cut into bite-sized pieces

6 knobs harissa

6 pinches ground cumin

extra-virgin olive oil

2 lemons, quartered

1 Drain and rinse the chickpeas and put in a saucepan. Add 5½ cups water and place over medium-high heat. Bring to a boil, then reduce the heat to low and simmer, covered, for 1 hour, or until the chickpeas are tender. (If you forgot to add the baking soda to the soaking water, the cooking time will be much longer, 2 hours or more.)

2 Once the chickpeas are tender, stir in the oil, lemon juice, harissa, crushed garlic, cumin, and salt to taste; simmer for another few minutes. Taste and adjust the seasoning.

3 Scatter the bread over the bottom of 6 individual soup bowls. Ladle the soup onto the bread and place a knob of harissa in the middle of each bowl of soup. Top with a pinch of cumin, then drizzle a little olive oil all around. Serve very hot with the quartered lemons.

A pot of beyssara with bread stacked on it to keep it warm

THIS SOUP IS FOUND both in Morocco and in Egypt, but it is in the former country that it is served on the street. In Marrakesh, beyssara is usually cooked in large, round earthenware jars that are balanced over charcoal fires in a tilted position, to make ladling out the soup easier. Even when it is cooked in aluminum pans, the vendors will tilt the pan over the charcoal fire.

Fava Bean Soup

❖

BEYSSARA

SERVES 4–6

1 cup dried peeled split broad beans, soaked overnight in plenty of hot water with 1 teaspoon baking soda

2 cloves garlic

1½ teaspoons ground cumin, plus more for the garnish

scant ½ teaspoon crushed red pepper flakes

1½ teaspoons paprika

salt

extra-virgin olive oil

1 Rinse and drain the beans and put in a large saucepan.

2 Add the unpeeled garlic cloves, cumin, red pepper flakes, and 4 cups water. Place over medium-high heat and bring to a boil. Cover the pan and cook for 30 minutes, or until the broad beans have turned into a mush.

3 Reduce the heat to low and simmer for another 10–15 minutes. Discard the garlic if you can find it and add the paprika and salt to taste. Pour into a shallow bowl, drizzle olive oil all over, and sprinkle with a little more cumin. Serve very hot with Moroccan bread (page 81) and more oil and cumin for those who like them.

Tripe Soup

◆

Iskembe Çorbasi

TRIPE, FROM BOTH SHEEP and cattle, is a prized meat in most Mediterranean countries. In Italy, Spain, and France, it is sold already cleaned and cooked. All you have left to do is dress it at home with your choice of sauce or garnish. In Middle Eastern countries, however, tripe is sold uncooked, although most of the time it is already cleaned. You will still need to clean it further at home by washing it in several changes of soap and water.

The following recipe comes from Turkey, where there are many restaurants and cafés that specialize in tripe soup. A similar version of this soup (patsas) is popular in Greece, where it is consumed early in the morning, after a night's drinking. If you are put off by the idea of eating variety meats, you can easily replace the tripe with lamb or chicken.

SERVES 6

1 10-ounce piece of uncooked sheep's tripe

salt

5 tablespoons unsalted butter

1½ tablespoons unbleached all-purpose flour

2 egg yolks

juice of ½ a lemon, or to taste

6 cloves garlic, crushed

½ cup white wine vinegar or champagne vinegar

¼ teaspoon cayenne

¼ teaspoon paprika

I Wash the tripe in several changes of soap and water and rinse well. Put in a large saucepan and add 1½ quarts water. Place over medium-high heat, add salt to taste, and bring to a boil. As the water comes to a boil, skim the surface clean. Cover the pan, lower the heat, and simmer the tripe for 1½ hours, or until tender. (If you are using cleaned, precooked tripe, simmer the tripe in 1½ quarts of chicken or vegetable stock for 15–20 minutes, then proceed.)

2 When the tripe is done, remove it and slice into thin strips. Strain the stock and set aside.

3 Melt 3 tablespoons butter in a clean saucepan and stir in the flour. Slowly add the strained tripe stock while continuing to stir. Add the tripe and simmer for another 5 minutes.

4 Beat the eggs with the lemon juice. Add a little of the hot soup liquid to the egg mixture, then pour the egg mixture into the soup, stirring constantly. Remove from the heat and stir in the garlic and vinegar. (Usually the garlic and vinegar are mixed together and served on the side for people to help themselves, but I prefer to mix them in.) Taste and adjust the seasoning.

5 Melt the rest of the butter in a frying pan. Stir in the cayenne and paprika.

6 Pour the soup into a preheated tureen and drizzle the flavored butter all over. Serve very hot with good bread.

Snail Soup

◆

BABOUCH (GHLALA)

SNAILS ARE CONSIDERED A delicacy throughout the Mediterranean. In Spain, where they are called caracoles, they are stewed with tomatoes and onions and served as a tapa. In Sicily they are known as either babalucci or lumache and are eaten on the feast of Santa Rosalia in July. There you are expected to suck the meat out of the shell instead of prying it out with a pin. In Crete I saw snails being sold in Chania's central market and tried them in a nearby café, stewed with zucchini and potatoes. In Lebanon they are sold on the street but prepared and eaten at home. The vendors collect them in the open countryside after the first rains and simply dump them on wooden trestle tables by the roadside. When the snails are really fresh, you will notice the seller having trouble controlling his hoard as they crawl all over the table, trying to get back to ground level.

Snails need to be cleaned thoroughly before cooking. In France they are purged on herbs, in Sicily on grain, and in Lebanon, Greece, and Morocco, they are washed in several changes of water until they stop releasing their slime. The Lebanese simply boil them and serve them hot with tahini tarator (see page 71), while the Moroccans make the healthful, aromatic soup for which I give the recipe below. In most places the soup is ladled from huge metal pots ferried around on wooden carts. Alongside the pot is a large white enamel bowl where the customers discard the gorgeous striped shells.

This broth is just as good prepared with lamb instead of snails or with no meat at all.

SERVES 6

Snails for sale in Chania's central market, Crete

4 pounds small snails or 1 pound cubed lamb
    from the shoulder

coarse salt

1½ tablespoons caraway seeds

½ tablespoon anise seeds

½ tablespoon paprika

3–4 small hot chili peppers, or to taste

2–3 small grains mastic, available in Middle Eastern markets

1 small piece of licorice root

2½ tablespoons dried thyme

½ teaspoon green tea leaves

3 sprigs mint

peel of 2 oranges

salt

1 Rub the snails in coarse salt and wash in plenty of cold water. Repeat three or four times, then rinse out the salt in several changes of cold water.

2 Place the snails in a large cooking pot. Add 2½ quarts water and the rest of the ingredients and place over medium-high heat. Bring to a boil. Lower the heat and simmer, covered, for 1½ hours. The snails should be completely detached from their shells but not rubbery. Taste and adjust the seasoning if necessary and serve hot or warm. If you are going to make the soup with meat, bring the water with the meat to a boil before adding the seasonings so that you can skim the water clean before finishing.

A boiled egg stand in Jame' el Fna, Marrakesh

SNACKS, SALADS, and DIPS

SPANISH POTATO OMELET ✦ *Tortilla de Patatas*

ITALIAN SPINACH OMELET ✦ *Frittata di Spinaci*

VEGETABLE LOAF ✦ *Polpettone*

TUNISIAN TAGINE WITH PARSLEY ✦ *Tajine Ma'danüs*

CHICKPEA SNACK ✦ *Farinata*

ITALIAN STUFFED VEGETABLES ✦ *Ripieni*

FETA CHEESE SALAD ✦ *Çingene Pilavi*

FAVA BEAN SALAD ✦ *Fül Müdammas*

CANNELLINI BEANS WITH SAFFRON ✦ *Fassüliah K'dra*

TOMATO AND ONION SALAD ✦ *Shlada Matecha*

WHITE CABBAGE SALAD ✦ *Salatet Malfüf Abyad*

GRILLED PEPPER AND TOMATO SALAD ✦ *Chakchüka*

MOROCCAN EGGPLANT SALAD ✦ *Za'lüq*

TUNISIAN GRILLED PEPPER AND TOMATO SALAD ✦ *Mechwiyah*

ONION AND PARSLEY SALAD ✦ *Salatat Baqdüness wa Bassal*

CHILI SHRIMP ✦ *Gambas Pil-Pil*

MOROCCAN FRIED FISH ✦ *Hüt bel Chermüla*

BOILED FAVA BEANS WITH SPICED SALT ✦ *Fül Maslüq*

FRIED EGGPLANT FANS ✦ *Melanzane a Quaglia*

VEGETABLE FRITTERS ✦ *Frittelle di Verdure*

CHICKPEA FRITTERS ✦ *Panelle*

FRIED CALAMARI AND OTHER FISH ✦ *Calamares e Pescados Fritos*

"RED" RICE CROQUETTES ✦ *Arancini (or Arancine) al Ragù*

POTATO CROQUETTES ✦ *Cazzilli*

FRIED VEGETABLES À LA TUNISIENNE ✦ *Keftagi*

STUFFED MUSSELS ✦ *Midye Dolmasi*

HOT CHILI PASTE ✦ *Harissa*

HOMMUS ✦ *Hommus bi-Tahineh*

YEMENI CILANTRO CHUTNEY ✦ *Z'houg*

HAZELNUT DIP ✦ *Turkish Tarator*

TAHINI DIP ✦ *Lebanese Tarator*

GARLIC SAUCE ✦ *Thüm*

YOGURT DIP ✦ *Cacik or Tzatziki*

WHEN I THINK OF street food in Spain, I don't think of ambulant food sellers wheeling carts through the streets; rather, I think of bars, tapas bars. Some are tiny and dark, with only standing room, while others are huge and brightly lit, with several counters, each serving a different variety of tapas (*tapa* means "snack," a small portion of any kind of food, ranging from anything canned, cured, or cooked to fresh). You can duck into one of these bars for just a nibble or linger for a full meal. There you will

Spanish Potato Omelet

TORTILLA DE PATATAS

be able to sample almost the whole range of Spanish cuisine and nearly always a tortilla (an omelet that looks like a cake). Tortillas come with an endless variety of fillings. The one I give here is the most common but also one of the tastiest.

SERVES 4–6 AS A TAPA OR 2 AS A MAIN COURSE

¼ cup extra-virgin olive oil

3 cups diced new potatoes

¼ cup finely chopped onion

4 eggs, beaten

salt

1 Put the oil in an 8½-inch frying pan and place over medium-low heat. When the oil is hot, add the potatoes and cook for 15 minutes, stirring occasionally. Add the onion and cook for another 20–30 minutes, or until the potatoes and onion are completely done and lightly golden.

2 When the vegetables are done, pour the excess oil into a small bowl and stir the vegetables into the beaten eggs. Season with salt and pepper to taste. Wipe the frying pan clean and pour the oil back into it. Place over medium heat and, when the oil is hot, pour the egg mixture into it. Shake the pan to spread the eggs evenly and cook for 7–10 minutes, or until the bottom is golden. Carefully slide a spatula along the sides and underneath the omelet to make sure it is not sticking and place a plate over the pan. Hold it tightly with one hand and turn the pan over with the other. Slide the tortilla back into the pan and cook for another 3–5 minutes, or until the bottom is set but the inside still slightly moist. Serve warm or at room temperature.

Italian Spinach Omelet

◆

FRITTATA DI SPINACI

THIS IS AN ITALIAN version of the Spanish tortilla but made much thinner. It is sold in friggitorie (fry shops) for people to eat while standing at the counter, or they can buy a slice wrapped in thick paper to eat on the street.

SERVES 4

3 tablespoons extra-virgin olive oil

1 small onion, very finely chopped

1 tablespoon finely chopped flat-leaf parsley

1 pound spinach, stalks removed and thinly sliced

1 cup grated Parmesan cheese

1½ teaspoons dried marjoram, or 2–3 sprigs fresh marjoram, leaves only, finely chopped

4 eggs

salt

freshly ground black pepper

1 Put 1 tablespoon olive oil and the chopped onion in a 6-inch frying pan and place over medium heat. Cook until the onion is soft and transparent. Add the parsley and continue frying, stirring occasionally, until golden. Transfer to a large mixing bowl and wipe the pan clean.

2 Rinse the spinach and put it in a large sauté pan. Place over medium-low heat and cook, stirring regularly, until the spinach has wilted and is nearly done, 2–3 minutes. Drain off the liquid and add the spinach to the onion and parsley. Stir in the cheese, marjoram, and eggs; season with salt and pepper to taste. Combine well.

3 Heat ½ tablespoon of the remaining oil in the pan over medium heat. Pour in a quarter of the egg mixture. Lower the heat and cook for 2 minutes (or until the bottom is lightly browned and the top is nearly set). Slide the frittata onto a plate, then hold the pan over the plate and invert the plate and pan to drop the omelet back into the pan on the uncooked side. Cook for another minute or so, or until the omelet is done but still slightly moist inside. Remove to a serving platter and cook the other 3 frittate the same way. Serve at room temperature.

POLPETTONE IS A STAPLE of Ligurian friggitorie, where it is usually baked in large rectangular trays. The word actually means meat loaf, but in Genoa everyone knows that it refers to a loaf made with vegetables. Nadia Battini (page 27), who gave me the recipe, bakes hers in a round oven-to-table dish. The loaf can be varied by replacing the green beans with any of the following vegetables when in season: pumpkin, zucchini, eggplant, spinach, Swiss chard, potatoes, artichokes, mushrooms, onions, or cardoons. Some, like the zucchini, eggplant, or mushrooms, need to be fried before using, while the others need to be boiled.

Vegetable Loaf

◆

POLPETTONE

SERVES 4–6

2 pounds thin green beans, topped and tailed

salt

1 medium onion, very finely chopped

5 tablespoons extra-virgin olive oil, plus more for drizzling

1 clove garlic, very finely chopped

2 teaspoons dried marjoram, or 1 tablespoon finely chopped fresh marjoram leaves

3–4 tablespoons dried porcini, soaked in tepid water, then drained and finely chopped

1 cup grated Parmesan cheese

1¼ cups ricotta cheese

2 medium potatoes, boiled and mashed

6 eggs

freshly ground black pepper

2 tablespoons fine bread crumbs

2 tablespoons unsalted butter

I Boil the beans in plenty of water with salt to taste for 5–7 minutes, or until they are al dente. Then drain and spread to dry on a kitchen cloth. Finely chop the beans.

2 Fry the onion in the oil over medium-high heat, stirring occasionally, until golden. Add the garlic and marjoram and sauté for another minute or so before adding the beans. Sauté the beans for 2–3 minutes, then transfer to a large mixing bowl to cool. Add the mushrooms, both cheeses, potatoes, and eggs; season with salt and pepper to taste.

3 Preheat the oven to 350 degrees. Grease a 10-inch round baking dish with a little olive oil. Sprinkle half the bread crumbs over the bottom.

4 Spread the vegetable mixture in the pan. Level the top and decorate with a few shallow geometric incisions. Dot all over with butter, drizzle with a little olive oil, and sprinkle with the rest of the bread crumbs. Bake in the preheated oven for 20–30 minutes, or until the loaf has set but is still moist inside. Serve warm or at room temperature.

AT THE MENTION OF tagine, most people think of fragrant, subtly spiced Moroccan stews that often combine sweet with savory. But Tunisian tagine is a very different affair: a cross between a quiche and a tortilla, thicker and denser than either, and always served as a starter. Tunisian tagine comes in two versions: wrapped in thin pastry, when it is called tajine malsüqa (malsüqa being the filo-like pastry that in Morocco is known as warqa), or prepared plain, without the pastry. It is the latter version that you find on the street, prepared with different garnishes. The version below is one of the most common; it can be varied by using different seasonal vegetables.

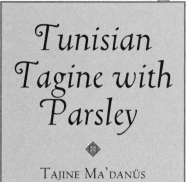

Tunisian Tagine with Parsley

TAJINE MA'DANÜS

SERVES 4–6

¼ cup extra-virgin olive oil

1 small onion, finely chopped

10 ounces chicken meat, both dark and white, cut into bite-sized pieces (1 heaping cup)

¼ cup dried cannellini beans, soaked overnight in plenty of water with ¼ teaspoon baking soda, or ½ cup drained canned

1½ teaspoons tomato paste

1½ teaspoons paprika

1 teaspoon unsalted butter

3 cups finely chopped flat-leaf parsley

1 scant cup grated Gruyère cheese

1 cup fine bread crumbs

8 eggs, beaten

¼ teaspoon ground cinnamon

¼ teaspoon ground dried roses (optional)

salt

freshly ground black pepper

1 Put the olive oil and onion in a saucepan and place over medium heat. Fry until the onion is slightly colored, then add the chicken and stir until browned. Add the beans, tomato paste, paprika, and 1 cup water. Bring to a boil, lower the heat, and simmer for 45 minutes, or until the beans are tender. If you are using canned beans, add them toward the end of cooking. Stir occasionally and, if the sauce is becoming too dry, add a little more water, but remember that you want the sauce to be very thick at the end.

2 Preheat the oven to 350 degrees. Grease a 9-inch round baking dish with the butter.

3 Let the chicken and beans become lukewarm before adding the remaining ingredients. Season with salt and pepper to taste. Mix well, taste, and adjust the seasoning if necessary. Pour the mixture into the baking dish. Spread it evenly and bake in the preheated oven for 15–20 minutes, or until the top of the tagine is lightly crisp and the eggs are just set. Serve warm or at room temperature, cut into wedges.

FARINATA, KNOWN AS SOCCA in Nice, is generally sold in friggitorie (page xvii), where it is baked in wood-fired ovens. The fire is lit to one side, and the huge tray of farinata is rested on two long metal rods. These are used to lift and turn the tray as soon as the side next to the fire starts to color. When the farinata is ready, it is bubbling all over and the top is crisp and golden, with small dark peaks where it has burned a little. Sadly, there is not much chance you can achieve the same effect in a domestic oven. However, you should still be able to produce a good result if you spread the chickpea mixture very thinly in your baking dish.

The best farinata I've ever eaten was in a little friggitoria on the Ripa, the arcaded promenade by the port in Genoa. I walked in there late one morning just as they were taking their first farinata out of the oven—the perfect time to have it. It was scrumptious, with a loose, crisp crust over a thin, silky layer of chickpea paste. A day later I had it at another friggitoria. Theirs was slightly drier but had the unmistakable taste of chickpeas, which reminded me of the advice of a Genoese friend, Giulio Frezza. According to him, you need to use chickpea flour that is less than a year old for a really good farinata. I am not quite sure how you can ascertain such a thing in shops outside Italy, unless your supplier is very "au fait" as to the age of his stock.

SERVES 4–6

Chickpea Snack

◆

FARINATA

Farinata tray in a friggitoria in Genoa, with pizze on top

just under 1 cup chickpea flour

salt

3 tablespoons extra-virgin olive oil

I Put the chickpea flour in a large mixing bowl, stir in 2 cups water, and add salt to taste. Stir well until the mixture is very smooth and has the consistency of milk. Cover with a clean towel and leave to rest for up to 3 hours. Stir it again after this time, then blow the bubbles on the surface to one side and pour them out.

2 Preheat the oven to its maximum heat.

3 Pour the oil into a 20-inch shallow round baking dish; add the chickpea mixture. Stir well to incorporate the oil and bake in the preheated oven until the surface of the farinata is colored and bubbling all over.

THIS IS ANOTHER GENOESE specialty that seems far too elaborate to belong to the street. Yet you will find it in many Ligurian friggitorie alongside the ubiquitous frittate, polpettone, and various vegetable torte (pies). Some of the tastiest ripieni I have had were served in a little place called Antica Sà Pesta ("ancient crushed salt," so named because it is the area where salt was sold), situated in Genoa's old town near the church of San Torpette. Looking through the window, I noticed a tray of ripieni being taken out of the wood-fired oven, a common feature of these places. They looked irresistible, so I went in to have some, even though ripieni are better either just warm or at room temperature. The handsome young cook handed me my order on a small cardboard tray lined with rough paper. The stuffing was very moist, with plenty of cheese. Sadly, he was too busy to discuss recipes with me, as was his beautiful wife.

Italian Stuffed Vegetables

RIPIENI

Luckily, I was staying with my friend Max Rabino, whose housekeeper, Nadia Battini, is an excellent cook. She was willing to show me how to make ripieni, and I spent the whole afternoon helping her make them and torta pasqualina (page 102) for our lunch the following day. Nadia steamed the vegetables instead of boiling them, explaining that it made them less soggy, and cooked them only until al dente because they would cook further in the oven. Also, she used mashed potato in the stuffing instead of bread crumbs for a softer texture. That afternoon we made stuffed onions, zucchini, and tomatoes, a particularly good combination, but you can also use peppers or anchovies, which are what I had at Sà Pesta. To serve six, choose any combination of three of the following ripieni.

SERVES 6 AS A STARTER

Stuffing

NADIA FRIES EACH INGREDIENT for the soffrito separately because she combines the ingredients slightly differently for each stuffed vegetable, but I fry all the ingredients together. If I lose a little delicacy in the balance of the stuffing, I gain time in the preparation.

FOR THE SOFFRITO:

> 3 tablespoons extra-virgin olive oil
>
> 1 medium onion, very finely chopped
>
> 1 small stalk celery, very finely chopped
>
> 1 small carrot, very finely chopped
>
> ¼ cup finely chopped flat-leaf parsley

TO FINISH:

> pulp or inside of whichever vegetable you are stuffing, squeezed very dry with your hands, then chopped very fine
>
> ½ teaspoon dried marjoram, or 1 teaspoon finely chopped fresh marjoram leaves
>
> 1 egg, beaten
>
> ¼ cup grated Parmesan cheese
>
> ¼ cup minced ham
>
> 1 small potato, cooked and mashed
>
> salt
>
> freshly ground black pepper

1 Put the olive oil, onion, celery, and carrot in a frying pan and cook over medium heat, stirring occasionally, for 10–15 minutes, or until soft and golden. Add the parsley and sauté for a few more minutes.

2 Transfer the soffrito to a mixing bowl, add the rest of the ingredients (if you are making stuffed peppers, chop one of the grilled peppers to use in the filling), and season with salt and pepper to taste. Taste and adjust the seasoning if necessary and use as indicated in the following recipes.

Stuffed Zucchini

ZUCCHINI RIPIENI

HERE I LIKE TO use very small, pale green zucchini. In London they are imported from Cyprus or Lebanon. Nadia uses the dark green variety. Whichever you choose, be sure they are small and more or less the same size for an attractive presentation.

> 8 small zucchini
>
> stuffing (preceding recipe)
>
> extra-virgin olive oil to grease the baking dish
>
> 1–2 tablespoons fine bread crumbs

1 Cut and discard the stem of each zucchini and slice off the brown skin on the bottom. Wash and cut the zucchini in half lengthwise and put in a steamer over boiling water. Steam for 8–10 minutes, or until they are just done. Once the zucchini are done, neatly scrape out the centers and reserve.

2 Prepare the stuffing, being sure to squeeze the zucchini pulp very dry before chopping.

3 Preheat the oven to 350 degrees and grease a baking dish with a little olive oil. Fill the zucchini, piling the stuffing high and smoothing it into a round shape with your fingers. Arrange the zucchini on the baking dish and sprinkle the tops with a few bread crumbs. Bake in the preheated oven for 20–25 minutes, or until crisp and lightly golden on top. Serve warm or at room temperature. These zucchini and the following stuffed vegetables can be made up to one day ahead of time. Simply remember to remove from the refrigerator an hour before serving so that they come to room temperature.

Stuffed Onions

CIPOLLE RIPIENE

IN GENOA, NADIA USED scallions that had a flat, wide white part that she left whole, only removing a few inner layers to make space for the stuffing. It is not easy to find similar scallions, and here I suggest using small red onions, which are slightly sweeter.

>   10–12 small red onions
>
>   stuffing (page 28)
>
>   extra-virgin olive oil to grease the baking dish
>
>   2 tablespoons fine bread crumbs

1 Peel the onions, cut them in half lengthwise, and put in a steamer over simmering water. Cover the pot and steam for 8 minutes, or until they are just done. Remove the inside layers, leaving 2 or 3 outer ones, depending on how thick they are. Chop the inside layers very fine.

2 Prepare the stuffing, using the chopped onion as the vegetable pulp.

3 Preheat the oven to 350 degrees and grease a baking dish with a little olive oil.

4 Arrange the onion shells in the baking dish and spoon as much stuffing as you can into each one without letting it spill over. Sprinkle with a few bread crumbs and bake in the preheated oven for 20–25 minutes, or until slightly crisp and golden on top. Serve warm or at room temperature.

Stuffed Tomatoes

POMODORI RIPIENI

> 6 medium tomatoes
>
> stuffing (page 28)
>
> 1½ tablespoons fine bread crumbs, and a little more for garnish
>
> extra-virgin olive oil to grease the baking dish

1 Put the tomatoes in a large bowl and pour over boiling water to cover. Leave for 30 seconds, then lift out of the water and cut off and reserve the tops. Remove and discard the seeds. Peel the tomatoes and salt the insides. Invert the tomato shells on your chopping board to drain off the excess moisture.

2 Prepare the stuffing, using the peeled tomato tops as the vegetable pulp. Add the bread crumbs. Taste and adjust the seasoning.

3 Preheat the oven to 350 degrees and grease a baking dish with a little olive oil.

4 Fill the tomatoes with as much stuffing as they will hold. Do not worry about letting the stuffing mound up at the top but do not let it spill over the sides. Arrange the tomatoes in the baking dish and sprinkle the tops with a few bread crumbs. Bake in the preheated oven for 25–30 minutes, or until the tomatoes are quite soft and the stuffing is crisp and golden on top. Serve warm or at room temperature.

Stuffed Grilled Peppers

RIPIENI DI PEPPERONI

> 4 medium red or yellow bell peppers
>
> stuffing (page 28)
>
> extra-virgin olive oil to grease the baking dish
>
> 1–2 tablespoons fine bread crumbs

1 Put the peppers under a preheated hot broiler, turn them over at regular intervals for 10–15 minutes, or until the skin is charred and blistered on all sides and the flesh is softened. Peel them, remove the seeds, and carefully cut 3 of the peppers lengthwise into 3–4 pieces. Chop the remaining one very small. Set aside.

2 Prepare the stuffing, using the chopped pepper as the vegetable pulp.

3 Preheat the oven to 350 degrees and grease a baking dish with a little olive oil.

4 Arrange the pieces of grilled pepper in the baking dish and spoon as much stuffing as you can into each piece, piling the stuffing into a mound without letting it spill over the sides. Sprinkle with a few bread crumbs and bake in the preheated oven for 20 minutes or until slightly crisp and golden on top. Serve warm or at room temperature.

THE TURKISH NAME FOR this salad is rather confusing: çingene pilavi means "gypsy pilaf," but the dish contains no rice. According to Nevin Halici, author of the *Turkish Cookbook*, it is named after gypsies because of their predilection for raw food. Ideally, you should use the long Turkish peppers that have a thin flesh, but you may not find them, in which case use half a green bell pepper and dice it. You can serve this salad as is or make it into sandwiches.

Feta Cheese Salad

◆

ÇINGENE PILAVI

SERVES 4

1¼ cups crumbled feta cheese

1 medium red onion, very finely chopped

2 medium firm ripe tomatoes on the vine, seeded and diced into ½-inch cubes

1 long pointed green pepper, halved, seeded, cored, and thinly sliced

3 tablespoons extra-virgin olive oil

salt

1–2 tablespoons finely chopped flat-leaf parsley for garnish

Put the feta cheese, onion, tomatoes, and pepper in a large mixing bowl. Add the olive oil and toss carefully. Taste before adding any salt, then transfer to a serving dish. Garnish with parsley and serve with good bread.

Fava Bean Salad

◆

FÜL MÜDAMMAS

FÜL IS WHAT MOST Egyptians have for breakfast every day. It's a rather pungent choice so early in the morning, but Arabs are not particularly known for being squeamish. In Egypt fül is generally sold from wooden carts that are designed especially to accommodate the huge copper or aluminum jar in which the beans are kept simmering. People gather around the cart to eat fül in deep bowls or inside whole-wheat pita bread, or they bring their own receptacle that the vendor fills for them to take home. Often the fül vendor will also offer ta'miyah (falafel, page 152). Fül is also very common on the streets of Lebanon and Syria. In Lebanon it has chickpeas added to it, while in Syria it is made more or less the same way as in Egypt.

SERVES 4

1½ cups dried small fava beans, soaked overnight in plenty of water
    with 1 teaspoon baking soda

salt

1–2 teaspoons ground cumin

FOR THE DRESSING:

2 cloves garlic, crushed

¼ cup extra-virgin olive oil

juice of 1 lemon, or more to taste

FOR THE GARNISH:

1 tomato, diced

a few sprigs flat-leaf parsley, coarsely chopped

4 scallions, trimmed and thinly sliced

1 Drain and rinse the soaked beans, then put them in a saucepan. Cover by about 2 fingers with cold water and place over medium heat. Bring to a boil, reduce the heat to low, and simmer, covered, for 1½ hours, or until the beans are very tender and quite mushy. Stir occasionally. Five minutes before the beans are ready, add salt and cumin to taste.

2 Beat the dressing ingredients together in the serving bowl, then add the beans. Stir together. Taste and adjust the seasoning if necessary. Serve warm or at room temperature, drizzled with olive oil and garnished with tomato, parsley, and scallions.

Note: To make fül sandwiches, cut small round pita breads in half-moons and fill with as much fül as you like. Garnish with chopped tomatoes, hard-boiled eggs, and ground cumin.

A fül and ta'miyah cart in Cairo, Egypt

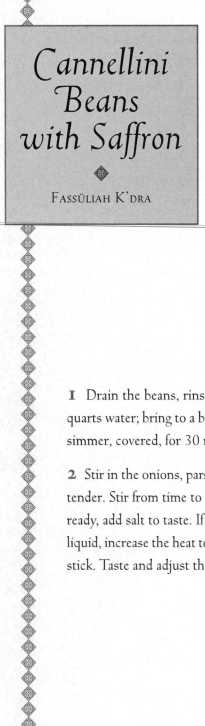

Cannellini Beans with Saffron

FASSÜLIAH K'DRA

YOU GENERALLY FIND THIS dish in the same stalls that sell beyssara (page 11), but I would be very surprised if street cooks used expensive saffron to color the beans. Instead, they probably add the much cheaper safflower or turmeric to impart the pale yellow hue that is so typical of this dish.

SERVES 6

2½ cups dried cannellini beans, soaked overnight in plenty of
    water with ½ teaspoon baking soda

large pinch saffron threads

5 tablespoons unsalted butter

3 medium onions, thinly sliced

¼ cup finely chopped flat-leaf parsley

1 teaspoon finely ground white pepper

salt

1 Drain the beans, rinse well, and place in a large saucepan. Add the crushed saffron and 1½ quarts water; bring to a boil over medium-high heat. Add the butter, reduce the heat to low, and simmer, covered, for 30 minutes.

2 Stir in the onions, parsley, and pepper and cook for another 30 minutes or until the beans are tender. Stir from time to time to make sure the beans are not sticking. Just before the beans are ready, add salt to taste. If the sauce is too thick, add a little water. If, on the other hand, it is too liquid, increase the heat to high and boil until thickened, stirring regularly so that the beans don't stick. Taste and adjust the seasoning if necessary. Serve hot, warm, or at room temperature.

IN MOROCCO YOU WILL automatically get a helping of this salad whenever you order grilled meat, offal, or fish. In some places the tomatoes and onions are reduced to a mush and the mixture looks more like a sauce than a salad. In others the tomatoes are cut in wedges and the onions sliced; and in still other places both are chopped quite small.

Tomato and Onion Salad

◈

SHLADA MATECHA

In the south of Morocco, you might be served this salad dressed with argan oil, which gives it a delicate nutty taste. Argan oil is extracted from the fruit of the argan tree, which grows in the southern Souss valley. The oil is produced in an extraordinary way with the help of goats. The animals graze on the fruit, which look like apricots, and because they are unable to digest the pits, they expel them the "natural way," polished of all flesh. The pits are then picked off the ground, broken, and the nuts removed to be pressed like olives. It was in the old port of Essaouira, where Orson Welles filmed *Othello*, that I first tasted argan oil. A large section of the port is taken up by fishmongers' stalls where you not only can buy fish but can also have it cooked for you to eat on the spot, seated at large trestle tables. The fishmonger who cooked my fish triumphantly produced a bottle of argan oil from under his display and proceeded to dress my tomato salad with it.

SERVES 4–6

10 medium firm ripe tomatoes on the vine, seeded and diced into small cubes

½ cup finely chopped flat-leaf parsley

2 medium red onions, very finely chopped

1 teaspoon ground cumin

½ teaspoon paprika

1 teaspoon finely ground black pepper

juice of 2 lemons, or to taste

4–5 tablespoons extra-virgin olive oil or argan oil

salt to taste

Toss the ingredients together and serve at room temperature.

White Cabbage Salad

SALATET MALFÜF ABYAD

THIS SALAD IS USED as an accompaniment to such Lebanese dishes as shish tawüq (page 163) or the french fries sandwich (page 151). Ideally, you should use tender-leaf flat-topped cabbage. A good alternative is organically grown cabbage, which is both tastier and more tender than mass-farmed cabbage. You can also dress this salad with lemon juice, oil, and crushed garlic.

SERVES 4–6

FOR THE MAYONNAISE DRESSING:

1 egg yolk

1 teaspoon Dijon mustard

salt

½ cup extra-virgin olive oil

1 clove garlic, crushed

juice of 1 lemon, or to taste

freshly ground black pepper

TO FINISH:

6 cups finely shredded white cabbage (about 1 small)

1 Put the egg yolk, mustard, and a pinch of salt in a mixing bowl and whisk until well blended. Drizzle in the oil very slowly at first, whisking all the time until the mixture starts thickening. After ¼ cup has been added, you can pour in the oil a little more quickly. When you have added all the oil, stir in the crushed garlic and lemon juice and season with pepper to taste. Taste and adjust the seasoning if necessary.

2 Place the shredded cabbage in a large mixing bowl, add the mayonnaise, and mix well. Adjust the seasoning again if need be and serve as a salad or use in the sandwiches suggested above.

STREET FOOD IN MOROCCO is very much like the food you eat in people's homes. The only difference is that on the street, it is usually cooked by men, while in homes it is invariably cooked by women. And of course, the choice is not as varied on the street except for the salads, an assortment of which is always present at stalls that sell fried fish or grilled meats.

Grilled Pepper and Tomato Salad

◆

CHAKCHŪKA

SERVES 4–6

3 medium yellow or green bell peppers

¼ cup extra-virgin olive oil

2 28-ounce cans peeled tomatoes, drained and coarsely chopped

1 clove garlic, crushed

¼ teaspoon crushed red pepper flakes, or to taste

¾ teaspoon paprika

salt

⅓ cup chopped flat-leaf parsley

1 Put the peppers under a preheated hot broiler; turn them over at regular intervals for 10–15 minutes, or until the skin is charred and blistered on all sides and the flesh is softened. Leave until cool enough to handle, then peel the peppers and remove the seeds and core. Cut the flesh into medium-thin strips.

2 Combine the olive oil, tomatoes, garlic, red pepper flakes, and paprika in a large frying pan. Add salt to taste and cook over medium-high heat for 20–30 minutes, stirring occasionally, until the tomatoes have reduced and lost almost all their liquid.

3 Add the peppers and parsley to the tomato sauce and cook, stirring occasionally, for a further 5–10 minutes, or until the sauce has become very concentrated. Leave to cool, then serve at room temperature with good bread.

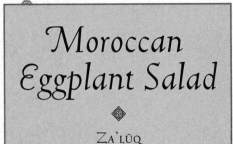

Moroccan Eggplant Salad

Za'lüq

THERE ARE CERTAIN DISHES that, even if they are sold on the street, are too fine for me to think of as street food, and this is one of them. The version you will eat on the street, however, is likely to be quite different from that made at home. It will have less cilantro, for instance, and the spicing will be less subtle. Also, the eggplants will inevitably have been boiled instead of steamed, resulting in a more watery taste.

SERVES 4–6

2 medium eggplants (about 14 ounces total weight)

4 cloves garlic, peeled

6 tablespoons extra-virgin olive oil

1 28-ounce can peeled tomatoes, drained and coarsely chopped

1 cup finely chopped cilantro

½ teaspoon ground cumin

juice of ½ lemon, or to taste

¼ teaspoon paprika

¼ teaspoon crushed red pepper flakes, or to taste

salt

1 Peel the eggplants lengthwise leaving thin strips of skin, and cut into small chunks. Steam the eggplant pieces together with the garlic for 30 minutes, or until very soft.

2 While the eggplant and garlic are cooking, put the oil in a sauté pan; add the chopped tomatoes, cilantro, and cumin and mix well. Place over medium-high heat and cook for about 15 minutes, or until the excess liquid has evaporated and the sauce looks fresh and chunky. Stir occasionally.

3 When the eggplant and garlic are ready, mash them with a fork or potato masher. Don't use a food processor, or the eggplant will become too mushy. The salad should have a soft but chunky texture. Add the mashed vegetables to the tomato sauce along with the lemon juice and the rest of the seasonings. Mix well and simmer over low heat for another 15 minutes, stirring regularly. Taste and adjust the seasoning if necessary and let cool. Serve at room temperature.

YOU CAN SERVE THIS salad as an appetizer with the traditional garnishes of tuna, hard-boiled eggs, and olives. It's also a popular sandwich spread in Tunisia, where vendors often couple it with harissa the way the French couple butter and mustard in their sandwiches.

SERVES 4

2 medium red bell peppers

salt

3 medium tomatoes, cut in half

1 medium onion, cut in half

1 clove garlic, crushed

juice of ½ lemon, or more to taste

2 tablespoons extra-virgin olive oil

1 teaspoon ground caraway seeds

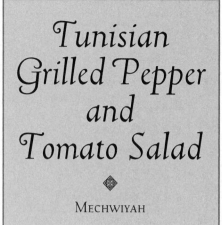

Tunisian Grilled Pepper and Tomato Salad

MECHWIYAH

1 Put the peppers under a preheated hot broiler; turn them over at regular intervals for 10–15 minutes, or until the skin is charred and blistered on all sides and the flesh is softened.

2 Sprinkle salt on the cut side of the tomatoes and broil them, cut side facing the heat, until slightly charred, about 25–30 minutes.

3 Broil the onion halves, skin side up first. When the skin is very charred, turn them over and broil, cut side up, for another 30 minutes, or until well charred.

4 When the peppers are ready, remove the stems, seeds, and ribs and either chop them very fine by hand or pulse in a food processor until very finely chopped but not completely puréed. Remove and drain in a sieve.

5 Skin the tomatoes and onions and chop them fine by hand or pulse in the food processor. Remove and drain them in a sieve. Once the vegetables are ready and well drained, transfer them to a mixing bowl and add the rest of the ingredients. Mix well; taste and adjust the seasoning if necessary. Serve at room temperature with or without the garnishes mentioned above, or use in the sandwiches on pages 126, 127, and 142.

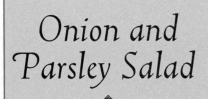

Onion and Parsley Salad

◆

Salatat Baqdüness wa Bassal

THIS SALAD IS COMMON throughout the eastern and southern Mediterranean from Turkey to Egypt. It is always laid on the bread on which grilled meat and poultry are served. In Turkey the salad is seasoned with only sumac; in Egypt, with lemon juice; and in Syria, Lebanon, and Israel it is seasoned with both. A chef friend of mine, Sami Tamimi, whose recipe this is, taught me to soak the sliced onions in boiling water for a few minutes before using. This softens them slightly and, more significantly, takes away some of the sharpness. Be sure to dry the onions well before adding the seasonings.

SERVES 4

2 medium onions, thinly sliced

2 tablespoons coarsely chopped flat-leaf parsley

2 tablespoons ground sumac

1 tablespoon lemon juice

1 tablespoon extra-virgin olive oil

salt

freshly ground black pepper

Soak the onions in 2 cups hot water for 5 minutes. Drain and spread to dry on paper towels. Transfer the onions to a mixing bowl. Add the remaining ingredients and mix together. Taste and adjust the seasoning if necessary and serve with any of the barbecues on pages 157–69.

THIS IS A WONDERFUL tapa or light meal that takes no time at all to prepare. You could peel the shrimp before frying, but I prefer the presentation of the shrimp unpeeled, even if they are a little messy to eat. The lemon juice is not particularly Spanish, but it does lift the taste of the shrimp as well as deglaze the pan to produce a luscious sauce.

SERVES 4 AS A STARTER OR 2 AS A MAIN COURSE

¼ cup extra-virgin olive oil

4–6 small cloves garlic, sliced in half lengthwise

4–6 small dried red chilies, or ½ teaspoon red pepper flakes

12 large fresh shrimp

½ lemon

salt

Put the oil, garlic, and chilies in a large frying pan and place over medium-high heat. When the oil is hot and starts sizzling around the garlic and chilies, add the shrimp and fry for 1 minute on each side. Remove the pan from the heat and squeeze a little lemon juice over the shrimp. Sprinkle with salt to taste and serve very hot with good bread to mop up the juices.

Chili Shrimp

❖

GAMBAS PIL-PIL

Moroccan Fried Fish

◆

Hüt bel Chermüla

FRIED FISH, ESPECIALLY FRIED sardines, are typical street foods in Morocco. The sardines are boned, butterflied, marinated, and sandwiched together with a little chermüla spread on the inside. They are then dipped in flour and fried. You will find platters of these sardines displayed in most of the food stalls in the medina. Moroccans will eat them standing around the stall or sitting side by side at a communal table. You can also take them away to eat on the run. It is not often that one can buy very fresh sardines, and even if you do find them, the preparation is rather tedious unless your fishmonger does it for you. So I use fillets of white fish instead.

SERVES 4–6

FOR THE CHERMÜLA:

> 3–4 cloves garlic, crushed
>
> 1 medium onion, thinly sliced
>
> 1 cup finely chopped cilantro
>
> 1 teaspoon ground cumin
>
> ½ teaspoon paprika
>
> ¼ teaspoon crushed red pepper flakes
>
> 6 tablespoons extra-virgin olive oil
>
> juice of 2 lemons, or to taste
>
> salt

TO FINISH:

> 2 pounds fillets of fresh white fish, such as sole, snapper, flounder, catfish, or cod, cut into manageable pieces
>
> vegetable oil for deep-frying
>
> 1 cup all-purpose flour

I Mix the chermüla ingredients together and marinate the fish in it in the refrigerator for 2–4 hours, stirring regularly.

2 Pour enough vegetable oil to deep-fry the fish into a large deep-frying pan and place over high heat. Remove the fish from the marinade, drain well, and dip into the flour. When the oil is very hot—to test, dip a piece of fish in the oil; if it bubbles around the fish, the oil is ready—slip in the fish pieces and fry for 1–2 minutes on each side, or until golden all over. Remove with a slotted spoon and drain on several layers of paper towels. Serve hot or warm with a salad of your choice.

Boiled and Grilled Snacks

Boiled and grilled snacks are an integral part of Mediterranean street food. In Morocco you can stop by a cart laden with boiled acorns—a strange but good thing to eat, a little like chestnuts. If you are lucky enough to be there at the same time as a veiled Berber lady, you will get a lesson in how to eat gracefully without uncovering your face. No easy feat! Or you can snack on hard-boiled eggs that you dip into a mixture of salt and cumin—2 parts salt to 1 part cumin. Or you can ask the vendor to make you a sandwich with the boiled eggs, potatoes, and harissa. In Egypt and Israel you will also come across hard-boiled eggs, which are known as beyd hamine or haminados. They are simmered for hours with onion skins, broad beans, or coffee beans until the shells become very brown. Inside, the egg whites turn a rust color and the yolk becomes very creamy. I personally have never noticed that the egg yolk was anything other than overcooked. The eggs are also dipped in salt and cumin, as in Morocco. In some places in the old city of Jerusalem, the eggs are baked in the oven with wood shavings and served with a sesame bagel and za'tar (page 89).

In Sicily the choice of boiled and grilled snacks is wider: boiled potatoes, zucca lunga (a kind of long zucchini), or artichokes are handed to you on a piece of paper; the vendor adds a sprinkling of salt and a squeeze of lemon juice to pep up the taste. More exciting, you may be offered boiled octopus, or purpu as it is known there. All along the seafront in Mondello, a suburb of Palermo, there are fish restaurants that have a counter on the street where you can stop for a plate of sea urchins or purpu. Depending on how large the octopus is, you will get a whole one or just a few tentacles. As the stock of boiled octopus dwindles, the seller will slip a few more into the large pot

Finishing an egg-and-jpotato sandwich in Marrakesh

where the water is barely simmering. When they are ready, he will use a long metal hook to fish them out.

Purpu is also available at stalls in food markets such as the Vucciria in Palermo, where you will also find boiled veal gristle. The last time I was in Palermo, I sampled the latter "delicacy" from a very old man who sat behind a small trestle table on which there was a large wicker basket lined with heavy cotton; next to the basket was a row of containers: sliced onion, boiled potatoes, and salad. Every time he had a customer, he would slip his hand under the cotton blanket covering the basket to grab a handful of meat. He stuffed the meat into a bun called guasteddi, garnished it with potatoes, salad, and onion, and finished the sandwich with a squirt of lemon juice. The meat is known as caldume or frittola and is not commonly available anymore. I wonder if, when the old man dies, there will be anyone to take his place handing out frittola sandwiches to the regulars at the Vucciria, though the Vucciria itself may not be there either. Sadly, it is a dying market.

As for grilled snacks, again you will have embarrassment of riches in Sicily: grilled peppers, onions, or artichokes. These are sold for people to eat on the spot or to take home. My favorite is grilled artichokes. The hard tops of the leaves are trimmed before the artichokes are banged against a hard surface to open them up. A teaspoon of finely chopped mint mixed with crushed garlic is stuffed into the heart, and a good drizzle of olive oil is poured into the artichoke. The seasoned artichokes are then set

upon a bed of burning charcoal for about 20 minutes or until the hard outer leaves become charred and the inside turns tender. They are then eaten like boiled artichokes, leaf by leaf. Rather messy—be sure to ask the vendor for plenty of paper napkins.

Grilled corn is common to most Mediterranean countries, but it is in Morocco that it is most fun to buy. You will see it sometimes set directly on embers on the pavement, and before the seller hands you the ear of corn, he will dip it in salted water, a wonderful way of moistening and salting it at the same time. Sweet potatoes in Egypt are baked in a portable wood-fired oven. The blazing oven stands in one corner of the cart with the baked potatoes arranged on top to keep them warm, while the rest of the cart is covered with a mountain of knobbly sweet potatoes waiting to be baked.

The most unusual of Mediterranean grilled street fare is intestines. In Sicily these are known as stigghiole. The intestines are baby lamb's—far better than those of grown lamb—seasoned with spices and herbs, wrapped around skewers, and barbecued over charcoal. Elsewhere the intestines are those of grown lamb or sheep. In Turkey and Greece the name is almost the same: kokoreç in Turkish and kokoretsi in Greek. In the Turkish version the intestines are wrapped around fat from the sheep's tail and left to grill on skewers, either on small carts wheeled through the streets or at stalls in the bazaars. Once the intestines are cooked, the vendor chops a section very fine and sautés the minced intestine on a hot griddle. He then seasons it with salt and dried herbs and stuffs it into a half or quarter of a fat baguette-like bread to serve as a sandwich. You can also buy kokoreç "to go," wrapped in paper.

In the Greek version the intestines are wrapped around the heart, liver, and lungs of the lamb and grilled. Moroccan street cooks make a similar but much larger version that they call kordas and bake it in the same pit oven as the whole lamb (mechoui); it is then cut into pieces to eat off the counter, as is done with mechoui (page 190).

Grilled chestnuts can be enjoyed pretty much everywhere. In Sicily the shells look as if they have been dipped in ashes, but that is because the chestnuts are salted before grilling; in other countries they are roasted plain. The only thing that changes from one place to another is the display and, of course, the price, although one thing is for certain—they will be expensive everywhere you have them.

THIS DELIGHTFUL AND WARMING snack is sold off large wooden carts on the streets of Damascus, Syria. In the middle of the cart is a large pot containing the simmering fava beans, and all around or on the cover of the pot is a neat arrangement of small porcelain bowls. The vendor serves the beans in one bowl and pours a little broth into another. To the broth he adds lemon juice and spices. People stand around the cart dipping the beans in a spiced salt mixture and sucking the flesh out of the skin. Between every few mouthfuls, they take a sip of the warm broth. The last time I had these beans, I found myself buying three bowls, one after the other, to the delight of the vendor, Zohair Qabbab, who gave me the following recipe. Be sure to use very large fava beans, which are available in Middle Eastern stores. The small ones become mushy and do not work. Boiled fava beans are also sold on the streets in other Mediterranean countries, including Morocco, Tunisia, and Lebanon, but they are served simply salted and often poured into paper cones and the cooking broth is discarded.

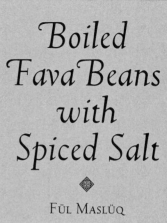

Boiled Fava Beans with Spiced Salt

◆

FÜL MASLÜQ

SERVES 4–6

2 cups large fava beans in their shells

2 tablespoons cardamom seeds, wrapped in cheesecloth

1½ tablespoons salt

¾ teaspoon ground cumin

⅛ heaped teaspoon ground cinnamon

2 lemons

I A day ahead of serving, rinse the beans several times in cold water. Zohair Qabbab rinses his 10 times. The reason for so many rinses is that the cooking broth, which is served to drink with the beans, must be very clear. Once you have cleaned the beans, leave them to soak in plenty of cold water for 24 hours.

2 Drain the beans and rinse very well before transferring to a large pan. Cover with water and place over medium-high heat. Bring to a boil, reduce the heat, add the wrapped cardamom seeds, and simmer, covered, for 1½ hours, or until the beans are very tender but not mushy.

3 Shortly before the beans are ready, mix the salt and spices together and put in a small bowl. Don't put the spice jars back in your cupboard, as you will need more to season the broth if you intend to use it.

4 Remove the beans with a large slotted spoon and put them in one large bowl or divide equally among 4 to 6 individual ones. Serve the beans hot with the spiced salt and, if desired, the seasoned broth on the side. If you are using the broth, strain it and season with lemon juice, cumin, cinnamon, and salt to taste.

THE ITALIAN NAME OF this dish, eggplant in quails, is somewhat misleading. There are no quails in it, but because of the way the eggplants are cut and open up during frying, they end up looking like a quail's tail; hence, the name. I am not sure how accurate the comparison is, but even if your eggplants do not end up looking like a bird's tail, they will still make a great, and fun-looking, snack.

Allow at least 2 or 3 small eggplants per person. Peel off the hard skin around the stem, keeping a short length of stalk on, then slice each eggplant into 3 segments lengthwise to about 1 inch from the stem. Slice across in the same way. The eggplants should end up cut into 9 segments, each about ½ inch thick and all still attached at the top. The slices will spread open during frying to achieve the tail effect. Heat enough vegetable oil in a large frying pan to deep-fry the eggplants, and when it is hot—test with the tip of one eggplant; if the oil bubbles around it, it is ready—fry as many eggplants as will fit comfortably in the pan, turning them until they are golden all over. This should take 3–4 minutes. Remove to drain on several layers of paper towels. Sprinkle with sea salt to taste while still warm and serve warm or at room temperature as is or as a sandwich filling (in which case, be sure to discard the stalk end).

In Morocco you will see plenty of fried eggplants on the street, but they will be cut in thick round slices and piled rather unattractively on large platters. Another vegetable that is fried and sold on the street in Sicily is cauliflower. The vegetable is divided into florets, blanched, and then deep-fried. If the cauliflower is young and tender, you won't need to blanch it.

Fried Eggplant Fans

MELANZANE A QUAGLIA

Vegetable Fritters

◆

VEGETABLE FRITTERS ARE ANOTHER staple of Genoese friggitorie. The choice is varied: salad or borage (these sound exciting but they are mostly batter speckled with a few strips of lettuce or herbs), zucchini, eggplant, carrot, or cauliflower. You can eat them at the counter as many Italians do, served on cardboard trays lined with rough paper, or take them away, wrapped in paper, to eat at home or on the street—the paper is thick enough to prevent the oil from seeping through.

The frying pans in which the fritters are cooked are large cauldron-like cast-iron pans with high, round handles. Most friggitorie will have two going at the same time, as well as a wood-fired oven. Sometimes one of the pans is pushed aside to make space for a copper pot in which the panissa (page 54) is cooked. You need to be quite choosy about which friggitoria you buy your fritters from. I always rely on the advice of my local friends.

SERVES 4–6

TO MAKE THE PASTELLA (BATTER):

  1 cup flour

  1 egg

  2 tablespoons extra-virgin olive oil

  1 cup light beer

  salt

FOR THE VEGETABLES:

  vegetable oil for frying

  1 medium zucchini, cut crosswise in half and thinly sliced lengthwise

  1 medium eggplant, cut crosswise in half and thinly sliced lengthwise

  2 medium carrots, cut crosswise in half and thinly sliced lengthwise

  1 green bell pepper, seeded, cored, and ribs removed then cut
    lengthwise into 8 pieces

1 Make the batter by whisking all the ingredients together until smooth. This batter is very light and transparent; you can make it thicker by reducing the beer to ¾ cup, although you will end up with less than you need for the amount of vegetables given above.

2 Pour the oil in a large frying pan until 1½ inches deep and place over medium-high heat. When the oil has reached 375 degrees, dip the vegetables in the batter and drop in the oil. Fry for 1–2 minutes on each side, or until golden all over. Remove with a slotted spoon or tongs and drain on several layers of paper towels. Be sure to skim the oil between each batch to get rid of the floating bits of batter, or else they will burn and cling unattractively to the vegetable fritters. Serve immediately or they will get soggy.

LEFT: *A platter of vegetable fritters and panissa alongside a tray of polpettone in a Genoese friggitoria*

RIGHT: *Stirring the panissa, Genoa*

Chickpea Fritters

◆

PANELLE

PANELLE, PANISSE, AND PANISSA are all different names for the same concoction, a paste made with chickpea flour, water, and salt that is first boiled, then left to set before being cut into different shapes, depending on where you are, and deep-fried. In Sicily panelle are crescent shaped or rectangular; in Genoa and Nice panissa or panisse are cut into sticks like French fries. In Nice the fritters are can also be made with cornmeal. The recipes vary only slightly from country to country. The one below is Sicilian. Both the Genoese and French do not use parsley in the mixture; instead, they add 2–3 tablespoons olive oil. The French also cut their panisse into round discs and serve it as a dessert, sprinkled with sugar or dipped in jam.

MAKES 20–22

> 2 cups chickpea flour
>
> salt
>
> finely ground white pepper
>
> a few sprigs flat-leaf parsley, most of the bottom stalk discarded, then
>   finely chopped
>
> vegetable oil for frying

1 Put the chickpea flour in a saucepan and gradually add 3 cups water, stirring continuously. The mixture needs to be very smooth; if necessary, use a whisk. Add salt and pepper to taste and place over medium heat. Cook for about 10–15 minutes, stirring constantly. Stir in the parsley and turn out onto an oiled surface. Quickly spread the mixture with an oiled spatula to a thickness of about ½ inch. Let set, then cut into smallish triangles or rectangles about 2 inches wide and 3½ inches long.

2 Heat enough vegetable oil to deep-fry the panelle, and when it is hot—test by dipping the tip of a panelle in the oil; if it bubbles around the panelle, the oil is ready—fry as many panelle as fit comfortably in the pan until crisp and golden on both sides. Remove with a slotted spoon and drain on several layers of paper towels. Serve hot with more salt on the side.

FRIED CALAMARI RINGS ARE a universal Mediterranean snack. Whether you go to a Spanish tapas bar, an Italian friggitoria, a Greek taverna, or an Egyptian beach shack, you will be able to nibble on a serving of scrumptiously crisp calamari rings. And they are never as good as when they have just been scooped out of the frying pan and served to you on a scrap of thick paper, sprinkled with coarse salt.

Fried Calamari and Other Fish

❖

CALAMARES E
PESCADOS FRITOS

Squid needs to be fried for a very short time, or else its juicy, yet softly resistant flesh will turn to tasteless rubber. The Spaniards also fry whole baby squid, which they call chipirones, while Italians offer a choice of other small fish. The Italian system of draining oil off the fried fish is to remove the fish to a round, shallow metal bowl in the middle of which sits a kind of inverted sieve. After the first batch of fried fish has drained on the sieve part, it is pushed onto the sides of the bowl so that the second batch can go in its place; any excess oil still remaining in the first batch will trickle down the sides and out into a receptacle underneath.

There is no need for a precise recipe for fried squid rings, baby squid, or any other small fish. Simply season some flour with sea salt, freshly ground pepper, and paprika if you like. Then rinse and dry whatever fish you intend to fry, toss it into the seasoned flour, shake off the excess flour, and fry quickly in very hot vegetable oil. Sprinkle with more salt if necessary and serve immediately with wedges of lemon.

A platter of fried calamari in Genoa

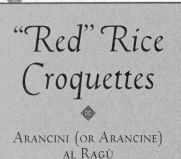

"Red" Rice Croquettes

Arancini (or Arancine) al Ragù

ARANCINI (OR ARANCINE, DEPENDING on whether you consider them male or female!) are a common staple of Sicilian bars and fry shops. If you travel to Sicily by ferry across the straits of Messina, arancini will be your first taste of the island—they are a fixture on the ferry's bar menu. Once there, you will see them everywhere: rossi (red), filled with ragù (meat sauce), or bianchi (white) when the filling is simply butter and cheese.

Commercial arancini are shaped bigger than those made at home, and often they are not as good. A friend of mine told me of a recent scandal when an arancini supplier was found to be using pet food instead of ragù. Since I heard that story, I've stayed away from store-bought "red" arancini.

Some people cook the rice like a risotto, while others add all the water in one go and, when the rice is done, mix in the cheese and eggs. I find the latter method easier, and I learned from a friend to add a little saffron, both for color and taste. Arancini keep well for a day but it is better not to refrigerate them unless the weather is very hot. Preheat your oven to 400 degrees just before you want to serve them, and put the arancini in to heat for 15–20 minutes.

SERVES 6–8

FOR THE RAGÙ:

> 2 tablespoons extra-virgin olive oil
>
> 1 small onion, very finely chopped
>
> 1 celery stalk from the heart, diced very small
>
> 1 clove garlic, very finely chopped
>
> 5 ounces lean ground beef (about ¾ cup)
>
> 1 14-ounce can peeled tomatoes, drained and finely chopped
>
> 1 teaspoon estrattu (Sicilian sun-dried tomato paste) or, if not available, 2 teaspoons tomato paste
>
> ¼ teaspoon crushed red pepper flakes
>
> ½ cup frozen petits pois, thawed in boiling water and drained
>
> salt
>
> freshly ground black pepper

TO MAKE THE ARANCINI:

> 2 cups arborio rice
>
> pinch saffron threads
>
> salt
>
> freshly ground black pepper
>
> ¾ cup grated Parmesan cheese
>
> 5 eggs
>
> ½ cup caciocavallo or pecorino cheese, diced into small cubes
>
> 1½ cups fine bread crumbs
>
> vegetable oil for frying

1 To make the ragù, place the oil, onion, celery, and garlic in a saucepan over medium-high heat. Cook until the vegetables are lightly golden. Add the ground beef and cook, mashing the beef with a wooden spoon to break up any lumps, until the meat is no longer pink. Add the tomatoes, estrattu (or tomato paste), and red pepper flakes and simmer for 15–20 minutes. Add the peas, season with salt and pepper to taste, and cook for another 5 minutes, or until the peas are tender. The sauce should be very dry. If it is not, increase the heat to high and boil off any excess liquid, not forgetting to stir regularly so that the meat does not stick to the bottom of the pan. Taste and adjust the seasoning if necessary. Let cool.

2 While the ragù is cooking, prepare the rice. Put the rice in a saucepan and cover with 4 cups water. Add the saffron, season with salt and pepper to taste, and place over medium-high heat. Bring to a boil, lower the heat, cover the pan, and simmer for 13–15 minutes, or until the rice has absorbed all the liquid (check the rice after 10 minutes to make sure it is not sticking; if it is, remove from the heat, wrap the lid with a kitchen towel, and leave to sit for 3–5 minutes). Stir in the Parmesan cheese and 1 beaten egg and turn the rice onto a shallow platter. Spread the rice, cover with a clean kitchen cloth, and leave until it is warm.

3 Now comes the difficult part. Lightly dampen your hands and pinch off a handful of rice. Flatten it on the palm of one hand to just under ½ inch thick, put a full tablespoonful of ragù in the middle and press 1 or 2 cubes of caciocavallo or pecorino in the middle of the meat. Cup the rice around the meat. If you need to use more rice to cover the filling completely, lightly dampen your hand again and pinch off a little more. Flatten it and cover the meat with it. Cup your free hand around the arancino and form it into a round ball the size of a tangerine—do not roll the ball of rice in between the palms of your hand; it will crack. Make sure that there are no cracks in the rice shell; if there are, seal them with a few grains of rice. Make the rest of the arancini. Then roll each into the beaten egg first, then in the bread crumbs. Repeat one more time to make sure the arancini are completely covered with bread crumbs. Leave to sit for 30 minutes. Gently roll the arancini between your hands to get rid of the excess crumbs.

4 Heat enough vegetable oil to deep-fry the arancini. When the oil is hot—test with the corner of an arancino; if the oil bubbles around it, it is ready—fry as many arancini as will fit comfortably in the pan for about 5–6 minutes, turning them over, or until crisp and golden all over. Serve hot or warm as a snack or accompanied by a green salad for a light meal.

White Rice Croquettes

❖

ARANCINI IN BIANCO

THIS VERSION IS SIMPLER and quicker to make. Omit the ragù. Prepare the rice the same way as above but without adding saffron. For the same amount of rice you need 3 tablespoons butter, diced into small cubes, and 1¼ cups diced caciocavallo or pecorino cheese. Fill each arancino with 1 cube butter and 3–4 cubes cheese, depending on how small the pieces are. Coat with bread crumbs and fry and serve as above.

THE WORD *CAZZILLO* MEANS "little prick," an amusing and rather appropriate name for these Sicilian potato croquettes. In Genoa they make similar croquettes, which they call cuculli (from the Roman word *cuculus*, meaning "hood"; this does not really explain why the word has come to describe fritters, which can also be made with chickpea flour or onion or stoccafisso fish), while in Morocco they make potato cakes instead of croquettes (ma'qüda), with a different, spicier mash. For the Moroccan version, use the same amount of potatoes, but add 2 crushed garlic cloves, 1 whole egg, and 2 table-spoons each finely chopped cilantro and flat-leaf parsley; instead of black pepper, use ¼ teaspoon crushed red pepper flakes and 1½ teaspoons each ground cumin and paprika. Shape the mash into flat round cakes, dip in egg yolk, and pan-fry in a little vegetable oil.

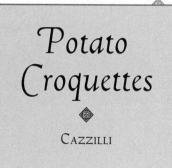

Potato Croquettes

CAZZILLI

MAKES 24

> 1 pound potatoes
>
> 1 egg
>
> 3 tablespoons grated caciocavallo or pecorino cheese
>
> 1 clove garlic, crushed
>
> 2 tablespoons finely chopped flat-leaf parsley
>
> salt
>
> freshly ground black pepper
>
> ½ cup fine bread crumbs
>
> vegetable oil for frying

1 Boil the potatoes for 25–30 minutes, or until done but not splitting. When they have cooled slightly, peel and pass them through a fine food mill.

2 Separate the egg; lightly beat the yolk. Add it to the potatoes, along with the grated cheese, garlic, and parsley. Season with salt and pepper to taste. Shape the mixture into small sausage-like shapes about 2½ inches long and 1 inch thick.

3 Roll the croquettes in the lightly beaten egg white first, then in the bread crumbs.

4 Heat enough oil to deep-fry the croquettes. When it is very hot—test by dipping a croquette in the oil; if it bubbles around the croquette, the oil is ready—fry as many as will fit comfortably in the pan until crisp and golden all over, about 3–4 minutes. Remove with a slotted spoon and drain on several layers of paper towels. Serve hot or warm.

Fried Vegetables à la Tunisienne

KEFTAGI

THERE IS A MARVELOUS place right behind Tunis's central market where they specialize in keftagi: a mixture of fried vegetables that are chopped very small, topped with a fried egg, and served with French fries. In the kitchen, cooks gather around a long table within reach of a large dish of fried vegetables. Each grabs a large handful, puts it in a metal tagine dish (a Tunisian tagine is a medium round, deep metal dish, quite unlike the Moroccan one, page 192), and chops the vegetables with a mezzaluna. They work very fast, each with a different rhythm. (Listening to the sounds they made reminded me of a contemporary piece of music composed by Giorgio Batistelli, who based a whole work on the sounds made by various artisans at work—knife grinders, cobblers, barrel makers, and so on.) Once the vegetables are chopped, they are transferred to small earthenware bowls. The cooks then drop eggs in hot oil and, when fried, scoop them out and slide one on top of each bowl. A few French fries are placed on the side, and the plates of keftagi are ready to be taken to the diners outside. On the tables or counter, the places are already set with knife and fork, a wedge of lemon pricked through the prongs of the fork, and a thick slice of bread. The plate in front of you is a mixture of warm and hot, the vegetables barely warm, and the egg very hot; the whole mixture is slightly greasy and in need of a splash of lemon juice to refresh it. Nevertheless, keftagi is pretty delectable and has a rather voluptuous texture.

SERVES 4

vegetable oil for frying

3 medium tomatoes, cut in half and seeded

3 medium potatoes, 2 sliced into medium-thin discs and 1 cut into
    sticks for French fries

1 large red bell pepper, seeded and ribs removed, then quartered
    lengthwise

1 long hot chili, seeded and cored

2 medium zucchini, cut crosswise in half and thinly sliced lengthwise

1 medium eggplant, cut crosswise in half and thinly sliced lengthwise

salt

freshly ground black pepper

4 eggs

2 tablespoons chopped flat-leaf parsley

1 lemon, quartered

French bread

1 Heat enough vegetable oil (or olive oil) in a large frying pan to deep-fry the vegetables. To test the heat of the oil, dip a corner of the vegetable into it; if bubbles surround it, the oil is ready. Fry the vegetables, each type separately (keep the French fries until very last), and drain on several layers of paper towels. Peel the tomatoes and peppers while still hot and sprinkle with salt and pepper to taste.

2 Chop the fried vegetables, but not the French fries, very small and divide among 4 shallow bowls.

3 Fry the eggs in the same oil and put one in the middle of each bowl. Pile a few French fries on the side and sprinkle with a little chopped parsley. Serve immediately with a wedge of lemon and a thick slice of French bread.

Busy cooks at work in the kitchen

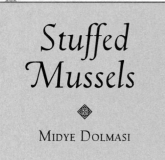

Stuffed Mussels

◆

MIDYE DOLMASI

I DISCOVERED MIDYE DOLMASI on my first visit to Istanbul in the mid-1970s. I was there primarily to explore the Islamic treasures of the city, although I ended up spending far more time exploring the spice bazaar and sampling Turkish street food than trying to learn about Islamic art. The stuffed mussels were a revelation. So scrumptious and unexpected that I ended up stopping at every street vendor carrying a tray or basket of midye dolmasi to see how their taste changed from one hawker to another. Some were drier, others not so well seasoned, and others not so fresh. But it was in Fethiyé, a rather ugly modern tourist resort, where many years later I found the ultimate stuffed mussels. They were all beautifully lined up on a large round metal tray. The street vendor—a very old man accompanied by a young urchin, his grandson perhaps—rested the tray on a trestle table whenever he had a customer. I wondered who had made them. The old man or his wife back home? I never found out. I spoke no Turkish, and they no foreign languages. So we just smiled at each other every time I pointed to another mussel. I must have eaten more than a dozen, all the time wondering why such a refined and elaborate dish should be sold so cheaply on the street. It is not so easy to find mussels that are large enough for stuffing. If you can't find any, just change the dish to a pilaf by preparing twice or three times the amount of rice stuffing. Cook the rice completely, then steam the mussels separately and spike them, half shelled, into the cooked rice.

SERVES 4

¼ cup extra-virgin olive oil

1 tablespoon pine nuts

2 small onions, finely chopped

½ cup Spanish Calasparra or paella rice or other short-grained rice, soaked in warm water

1 tablespoon raisins

1½ tablespoons tomato paste

¼ teaspoon ground cinnamon

¼ teaspoon ground allspice

¼ teaspoon paprika

pinch cayenne

pinch ground cloves

1 tablespoon chopped flat-leaf parsley

1 tablespoon chopped dill

salt

freshly ground black pepper

about 40 medium to large mussels

2 lemons, cut into wedges

A stuffed mussel stall in the fish market in Izmir; the smaller ones are on the left, and the larger, more expensive ones are on the right.

I Put the oil, pine nuts, and onions in a saucepan and sauté, stirring occasionally, until lightly golden. Drain the rice and stir into the pan. Add the raisins, tomato paste, spices, parsley, and dill. Season with salt and pepper to taste and barely cover with water, about 1 cup. Bring to a boil, reduce the heat to low, and simmer, covered, for 8–10 minutes, or until the water is absorbed and the rice is barely done. Remove the pan from the heat, wrap the lid with a kitchen cloth, and put it back over the pan. Let cool.

2 To prepare the mussels, first pull and discard the beards if there are any and rinse the mussels under cold water—do not let them soak or they will die. Lay 1 mussel on a kitchen towel on your work surface and insert the tip of a small sharp knife between the shells at the nerve end of the slanted bottom. Slide the knife downward and all around the shell until you cut into the muscle—the mussel will open easily, with the two halves remaining attached. Open the rest of the mussels in the same way. Do not rush this part of the preparation or you will either break the shells or hurt yourself with the knife.

3 Once you have opened all the mussels, stir the rice with a fork and fill each mussel with a teaspoon or more of rice, depending on how large they are. Close them well, wipe away any rice grains sticking out, and arrange in 2 or 3 layers in the top part of a steamer. Weigh down the filled mussels with a plate and steam for 20–25 minutes. Remove the steamer section and let the mussels cool. Serve at room temperature with wedges of lemon.

Hot Chili Paste

❖

HARISSA

IF YOU ORDER A sandwich in Tunisia, the vendor will automatically spread the bread with harissa the way Westerners spread theirs with butter, mayonnaise, or mustard. Some people ask for the harissa to be mixed with creamy processed cheese triangles (La Vache Qui Rit is a favorite brand). Harissa is also eaten as a dip, drizzled with olive oil. In homes it is generally served plain, while in restaurants it is topped with canned tuna and olives. The plate of harissa is brought to the table before any other food for you to dip your bread into while waiting for your order. Commercial harissa, especially that in tubes, does not compare to the real or homemade version. It is well worth finding good chili peppers to make your own.

MAKES JUST OVER 2 CUPS

> 8 ounces large dried chilies
>
> 15–20 cloves garlic
>
> salt
>
> ½ cup ground caraway seeds
>
> extra-virgin olive oil to cover the harissa

1 Pull off the stalks of the chilies and shake out and discard the loose seeds. Rinse the chilies under cold water and soak them in hot water for about 20 minutes.

2 Peel the garlic and put in a food processor with a little salt. Process until very smooth.

3 Drain the chilies, add to the garlic, and pulse until you have a lightly textured paste. The chilies should not be pulverized.

4 Transfer to a mixing bowl. Add the ground caraway and more salt if necessary and mix well. Spoon into a container and cover with olive oil. The oil will preserve the harissa. Make sure you top up the oil every time you use some of the harissa. Well covered in oil, it will keep for months in the refrigerator.

Hommus

❖

Hommus bi-Tahineh

HOMMUS IS NOW PART of the global menu, sold in most Western supermarkets neatly spooned into hygienic plastic tubs with trendy labels. But when hommus is sold on the streets in Syria, it is squeezed into plastic bags that, in some places, are stamped with the maker's name. Not perhaps the safest way to package such a creamy concoction but an amusing one, especially when the bags are stacked on top of each other on wooden carts or in stall windows. I wonder how people manage to pack the hommus bags with the rest of their shopping without puncturing them, or if they ever walk around eating from the bag. Perhaps they simply take the bags back to their nearby stalls to eat for lunch.

SERVES 4

just over 1 cup dried chickpeas, soaked overnight in plenty of water
    with 1 teaspoon baking soda

¾ cup tahini

salt

juice of 2 lemons, or to taste

1 clove garlic, crushed

paprika and olive oil, for garnish

1 Drain and rinse the chickpeas. Place them in a saucepan, cover well with cold water, and place over medium-high heat. Bring to a boil, reduce the heat to low, and simmer, covered, for 1 to 1½ hours or until very tender.

2 Drain the chickpeas and place in a food processor. Process to a smooth purée and transfer to a mixing bowl. Stir in the tahini and salt to taste and blend well. Pour in the lemon juice. Mix in the crushed garlic. If the purée is too thick, use a little of the cooking water to thin it down—the purée should be creamy but not runny. Taste and adjust the seasoning if necessary, then pour into a shallow round or oval bowl. Spread across the dish, raising the purée slightly at the edges. Sprinkle the raised edges and center with paprika, and trickle a little olive oil in the dip in between the whole peas.

Z'HOUG IN ISRAEL IS the equivalent of harissa in Tunisia, a spread used like butter in almost all sandwiches. You can use green chilies here instead of red ones, but be sure to use a mixture of mild and hot peppers; otherwise, the z'houg will be too fiery.

SERVES 6

Yemeni Cilantro Chutney

◆

Z'HOUG

4 ounces mild red chilies seeded, cored, and cut into chunks (about 1 cup)

4 ounces hot red chilies seeded, cored, and cut into chunks (about 1 cup)

4–5 cloves garlic

1½ cups cilantro leaves

1½ cups flat-leaf parsley leaves

1 teaspoon ground cumin

1 teaspoon salt

1 teaspoon freshly ground black pepper

pinch ground cardamom

2 tablespoons extra-virgin oil

Put the chilies and garlic in a food processor and grind until coarse. Add the herbs, seasonings, and oil and continue processing until you have a lightly textured paste. Serve or transfer to a glass jar with a tight-fitting lid. This chutney will keep in the refrigerator for about a month.

Hazelnut Dip

Turkish Tarator

TURKISH TARATOR IS QUITE unlike the Lebanese one, which is made with tahini. You can use walnuts, almonds, or pine nuts instead of hazelnuts. Walnuts or almonds should be soaked and peeled before using. Although you could make the sauce without taking the trouble of soaking or peeling the nuts, the texture would be less soft and the taste slightly different.

SERVES 4

1½ cups whole shelled hazelnuts

2 slices soft white bread, crusts removed

1 large clove garlic, peeled

⅔ to 1 cup extra-virgin olive oil

juice of 1½ lemons, or to taste

salt

Put the hazelnuts in a deep bowl, cover with boiling water, and let soak for 1 hour. Drain the nuts and put in a food processor along with the bread, garlic, and 1 teaspoon water. Blend until smooth, then start drizzling in the olive oil with the motor running. When the oil is completely absorbed, add the lemon juice and salt to taste. If you have the patience and energy, you can also make this dip by pounding the ingredients in a large mortar with a pestle. The texture will be finer. Taste and adjust the seasoning if necessary. Transfer to a serving bowl and serve at room temperature with fried mussels (page 139) or a choice of crudités.

I CALL THIS LEBANESE tarator but you will also find it in Syria, Jordan, Israel, and Egypt. In Egypt, where it is called tahina, it is always served in cafés and restaurants as part of the initial spread for the breaking of the fast of Ramadan. In Lebanon it is served plain with fried fish or mixed with chopped parsley or cilantro to use in falafel sandwiches (page 152).

Tahini Dip

❖

LEBANESE TARATOR

SERVES 4

½ cup tahini

juice of 1 lemon, or to taste

⅓ cup water

1–2 cloves garlic, crushed

½ cup finely chopped parsley or cilantro (optional)

salt

Put the tahini in a mixing bowl and gradually whisk in the lemon juice alternately with the water—this is to make sure that you get the right balance of taste while keeping the consistency as it should be, like creamy yogurt. The tahini will first thicken to a purée-like consistency before starting to thin again. If you decide to use less lemon juice, make up for the loss of liquid by adding a little more water or vice versa. Add the crushed garlic (and chopped herbs if you are using them) and salt to taste. Taste and adjust the seasoning if necessary and serve with the recipes on pages 146 and 152 or just with pita bread or a selection of crudités.

Garlic Sauce

Тнüм

THIS IS THE LEBANESE version of aïoli but without any egg. Thüm is a very pungent dip, so use it in moderation or it will make you a social leper for a day or two afterward.

SERVES 4–6

5 large garlic cloves

salt

⅓ cup extra-virgin olive oil

3–4 tablespoons strained yogurt (optional)

1 small potato, boiled and mashed (optional)

Put the peeled garlic cloves and a little salt in a mortar and pound with a pestle until reduced to a very fine paste. Drizzle in the oil very slowly, stirring constantly as if you were making mayonnaise. If you do not like your garlic sauce strong, add strained yogurt or mashed potato or a combination of both at the end.

THIS DIP IS FOUND, with slight variations, in Greece, Turkey, Lebanon, and Syria. In Greece it is often spooned over souvlaki (page 160) or served as part of mezedes, while in Lebanon and Syria, it is flavored with mint and served as a side dish or again as part of a mezze.

SERVES 4

4 Persian or Kirby cucumbers, peeled and grated

salt

16 ounces plain yogurt

2 cloves garlic, crushed

1–2 tablespoons chopped dill

extra-virgin olive oil for garnish

paprika for garnish

Sprinkle the grated cucumber with a little salt and leave for 30 minutes. With your hands, squeeze it very dry and place in a mixing bowl. Add the yogurt, garlic, and dill and mix well. Taste and adjust the salt if necessary and transfer to a serving dish. Drizzle with a little oil and sprinkle with a little paprika. Serve as a dip with pita bread or with the kebabs listed on page 157. This will keep, refrigerated, for 1 day.

A typical way of carrying bread in wooden cages in Cairo, Egypt

PIZZAS, BREADS, and SAVORY PASTRIES

LEMON AND OLIVE OIL FOCACCIA ✦ *Focaccia con Limone e Olio*

SICILIAN FOCACCIA ✦ *Sfincione*

MOROCCAN BREAD ✦ *K'sra*

YEMENI FRIED BREAD ✦ *M'lawwah*

MOROCCAN FLAT BREAD ✦ *R'ghäyef*

THYME BREAD ✦ *Manaqish bil-Za'tar*

TURKISH MEAT BREAD ✦ *Etli Ekmek*

SAJ BOREK WITH SPINACH AND CHEESE ✦ *Saç Boregi*

SPINACH TRIANGLES ✦ *Fatayer bil-Sabanegh*

CHEESE TRIANGLES ✦ *Fatayer bil-Qarish*

Potato Boreks ✦ *Borekas Tapükhay Adama*

Spinach Rolls ✦ *Spanakopitta*

Cheese Triangles ✦ *Tyropitta*

Artichoke Pie ✦ *Torta Pasqualina*

Swiss Chard Pie ✦ *Torta di Bietola*

Rice Pie ✦ *Torta di Riso*

Onion Pie ✦ *Torta di Cipolle*

Moroccan Doughnuts ✦ *Sfinge*

Easter Bread ✦ *Tsoureki*

Thursday Bread ✦ *Khobz al-Khamiss*

Ramadan Bread with Dates ✦ *Khobz Ramadan*

Turkish Sesame Galettes ✦ *Simit*

Greek Sesame Galettes ✦ *Koulouria*

Neapolitan Pizza ✦ *Pizza Napolitana*

French Pancakes ✦ *Crêpes*

IT WAS IN PORTO Ercole in Tuscany that I ate my first "real" focaccia, a thin flat bread rather like pizza, which can be simply flavored with olive oil and sea salt or garnished with a variety of savory ingredients, such as thinly sliced potatoes, anchovies, onion, or rosemary. Porto Ercole is one of the most popular summer resorts in Italy, but its main attraction for me (apart from my friend's house perched high over the sea in one corner of a massive Spanish fortress) is a tiny focacceria just off the port that produces some of the best focaccia, or schiacciata, as it is also known in Tuscany, found anywhere. Focaccia is usually eaten as a snack. In Italy it is usually made very thin, and I prefer it

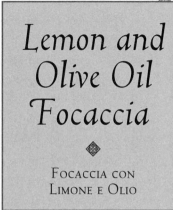

Lemon and Olive Oil Focaccia

❖

FOCACCIA CON
LIMONE E OLIO

this way, but you can also make it thick as bread, which is useful for sandwiches. The recipe below comes from Dan Lepard, coauthor of *Baking with Passion*, who makes his quite thick. You can make yours thinner by simply using a larger baking tray and stretching the dough as thinly as you can without breaking it.

SERVES 6–8

1½ teaspoons active dry yeast

4 cups unbleached all-purpose flour, plus more for kneading

1½ tablespoons cornmeal, plus more for the baking sheet

¼ cup orange juice

zest of 1 lemon

salt

⅓ cup extra-virgin olive oil

2–3 sprigs rosemary, leaves only

1 Whisk the yeast into 1¼ cups warm water with 1½ cups of the flour and leave in a warm place for 20–30 minutes, or until the mixture becomes frothy.

2 Place the remaining flour and the cornmeal in a large mixing bowl. Add the yeast mixture together with the orange juice, lemon zest, and 1 teaspoon salt. Stir with your hands, always in the same direction, until you have a rough, wet, and sticky ball of dough in the center of the bowl. Drip ⅓ of the olive oil over the dough and use a little to rub over your hands. Tuck the dough underneath itself, rotating the bowl slightly as you continue tucking until the dough becomes somewhat smoother on top. Cover the bowl with plastic wrap and leave in a warm place for 45 minutes.

3 Uncover and lightly press into the dough with your fingers, making dozens of indentations all over. Drip ⅓ of the oil over the dough and repeat the tucking operation, cover, and leave in a warm place for 30 minutes. Repeat the same procedure a total of 4 times, with a 30-minute interval between each time, until 3 hours have elapsed. By then the dough should be very smooth, with no visible flour lumps. This method might sound too fussy and time-consuming, but the focaccia will be much lighter than if you make the dough less wet and knead it only once or twice.

4 Brush a 12 × 18-inch baking sheet (or a larger one if you want your focaccia thinner) with olive oil and sprinkle with a thin layer of cornmeal. Place the dough on the pan and make indentations with your fingers all over. Do not attempt to cover the pan with the dough at this stage. Cover with plastic wrap and leave for 30 minutes. Then lift one side of the dough and stretch it until you reach the edge of the pan. Do the same if necessary with the other side until you have covered the pan. With the tips of your fingers, and using the remaining oil, lightly press into the dough at regular intervals to make little dips. These will eventually catch the sea salt and rosemary. Cover with plastic wrap and leave until the dough doubles in size, about 45 minutes.

5 Fifteen minutes before the dough is ready, preheat the oven as high as it will go.

6 When the dough has risen, uncover it and make more indentations all over. Sprinkle with the rosemary and coarse sea salt to taste and place on the middle shelf of the oven. After 5 minutes, reduce the heat to 350 degrees and bake for 35–40 minutes, or until quite brown and blistered and firm to the touch. If you are making the focaccia thin, bake for 20 minutes or until it is golden and slightly crisp. Remove from the pan and cool on a wire rack before serving.

SFINCIONE IS A SPECIALTY from Palermo, not unlike a regular focaccia but thicker and possibly lighter. It is found at various stalls in the city, but a fun place to have it, even if their sfincione is not the best, is Antica Focacceria San Francesco, in piazza S. Francesco in Palermo. The following recipe varies only slightly from the previous one but it is simpler and quicker to make.

SERVES 4

¾ teaspoon active dry yeast

1¾ cups unbleached all-purpose flour, plus more for kneading

juice of 1 lemon

1 tablespoon extra-virgin olive oil

½ cup grated Parmesan cheese

¼ teaspoon salt

¼ teaspoon freshly ground pepper

FOR THE TOPPING:

3 tablespoons extra-virgin olive oil

1 small onion, finely chopped

1 14-ounce can peeled tomatoes, finely chopped

2 tablespoons finely chopped flat-leaf parsley

4 salted anchovies, rinsed and boned if necessary, then cut into short pieces

5 ounces caciocavallo or pecorino cheese, thinly sliced

2 tablespoons fine bread crumbs

1 Stir the yeast into ¼ cup water and leave for a few minutes.

2 Sift the flour directly onto a clean work surface and make a well in the middle. Mix the lemon juice, olive oil, and grated cheese together, add the salt and pepper, and pour into the middle of the flour. Work the liquid in with your fingers, gradually adding the yeast water and another ¼

Sicilian
Focaccia

◆

SFINCIONE

cup water. Knead until you have a rather wet dough, about 10 minutes. Transfer to a floured bowl, cover with a damp towel, and leave to rise in a warm place for about 2 hours.

3 To make the topping, put the olive oil and onion in a saucepan, place over medium-high heat, and cook, stirring occasionally, until golden. Add the tomatoes and parsley and continue cooking for about 20 minutes, or until the sauce is thickened. Set aside.

4 About 10 minutes before the dough is ready, preheat the oven to 400 degrees and oil a 10 × 13-inch baking dish.

5 When the dough has risen, turn it out onto the work surface and knead for a couple of minutes. With your hands, spread the dough in the baking disk, pressing on the dough until it covers the whole dish. Press the bits of anchovy into the dough at regular intervals—you will eventually be cutting the sfincione into 4 portions, and each should have an equal quantity of anchovy on it. Cover the dough with the slices of cheese and spread the tomato sauce all over. Sprinkle with the bread crumbs.

6 Bake in the preheated oven for about 35 minutes, or until the sfincione is done. Let rest until warm and serve, or serve later at room temperature.

Trays of different sfincione at Antica focacceria, San Francesco

THERE IS NOTHING I like better than to buy bread from one of the Berber women who set up stalls in the medina. They bake the loaves in their home early in the morning—they must start very early to make so many—then swaddle them in cotton, leaving only a few showing to attract the attention of passersby. Morocco is an extraordinary country, only a few hours' flight from sophisticated London or Paris, yet completely unspoiled by modern life. Going there is like going back in time to the Middle Ages. Last time I was there, I was taken to a farm a few kilometers away from Marrakesh, where my friend's family lived without electricity or running water. The farm was spotlessly clean, and when the time came for lunch, one of the young girls set about making the bread. She kneaded the dough in a large earthenware dish, shaped it, wrapped it in cloth, and left it to rest. When it was time to bake it, her mother set another flat earthenware dish over a raging fire built with olive branches, and when the dish became really hot, she started baking the bread for our lunch. It was as much a delight to watch as it was to eat. Tunisian bread is similar to Moroccan but without sesame seeds and with ground fennel seeds in place of the anise seeds. In Algeria the bread is made with a mixture of flour and fine semolina and left plain.

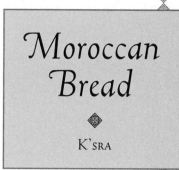

Moroccan Bread

◆

K'SRA

MAKES 1 MEDIUM LOAF

> 1½ teaspoons active dry yeast
>
> 2½ cups unbleached all-purpose
>   flour, plus more for kneading
>
> ¼ teaspoon salt
>
> 1 teaspoon anise seeds
>
> 1½ teaspoons sesame seeds

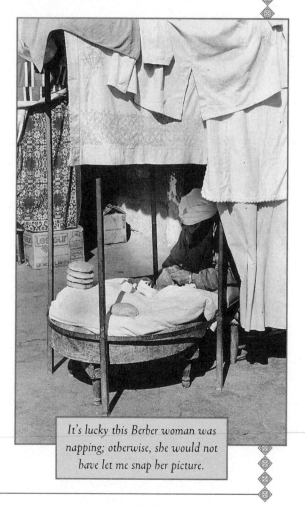

It's lucky this Berber woman was napping; otherwise, she would not have let me snap her picture.

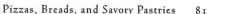

1 Stir the yeast into ¼ cup water and leave for 5–10 minutes.

2 Sift the flour into a shallow mixing bowl, add the salt, anise seeds, and sesame seeds, and gradually pour in the yeast water, then another ½ cup tepid water, incorporating it into the flour. Knead energetically for about 5 minutes, or until you have a firm, elastic dough.

3 Lightly flour your hands and roll the dough into a ball. Flatten it until you have a disk about 6 inches wide and 1 inch thick and place on a floured baking sheet. Leave to rise in a warm place for about 1½ hours, or until it has doubled in size.

4 Fifteen minutes before the dough is ready, preheat the oven to 400 degrees.

5 Bake the bread in the preheated oven for 45–50 minutes, or until the bread sounds hollow when tapped on the bottom. Leave to cool slightly on a wire rack and serve immediately or serve when it has cooled completely. This bread, like all others, freezes very well.

THIS VERY INTERESTING FLAT bread is fried instead of baked. It makes a wonderful starter served with z'houg, grated tomatoes, and haminados eggs. The best way to grate tomatoes for the recipe below is to cut them crosswise in half and then grate the cut side. The skin will stay in your hand for you to discard. You can make these breads well ahead of time and freeze them before step 3. Simply remember to take them out of the freezer a couple of hours before cooking and, after the dough has thawed, proceed as in step 3.

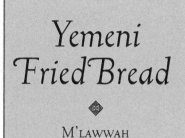

Yemeni Fried Bread

❖

M'LAWWAH

SERVES 6

> 3½ cups unbleached all-purpose flour
>
> 1 teaspoon sea salt
>
> 1 teaspoon sugar
>
> 1 tablespoon white wine vinegar
>
> 1 tablespoon vegetable oil
>
> 8 tablespoons (1 stick) unsalted butter, softened
>
> extra-virgin olive oil for frying

FOR THE GARNISH:

> z'houg (page 69)
>
> 10 medium vine-ripened tomatoes, grated and skins discarded
>
> haminados eggs (page 46), chopped
>
> salt
>
> freshly ground black pepper

1 Sift the flour into a big bowl. Add the salt, sugar, vinegar, oil, and 1 cup water. Knead for about 5 minutes, until you have a smooth, firm dough. Shape the dough into a ball and let rest for 30 minutes. Then knead the dough again and divide into 6 pieces. Shape each into a ball and let rest for another 30 minutes.

2 Divide the butter into 6 equal portions. Roll 1 ball of dough into a disc or oval about ¼ inch thick. Spread with 1 portion butter and fold the buttered dough into a narrow rectangle. Wrap in plastic wrap and set aside. Do the rest of the dough balls the same way and refrigerate for at least 2 hours.

3 Roll out each piece of dough into a round disk as thinly as you can, not paper-thin but thin enough for it to cook inside and out during frying without becoming too brown. Heat a little olive oil in a large frying pan over medium heat. When the oil is hot, put a disk in to fry, covered, for 2–3 minutes on each side. Remove, place on parchment paper, and keep warm. Fry the rest of the breads, placing parchment paper between them. Serve warm with z'houg, grated tomatoes, and chopped haminados eggs. Season the tomatoes and eggs with salt and pepper to taste.

IT IS NOT OFTEN that you see women cooking on the street in North Africa unless they are making this bread. They stand behind large flat griddles on which they cook the bread, flattening it further with their fingers, not seeming to mind the heat. Some occasionally dip their fingers in a small bowl of oil to drizzle on the bread while it is cooking—this slightly greasier version is definitely better. My Algerian food shop in London has a very similar version to r'ghäyef, which they call m'arek or m'hajjib. Theirs is larger and has a spicier filling. In Tunisia there is another, similar bread, m'lawi, which is left plain.

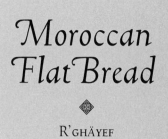

Moroccan Flat Bread

◈

R'GHÄYEF

SERVES 4

FOR THE DOUGH:

> ¼ teaspoon active dry yeast
>
> 1 cup unbleached all-purpose flour
>
> ½ teaspoon salt, plus more for the filling

FOR THE FILLING:

> 1 medium onion, very finely chopped
>
> ¼ cup finely chopped flat-leaf parsley
>
> 3 tablespoons unsalted butter, softened, plus more for greasing
>
> ½ teaspoon ground cumin
>
> 1 teaspoon paprika
>
> ⅛ teaspoon crushed red pepper flakes

1 Stir the yeast into a scant ½ cup tepid water and leave for about 5 minutes.

2 Sift the flour into a large mixing bowl. Add the salt and yeast water, gradually working it in, until the dough is slightly wetter than that for bread. Knead with your hands for 10 minutes, or until completely smooth and pliable.

3 Put all the filling ingredients in a mixing bowl, add salt to taste, and mix together well.

4 Smear your work surface and hands with butter and divide the dough into 4 equal portions. Flatten 1 portion with your fingers into a very thin square, stretching it as you finish—be careful not to tear it. Spread a quarter of the filling over one half and fold the plain side over. Fold again to form a square. Flatten as thin as possible with your fingers.

5 Grease a large nonstick frying pan with a little butter and place over medium-high heat. Place the folded dough in the pan and cook for 3–4 minutes on each side, or until lightly golden all over. Remove and place on parchment paper. Repeat the procedure to make the rest of the breads, buttering your hands, work surface, and pan before making each one. Serve hot or warm.

M'lawi and other bread at a stall in the medina in Tunis

Thyme Bread

◆

MANAQISH BIL-ZA'TAR

THERE ARE TWO TYPES of manaqish bil-za'tar: those baked in the oven and those cooked on the saj (a kind of inverted wok placed over charcoal or, in the modern places, a gas fire), the latter being thinner and slightly more crisp. The topping, za'tar, is a savory mixture made with powdered dried thyme, sumac, and raw or toasted sesame seeds. You can make your own za'tar or buy it ready-made in Middle Eastern stores. You can also vary the topping by using kishk (a mixture of bulgur and strained yogurt that is fermented, dried, and rubbed to produce a very fine powder); halloumi cheese, sliced thinly and spread over the dough (my favorite Lebanese restaurant in London, Al Waha, spreads the za'tar mixture over the cheese to produce unusual and scrumptious manaqish); or qawarma (lamb confit, which Lebanese mountain people use in winter when fresh meat is scarce). The following recipe is the saj version cooked in a nonstick pan. If you want to bake the manaqish, roll them out a little thicker and bake in 350 degree oven.

Manaquish on the saj, Byblos, Lebanon

SERVES 4

FOR THE DOUGH:

½ teaspoon active dry yeast

1¾ cups unbleached all-purpose flour, plus more for kneading

1 teaspoon salt

2 tablespoons vegetable oil

FOR THE TOPPING:

3 tablespoons za'tar (thyme mixture), available in Middle Eastern markets

just under ½ cup extra-virgin olive oil

1 small onion, finely chopped (optional)

1 Stir the yeast into ¼ cup tepid water and leave for 5–10 minutes.

2 Sift the flour and salt into a large mixing bowl, make a well in the center, and pour in the oil. Work it in with your fingertips until completely absorbed. Add the yeast water and knead with your hands for a couple of minutes. Gradually add another ¼ cup water and knead until the dough is smooth and elastic. Form into a ball, cover with a damp cloth, and leave in a warm place for 1 hour, or until doubled in size.

3 Put all the topping ingredients in a small bowl and mix together well.

4 Divide the dough into 4 equal portions and roll each into a ball. Dip the first ball of dough in flour on all sides, shake off the excess, and roll into a thin disk, about ⅛ inch thick. Make a few dimples across the flat dough, pressing hard with the tips of your fingers—this is done to stop the oil in the topping from running out during cooking. Spread a quarter of the topping over the disk of dough.

5 Place a nonstick skillet over medium heat. Cook the dough in the skillet, topping side up, for 3–5 minutes, or until the bottom is crisp and lightly golden. Repeat the procedure to make the rest of the breads. Serve hot or warm, either plain or with a bowl of labneh (strained yogurt) and another of olives.

FOR THE ZA'TAR:

>   2 parts powdered dried thyme
>
>   1 part sumac
>
>   ½ part toasted sesame seeds
>
>   Salt to taste

Put all the ingredients in a frying pan and place over medium heat. Stir continuously until the aroma rises and the mixture is slightly toasted. Let cool and store in a hermetically sealed container.

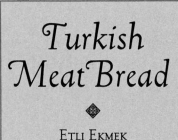

Turkish Meat Bread

ETLI EKMEK

THIS IS THE TURKISH version of the topped bread also found in Syria and Lebanon. There it is called lahm bil-ajine (meat in dough), and the meat mixture sometimes includes pine nuts. In some areas the seasoning contains pomegranate molasses. In Baalbek the bread is known as s'fiha; its crust is thicker and the shape small and square instead of round or oval. I prefer the Turkish version, for which the dough is flattened until very thin. You will find the best etli ekmek in Konya in Anatolia. It is sold at specialist bakeries or served in kebab restaurants. The most enjoyable of these restaurants are located behind the Mevlevi monastery, where old houses with large terraces overlooking the domes of the monastery have been converted into eateries serving local specialties.

SERVES 4

FOR THE DOUGH:

½ teaspoon active dry yeast

1¾ cups flour, plus more for kneading

¼ teaspoon salt

1 tablespoon extra-virgin olive oil

FOR THE FILLING:

1 medium onion, very finely chopped

1 large tomato, peeled and diced very small

7 ounces lean ground lamb (about 1 cup)

1 teaspoon lemon juice, or more to taste

½ teaspoon ground allspice

¼ teaspoon ground cinnamon

¼ teaspoon cayenne pepper

Salt

⅛ teaspoon finely ground black pepper

Making etli ekmek in a bakery in Konya

1 Stir the yeast into ¼ cup tepid water and leave for 10 minutes.

2 Sift the flour into a large mixing bowl and make a well in the center. Add the salt and olive oil and work in with your fingers, then add the yeast water and another ¼ cup water. Knead for 5 minutes, or until you have a smooth, elastic dough. Cover the bowl with plastic wrap and let rest in a warm place for 30 minutes.

3 While the dough is resting, combine all the ingredients for the filling.

4 Preheat the oven to its highest setting. Line a large baking sheet with parchment paper.

5 Divide the dough into 4 equal pieces and roll each into a ball. Take 1 ball, flatten it with your hand into a 5-inch disk, then pull and stretch into a long oval—the bread should be quite thin. Transfer to the lined baking sheet and, with your fingers, make deep indentations just inside the edges. Spread a quarter of the meat mixture all over. Repeat the procedure to make the other breads.

6 Bake in the preheated oven for 12–15 minutes, or until lightly golden. Serve immediately.

Saj Borek with Spinach and Cheese

SAÇ BÖREGI

THE MAKING OF SAJ boreks, an Anatolian specialty, has become a tourist attraction in Turkey. Walking down Istiklal Street in Istanbul, you see Anatolian ladies settled in the windows of some restaurants making saj boreks in full view of passersby. Sadly, their boreks can't hold a candle to those I had in Anatolia.

The traditional dough for saj borek is made with different flours, strong bread flour, all-purpose, and whole wheat. Mixing the flours produces a superior dough, but using just unbleached all-purpose flour, as in the recipe here, is fine—the texture may not be perfect, but it is good all the same. You can vary the filling below and use ground meat, in which case go to the recipe on page 90 but cook the meat before using. For a potato filling, grate two boiled potatoes and mix with a little chopped parsley and onion, then season with salt, pepper, and a pinch of crushed red pepper flakes. You can also use the cheese mixture below on its own.

SERVES 4

Making saç boregi in Meram, Konya

FOR THE DOUGH:

　　　1 cup unbleached all-purpose flour, plus more for kneading

　　　(or ⅓ cup each strong bread flour, unbleached all-purpose flour, and
　　　　　whole-wheat flour)

　　　½ teaspoon salt

FOR THE FILLING:

　　　¾ cup crumbled feta cheese

　　　2 tablespoons chopped flat-leaf parsley

　　　3½ ounces spinach, finely shredded (about 2½ cups)

　　　freshly ground black pepper

TO FINISH:

　　　2–3 tablespoons butter, melted

1 Sift the flour into a large mixing bowl, add the salt, and a touch over ⅓ cup water. Knead for 5 minutes, until you have a smooth, firm dough. Divide into 4 pieces and roll each into a ball. Let rest for 30 minutes.

2 Mix the cheese with the parsley.

3 Flour the work surface and a thin rolling pin. Take 1 ball of dough and roll it out as thinly as you can, flouring it all the time, to a 12-inch diameter. Sprinkle a quarter of the spinach over half the dough and then sprinkle a quarter of the cheese mixture over the spinach. Fold the plain side of the dough over the filling to make a half circle.

4 Heat a nonstick griddle or pan over medium heat. Place the filled dough on the hot griddle or pan. Cook for a minute or so on one side and again on the other until lightly crisp and golden on both sides. Transfer to a plate, brush with melted butter, and serve immediately. Repeat the procedure to make the other saj boreks.

Spinach Triangles

FATAYER BIL-SABANEGH

IN HOMES IN LEBANON, these triangles are made small and dainty, while those sold in bakeries and sandwich shops are much larger.

SERVES 4

FOR THE DOUGH:

1 cup unbleached all-purpose flour, plus more for kneading

¼ teaspoon salt

2 tablespoons vegetable oil

FOR THE FILLING:

5–6 ounces spinach, finely shredded (about 4 cups)

salt

1 small onion, very finely chopped

¼ teaspoon finely ground black pepper

1 tablespoon ground sumac

1 tablespoon pine nuts

juice of ½ lemon, or more to taste

1 tablespoon extra-virgin olive oil

1 Sift the flour and salt into a mixing bowl and make a well in the center. Pour in the oil and work into the flour with your hands until it is completely absorbed and the flour looks like grated cheese. Add ¼ cup water and knead until the dough is smooth and elastic. Form into a ball, cover with a damp cloth, and let rest while you prepare the filling.

2 Preheat the oven to 450 degrees and line a baking sheet with parchment paper.

3 Put the shredded spinach in a mixing bowl, sprinkle with a little salt, and rub with your fingers until it wilts.

4 Season the chopped onion with a little salt and the pepper and again rub with your fingers to soften it before adding to the spinach. Add the sumac, pine nuts, lemon juice, and olive oil and mix well. Taste and adjust seasoning if necessary—the filling should be quite strongly flavored to offset the mild pastry.

5 Divide the dough into 4 pieces and roll each into a ball between the palms of your hands. Flatten one slightly and dip all sides into flour. Shake off the excess flour and roll out into a 6-inch disk, about 1/16 inch thick.

6 Drain the spinach mixture of any liquid and put a quarter of it in the middle of the disk of dough. Think of the disk as having 3 sides, each 1/3 of the circumference. Lift 2 sides and pinch together, halfway down, to make a thin raised joint. Lift the third, open side and pinch it equally to both loose edges in order to form a triangle with a thin raised inverted *y* in the middle—be sure to pinch the pastry tightly together so that it does not open during baking. Carefully transfer the filled pastry to the lined baking sheet and make the rest of the triangles in the same way.

7 Bake in the preheated oven for 10–15 minutes, or until golden, and serve warm or at room temperature. These will freeze very well either before or after baking.

Cheese Triangles

◆

FATAYER BIL-QARISH

THIS FILLING IS TRADITIONALLY made with a Lebanese-Syrian cheese called qarish, which is not easily available anymore in Lebanon or Syria and even less so in the West. It is very easy to make at home, though. Just boil some yogurt with a little lemon juice until it separates, then pour into a colander lined with a double layer of cheesecloth and leave to drain for a couple of hours. Use 1 tablespoon lemon juice for every quart yogurt to produce about 1½ cups qarish. This homemade qarish makes a good substitute for myzithra in the recipe on page 232. Another good substitute for qarish is curd cheese.

SERVES 4

2 tablespoons unsalted butter

1 egg

1 cup qarish (see headnote) or curd cheese

½ cup finely chopped flat-leaf parsley

¼ cup finely chopped mint

2 tablespoons finely chopped scallions

½ teaspoon ground cinnamon

½ teaspoon ground allspice or 7-spice mixture (page 131)

salt

freshly ground black pepper

dough (page 94)

1 Melt the butter in a small frying pan over medium heat and soft-scramble the egg. Transfer the scrambled egg to a mixing bowl. Add the cheese, herbs, scallions, and spices and season with salt and pepper to taste. Mix well. Taste and adjust the seasoning if necessary. Set aside.

2 Make the triangles as in the previous recipe. Serve hot, warm, or at room temperature.

BOREKAS ARE SAVORY OR sweet pastries made with puff pastry and a variety of fillings and shaped in rectangles, squares, or triangles. They are found everywhere on the streets in Israel, often treated as if they were sandwiches. The vendor opens the boreka to add chopped eggs, tomatoes, and tahini sauce to the filling. He then presents it to you with pickles. At the Arab stalls borekas are sold with a garnish of za'tar (page 89) and salt. Whichever way you have them, plain or filled, they are totally irresistible.

MAKES 6

Potato Boreks

◆

BOREKAS TAPÜKHAY ADAMA

A medieval doorway in Cairo

1 medium onion, thinly sliced

1 tablespoon extra-virgin olive oil

2 medium potatoes, boiled and mashed

salt

freshly ground black pepper

3–4 tablespoons crumbled feta cheese (optional)

13-ounce package puff pastry, preferably fresh but frozen if necessary

1 egg yolk beaten with 1 tablespoon water

2 tablespoons sesame seeds

6 haminados eggs (page 46)

1 Fry the onion in the oil until lightly golden. Season the potatoes with salt and pepper to taste, add the onions and cheese if you are using it, and mix well. Set aside.

2 Preheat the oven to 400 degrees. Line a baking sheet with parchment paper.

3 Roll the puff pastry quite thinly, about ¼ inch or less, and cut into 6 equal squares.

4 Divide the filling into 6 parts. Place 1 portion in the middle of a square and fold into a triangle. Press hard on the sides to seal well and brush with the egg yolk. Repeat with the remaining dough and filling. Sprinkle the borekas with sesame seeds.

5 Bake on the middle shelf of the preheated oven for 25–30 minutes, or until crisp and golden. Check the bottoms to see if they are done; they should be brown. Serve warm or at room temperature with haminados eggs.

Notes: These cannot be refrigerated, but they can be frozen, preferably before baking. You can also shape these borekas into rectangles.

SPANAKOPITTA COMES IN DIFFERENT shapes and sizes and can be made with filo or puff pastry. There is an excellent bakery near the central market in Athens that offers crescent-shaped spanakopitta made with puff pastry. In Chania's central market in Crete, I found a bakery where the spanakopitta is made with filo, shaped in a large round pie, and sprinkled with sesame seeds. In another

Spinach Rolls

◈

SPANAKOPITTA

café/restaurant, it was made with filo but shaped into large individual rectangles. This is the shape that I found easiest to handle. The filling also varies from one region to another. In Crete it is spinach with myzithra (see page 230) and no eggs. Elsewhere feta is added. Whichever way you decide to make your filling, it is important you drain off the liquid from the cooked spinach in order to have a clean, crisp pie.

SERVES 6 (1 PIE PER PERSON)

2 tablespoons extra-virgin olive oil

1 medium onion, very finely chopped

8 medium scallions, trimmed and thinly sliced

1 pound spinach, tough stalks removed, then shredded into thin strips

salt

freshly ground black pepper

¼ cup coarsely chopped flat-leaf parsley

½ cup fresh dill, leaves only

½ cup crumbled feta cheese

4 tablespoons (½ stick) butter, melted

6 sheets filo pastry, about 11 × 18 inches

1 Put the olive oil, onion, and scallions in a large sauté pan and place over medium heat. Cook, stirring regularly, until the onion is soft and transparent. Increase the heat to high and stir in the spinach. Season with salt and pepper to taste and sauté for 2–3 minutes, or until the spinach is wilted. Drain the spinach of all excess liquid, then stir in the herbs. Taste and adjust the seasoning if necessary and set aside for 15–20 minutes. Press the spinach with a large spoon to extract the last of the excess liquid. Stir in the cheese.

2 Preheat the oven to 400 degrees. Line a baking sheet with parchment paper.

3 Take a sheet of filo pastry and brush it with butter—keep the others covered with a slightly damp cloth or plastic wrap so that they don't dry out. Put ⅙ of the spinach filling at the end nearest you, about 1 inch clear of the end and 2 inches clear of the sides. Fold the sides over the filling and brush with butter, then fold up the end; continue folding until you have a 3½ × 2-inch rectangle, brushing each fold except the first one with butter. Place on the lined baking sheet with the loose end down. Continue filling and rolling the spanakopittas until you have used up both the filling and the pastry. Brush the rolls with the rest of the melted butter.

4 Bake in the preheated oven for 25–30 minutes, or until crisp and golden. Serve hot or warm.

AS WITH SPANAKOPITTA, YOU can make a single pie with this recipe. If you do, increase the number of filo sheets to 12 and lay half on the bottom of a greased baking dish, brushing each with melted butter. Spread the filling over the pastry and cover with the rest of the filo, not forgetting to brush each sheet with butter. Brush the top with butter and bake as below or possibly a little longer. Once the pie is ready, let it rest for 5 minutes before cutting it into 8-inch squares and serving.

SERVES 6

Cheese Triangles

◆

TYROPITTA

2 cups crumbled feta cheese

¼ cup chopped flat-leaf parsley

⅛ teaspoon grated nutmeg

salt

freshly ground black pepper

2 eggs, beaten

4 tablespoons (½ stick) unsalted butter, melted

6 sheets filo pastry, about 11 × 18 inches

1 Put the cheese in a large mixing bowl. Add the parsley and seasonings—you might not need any salt if the cheese is already salty. Taste and adjust the seasoning if necessary, then stir in the beaten eggs.

2 Preheat the oven to 350 degrees. Cover a large baking sheet with parchment paper.

3 Take a sheet of filo and brush half of it lengthwise with melted butter. Fold it in half lengthwise and place 2½–3 tablespoons filling at the top end. Fold the pastry over the filling to form a triangle, then brush with melted butter and continue folding as you would fold a flag, brushing each fold with butter. Trim the loose end with a sharp knife, brush the top with butter, and place on the baking sheet. Continue filling and making the triangles until you have used up both the filling and the pastry.

4 Bake in the preheated oven for 35–40 minutes or until crisp and golden. Serve hot or warm.

Artichoke Pie

Torta Pasqualina

THIS PIE AND THE following ones are typical of Genoese street food. They are made and sold in the town's friggitorie and always baked in wood-fired ovens. In one of the friggitorie I went to, I watched the cook, Luigi, stretch the dough to a near transparent thinness. He first flattened the dough with a rolling pin, then picked it up, draped it around his wrists, and started rotating it until it stretched to more than triple its size. When I tried to repeat this feat at home, I got into a tangle, the way I usually do when I go fishing. After a couple of tries, I got it nearly right. Still, the sheets of dough were not as thin as Luigi's. So I changed tack and decided to simplify my life and use filo pastry instead. Not a bad substitution; the pie seemed very easy to make after that. However, if you feel like making your own dough, all you need is unbleached all-purpose flour, a little oil, and enough water to make a very supple dough; don't forget to add a little salt. The principle for making this and the following pies is the same. They have the same casing and are made in the same-size baking dish. Consider this recipe as the master recipe for filling and baking and the following ones as variations on the filling.

SERVES 4–6

FOR THE FILLING:

5 tablespoons extra-virgin olive oil

1 pound 12 ounces frozen artichoke hearts, defrosted and thinly sliced (see Note below)

doubled recipe for soffrito (page 28)

8–10 dried porcini mushroom slices, soaked in hot water, drained, and finely chopped

1 tablespoon dried marjoram (or 2 tablespoons finely chopped fresh marjoram leaves)

3 eggs, beaten

1½ cups crumbled ricotta cheese

1 cup grated Parmesan cheese

salt

freshly ground black pepper

TO FINISH:

5 sheets filo pastry, about 11 × 18 inches

3 tablespoons unsalted butter, ½ tablespoon melted

5 eggs

1 To make the filling, put the oil and artichokes in a large sauté pan and place over medium heat. Cover and cook for about 20 minutes, stirring regularly. Uncover and cook for another 5 minutes, or until the artichokes are slightly colored and done.

2 Place the soffrito in a large mixing bowl and add the cooked artichokes. Here you have the choice of keeping them in slices or chopping them very fine. I keep mine in slices, as I like the pie to have some crunch. Add the porcini, marjoram, eggs, ricotta, and grated Parmesan and season with salt and pepper. Mix well; taste and adjust the seasoning if necessary.

A torta pasqualina cooking in
a wood-fired oven in Genoa

3   Preheat the oven to 350 degrees. Grease the bottom and sides of a 10-inch round baking dish with a little olive oil. Try to find a dish with sides about 2 inches high.

4   Lay 2 sheets of filo pastry across the bottom of the dish in a cross pattern so that the pastry goes over the sides of the dish. Spread the filling evenly over the filo, then make 5 shallow wells in it, each large enough to hold an egg. Place a knob of butter in each well, then break an egg into it. Sprinkle the eggs with a little salt, then cover with the remaining 3 sheets of filo, again crossing them. With a pair of scissors, cut the edge of the pastry to about ½ inch of overhang and roll the loose pastry over the edge of the pie to make a slightly raised edge. Brush the top with the melted butter.

5   Bake in the preheated oven for 35–40 minutes, or until the top of the pie is golden. Serve warm or at room temperature.

Note: You can use fresh artichokes if you prefer. You will need 18 small Ligurian artichokes for this recipe. To prepare them, tear the leaves off. Peel the bottom, remove the choke, and slice thinly. If you are not going to use the hearts right away, soak them in acidulated water so that they won't discolor.

Swiss Chard Pie

◆

TORTA DI BIETOLA

YOU CAN TURN THIS pie into a torta pasqualina by simply adding eggs, as in the artichoke pie above. I remember once buying a portion of this pie in a little friggitoria in Genoa. The waitress served it to me on a cardboard tray covered with rough paper, as is usual in these places, and of course, she did not give me a fork. There was no way I could pick up the piece of pie with my fingers without the Swiss chard flopping out of the pastry—the pastry is so thin as not to count as a casing. I kept sliding the pie to the edge of the tray so that just enough of it protruded for me to take a bite. It was certainly not the most elegant way to eat it nor the most practical. Finally the lady realized I was having difficulties and mercifully handed me a fork.

SERVES 4

6 tablespoons extra-virgin olive oil

1 medium onion, very finely chopped

3 pounds Swiss chard, leaves only, cut into very thin strips

salt

freshly ground black pepper

5 sheets filo pastry, about 11 × 18 inches

1 cup crumbled ricotta cheese

2 tablespoons unsalted butter, melted

1 Put the oil and onion in a large sauté pan and place over medium heat. Cook until the onion is lightly golden. Add the Swiss chard, season with salt and pepper, and cook for 15–20 minutes, stirring occasionally, until the chard is soft. Drain off any excess liquid, then taste and adjust the seasoning if necessary. Set aside.

2 Preheat the oven, prepare the baking dish, and lay out the filo pastry as in the recipe for artichoke pie (page 102).

3 Spread the chard evenly over the filo. Scatter the ricotta all over the top and season with a little more salt and pepper. Cover with the rest of the filo pastry, again following the instructions for the artichoke pie. Prick the pastry in several places to let off the moisture from the chard and brush with the melted butter.

4 Bake in the preheated oven for 35–40 minutes, or until the pastry is crisp and golden. Serve warm or at room temperature.

Rice Pie

◈

Torta di Riso

YOU CAN PREPARE THIS Genoese pie in several different ways: in pastry or without, and with the rice cooked with tomatoes (al pomodoro) or in milk (bianco). Some friggitorie serve both, but more often than not, they serve one or the other. In the recipe below, which is the tomato version, I use dried porcini to give the pie a subtle, luxurious touch, a touch that you will not find on the street.

SERVES 4

8–10 dried porcini mushroom slices

1 tablespoon extra-virgin olive oil

1 tablespoon unsalted butter

1 small onion, very finely chopped

1 tablespoon finely chopped flat-leaf parsley

1 14-ounce can peeled tomatoes, finely chopped

1 cup Carnaroli or Vialone rice

salt

⅔ cup freshly grated Parmesan cheese

5 sheets filo pastry, about 11 × 18 inches

1 cup crumbled ricotta cheese

a little melted butter to brush the top of the pie

1 Soak the porcini in tepid water for 10–15 minutes. Drain, reserving the liquid. Finely chop the porcini.

2 Put the oil, butter, and chopped onion in a saucepan and place over medium heat. Cook, stirring occasionally, until the onion is lightly golden. Add the parsley and tomatoes and cook for 5–10 minutes, or until the sauce has reduced. Stir in the porcini and rice and add just under 2 cups water, including the porcini soaking water. Season with salt and simmer for about 12 minutes, or until the water is absorbed. Take the rice off the heat, add the grated Parmesan, and mix well. Cover with a clean towel and let cool.

3 Preheat the oven, prepare the baking dish, and lay out the filo pastry as in the recipe for artichoke pie (page 102).

4 Spoon the rice into the pastry, spreading it quite thinly, and cover with the ricotta. Finish and bake, following the same instructions for the artichoke pie. Serve hot, warm, or at room temperature.

AGAIN, YOU CAN USE porcini to upgrade this pie from humble street fare to rather refined home cooking. If you want to use them, soak 10–12 dried porcini mushroom slices in hot water for 10 minutes, then drain and chop before mixing in with the cooked onion.

SERVES 4

Onion Pie

❖

TORTA DI CIPOLLE

> 3 pounds red onions, thinly sliced (about 9 heaping cups)
>
> 5 tablespoons unsalted butter, ½ tablespoon melted
>
> ¼ cup extra-virgin olive oil
>
> ¼ cup grated Parmesan cheese
>
> salt
>
> freshly ground black pepper
>
> 5 sheets filo pastry, about 11 × 18 inches

I Blanch the sliced onions for 2–3 minutes and drain well.

2 Put 4 tablespoons butter and the oil in a large frying pan and place over medium heat. When the butter has melted, add the onions and cook, stirring regularly, until lightly colored. If you are using porcini, add them toward the end of cooking. When the onions are done, take off the heat and let cool slightly, then stir in the grated cheese and season with salt and pepper.

3 Preheat the oven, prepare the baking dish, and lay out the filo pastry as in the recipe for artichoke pie (page 102).

4 Spread the fried onions evenly over the pastry. Finish and bake following the instructions for the artichoke pie. Serve warm or at room temperature.

Moroccan Doughnuts

◆

SFINGE

SFINGE IS ONE OF the main street food staples in Morocco and, like much other street fare, requires special skills. You need to develop a knack not only to work the wet dough but also to shape and drop the rings into the boiling oil. That is not to say that they are particularly difficult to make, just that you have to be ready for the following recipe to require extra care in the preparation. All the sfinge makers I have seen are men, and not so long ago they were always situated next to the lamb's head bakers. Back then, people ate both for breakfast. Even now some old people will buy their sfinge to take to the nearest lamb's head stall to eat with the meat.

SERVES 6–8

1½ teaspoons active dry yeast

2 cups and 1 tablespoon unbleached all-purpose flour, plus more for kneading

1 teaspoon salt

vegetable oil for frying

1 Stir the yeast into ¼ cup tepid water and leave for a few minutes.

2 Sift the flour and salt and yeast water into a large mixing bowl and gradually add ½ cup water. Knead until you have a soft, sticky, stretchy dough—you may be tempted to add too much flour while working the dough; don't or the doughnuts will turn out dry and heavy. Place the dough in a lightly oiled bowl and cover with a clean cloth. Let rest in a warm place for 2–3 hours.

3 When the dough is ready, pour enough oil into a large frying pan to deep-fry the doughnuts. Place over medium-high heat.

4 Knead the dough again and, when the oil is very hot, smear your hands with a little cool vegetable oil. Divide the dough into 12 pieces and roll each into a ball between the palms of your hands. With your thumb, punch a hole through the middle of one ball of dough, stretch it to form a floppy ring, and slide it into the hot oil. Insert a wooden chopstick in the middle of the doughnut and swirl it in the oil as if you are trying to make the opening wider. This is to stop the hole from narrowing. Drop in as many doughnuts as will fit comfortably in the pan, not forgetting to lightly oil your hands every now and then. They will puff up, so do not overcrowd the pan. Fry for 2–4 minutes on each side, or until golden brown all over. Remove and place on several layers of paper towels. Finish making the doughnuts and serve hot, either plain or with honey or sugar.

Easter Bread

Tsoureki

THE TSOUREKI THAT ARE sold on the street are made a lot smaller than in this recipe. You can do the same by dividing the dough into four portions and twisting each rope of dough into a figure eight to produce loaves as in the photo opposite.

SERVES 6

1½ teaspoons active dry yeast

3 tablespoons warm milk

2 cups unbleached all-purpose flour, plus more to work the dough

⅓ cup sugar

⅛ teaspoon salt

1 teaspoon extra-virgin olive oil

scant ½ teaspoon ground mahlep, or ¼ teaspoon ground mastic, available in Middle Eastern markets

⅛ teaspoon ground cardamom

1 large egg

3 tablespoons unsalted butter, melted

1 egg yolk mixed with 1 tablespoon water

1 Put the yeast in a small mixing bowl and add ⅓ cup tepid water; stir until completely dissolved and leave for a few minutes. Stir in the warm milk and 1 cup flour and mix together to make what is called a sponge: a thick mixture that will become the raising agent. Cover the bowl and leave in a warm place for about half an hour, or until it has doubled in size.

2 Put the sugar, salt, oil, and spices in a large mixing bowl. Mix well. Stir in the egg. Stir in the sponge and add the remaining 1 cup flour in 2 parts. Knead until you have a soft, slightly sticky dough—you may need to add 1–2 tablespoons water if it is too firm. Gradually add the butter, working it into the dough but taking care not to overwork the dough. Cover the dough with plastic wrap and the bowl with a thick kitchen towel and leave for 2 hours, or until the dough has tripled in size.

3 Line a baking sheet with parchment paper and lightly flour your work surface and hands.

4 Divide the dough into 3 equal parts. Roll the pieces between the palms of your hands into strands measuring 13 inches long and 1½ inches wide. Place the strands on the baking sheet and braid them, forming a long loaf. Leave to rise again for another 30–45 minutes.

5 Fifteen minutes before the loaf is ready for baking, preheat the oven to 400 degrees.

6 Brush the loaf with the egg yolk, taking care not to let it pool in the crevices. Let rest for 15 minutes. Brush the loaf again with the remaining egg yolk and bake in the preheated oven for 20 minutes, or until golden. Remove from the oven and let cool on a wire rack before serving. Tsoureki is best eaten the same day, but it will freeze very well if you want to keep it for later. Simply reheat the loaf in a moderate oven and serve warm or at room temperature.

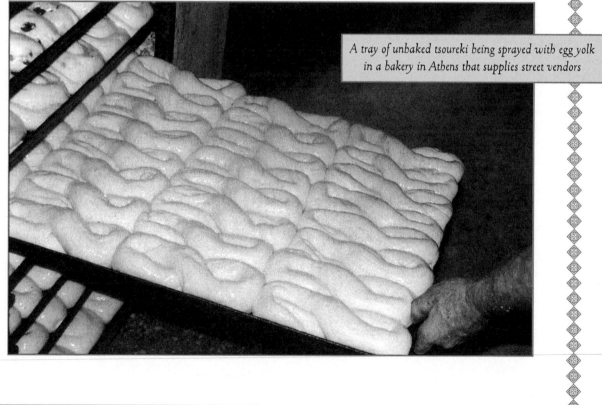

A tray of unbaked tsoureki being sprayed with egg yolk in a bakery in Athens that supplies street vendors

Thursday Bread

❖

Khobz al-Khamiss

DURING RAMADAN THIS STAMPED bread is sold off wooden carts wheeled through the streets of Tripoli, along with other breads such as the date one on page 114. Thursday bread is also sold in bakeries. It looks similar to qorban, the Holy Communion bread of the Greek Orthodox church, except the stamped pattern is different. The Orthodox pattern is made of Greek letters within a cross, while the Muslim one is made of round geometric designs. The breads themselves are also different. The Muslim variety is basically a thick pita bread flavored with mahlab (the kernel of a wild cherry, which adds an intriguing fragrant taste to breads and cookies), then brushed with water toward the end of baking and sprinkled with habbet al-barakeh (nigella seeds). The Christian bread, on the other hand, is more like a Western spongy bread and is flavored with orange blossom water. It is reserved for church use, while khobz al-khamiss is eaten throughout Ramadan, mainly for sühür (the last meal taken before the fast begins again), with cheese or labneh (strained yogurt) and olives.

When I was being brought up as a good Christian in Lebanon and Syria, I always looked forward to Communion on Sunday, not because I was devout but because I loved the fragrant taste of qorban, perfectly complemented by the sweet sip of wine from the chalice. My thoughts were not so much on the flesh and blood of Christ as on how to get more bread and wine. Only once was I able to indulge in more, and that was when the priest came to officiate at our home. My mother and aunt made the loaves at home, and the priest brought a whole bottle of Communion wine that he left behind. My sisters and I had a field day finishing the leftover bread and wine before our mother realized what we were up to.

MAKES 4

½ teaspoon active dry yeast

2 cups flour

½ teaspoon sea salt

¼ teaspoon ground mahlab, available in Middle Eastern stores

½ tablespoon extra-virgin olive oil

a little vegetable oil

⅛ teaspoon nigella seeds (habbet al-barakeh)

1 Stir the yeast into ¼ cup tepid water and leave for a few minutes.

2 Sift the flour into a large mixing bowl, then add the salt and mahlab; with the tips of your fingers, rub in the olive oil. Add the yeast water and gradually another ½ cup water and knead for about 5 minutes. Lightly oil a large bowl, put the dough in the bowl, and cover with a damp cloth. Let rest in a warm place for about 1 hour or until doubled in size.

3 Divide the dough into 4 pieces and roll each into a ball. Let rest for 30 minutes.

4 Preheat the oven to its highest setting, about 500 degrees. Place a baking sheet in the oven.

5 Roll each ball of dough into a 7-inch disk. Remove the baking sheet from the oven and quickly line it with parchment paper. Place 2 disks on it, brush them lightly with vegetable oil, and sprinkle with a few nigella seeds. Bake in the preheated oven for 10 minutes, or until the breads have puffed up and are golden. (You can also bake the breads on a baking stone that you will need to preheat as well; if you use a stone, reduce the baking time to 5–7 minutes.) When the breads are ready, remove from the oven and bake the remaining breads the same way. Serve immediately or leave to cool on a wire rack and freeze for later use.

Ramadan Bread with Dates

Khobz Ramadan

WHEN I WAS TESTING some of the baking recipes for this book with my friend Richard Hosking, author of *Dictionary of Japanese Food*, who is a far better baker than I, we decided that a good way to use up so many different breads and pastries was to have an old-fashioned tea party. This bread was on the menu of our first party. It was a great success, although it turned out quite differently from what I had eaten on the streets of Tripoli, Lebanon. The skill required for street food is, in some cases, so specialized that it is often impossible to replicate the food exactly in a home kitchen. A good approximation is all that one can hope for. Here is one of those approximations, in which the bread ends up more like a cookie than a bread.

MAKES 4

8 ounces pitted dates

½ pound (2 sticks) unsalted butter, softened

1½ teaspoons active dry yeast

3½ cups unbleached all-purpose flour

1 tablespoon sesame seeds

1 teaspoon anise seeds

1 egg yolk, beaten

1 Put the dates in a food processor and process until coarsely chopped. Add 4 tablespoons butter and continue processing until you have a smooth paste. Divide into 4 equal parts, cover with plastic wrap, and refrigerate.

2 Stir the yeast into ¼ cup tepid water and leave for 10 minutes in a warm place.

3 Sift the flour into a large mixing bowl and add the sesame and anise seeds and the remaining butter. Work the butter into the flour with your hands. Add the yeast water and ¾ cup tepid water. Knead until you have a supple, firm dough. Divide the dough into 4 equal parts, roll into balls, and let rest for 15 minutes.

4 Roll out each ball of dough into a disk about 7½ inches wide and ½ inch thick. Flatten one portion of date paste with your hands into a smaller disk, about 4½ inches wide. Lay it in the middle of the dough. Turn the edges of the dough over the filling and seal the dough. Turn over and lay on the baking sheet. Pat with your hands to make as perfect a circle as you can. Make the other breads in the same way, cover with plastic wrap, and let rest for another 15 minutes.

5 Preheat the oven to 400 degrees. Line a large baking sheet with parchment paper.

6 Brush the breads with egg yolk and bake for 25–30 minutes, or until golden. Remove to a wire rack to cool. This bread will keep for a couple of days, but it is best eaten on the day it is baked.

Turkish Sesame Galettes

Simit

SESAME GALETTES, IN ONE form or another, are a street staple throughout the eastern Mediterranean, starting in Greece and continuing all the way down to Egypt. In Greece, Turkey, and Egypt they are shaped into rings, and in Greece they are made slightly sweet. In Lebanon they are shaped like handbags, and the vendor will tear the fat "bag" part open to sprinkle the inside with a little za'tar (page 89). In Tripoli and Syria the galettes are shaped into flat disks and are often sold filled with halloumi cheese seasoned with sumac. It would be too repetitive to include recipes here for all the variations, so I have given recipes only for those in which the difference is noticeable or for which you can achieve a good result at home.

MAKES 4

FOR THE DOUGH:

> 1 teaspoon active dry yeast
>
> 2 cups unbleached all-purpose flour
>
> ¼ teaspoon salt
>
> a little unsalted butter

TO FINISH:

> ½ cup pekmez (Turkish grape molasses)
>
> ½ cup water
>
> ½ cup sesame seeds

1 Stir the yeast into 2 tablespoons tepid water and let stand for a few minutes.

2 Sift the flour and salt into a large mixing bowl and make a well in the center. Add the yeast water and gradually ½ cup water and knead for 5 minutes, until you have a very smooth, elastic dough.

3 Grease another bowl with a little butter and transfer the dough into it. Cover the bowl with plastic wrap and let rest for 1¾ hours.

4 Lightly flour the work surface and knead the dough again for a minute or so. Roll it into a thick cylinder and divide into 4 equal pieces. Roll each piece into a ball and let rest for another half hour. Then roll each piece of dough into a long sausage shape measuring about 14 inches long. Holding one end, twist it a few times. Bring the other end around and join the ends together. Place on a lightly floured surface and shape the other pieces in the same way.

5 Line a baking sheet with parchment paper.

6 Mix the pekmez and water together in a large bowl and spread the sesame seeds on a flat plate. Dip each simit ring in the pekmez water, then roll in the sesame seeds. Place on the lined baking sheet and repeat the process with the 3 remaining simit rings. Leave for another 20–30 minutes to rise a little more.

7 Preheat the oven to its highest setting.

8 Bake the simits in the preheated oven for 20–25 minutes, or until crisp and golden brown. Serve hot straight out of the oven or reheated later in the day. Simits do not keep, but like all breads, they freeze very well. Reheat before serving defrosted simits.

A simit and kumru vendor in Izmir

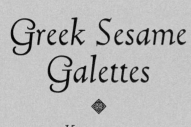

Greek Sesame Galettes

❖

KOULOURIA

SERVES 4

LAST TIME I WAS in Athens, a friend took me to a baker in Sarri who bakes koulouria, tsoureki, and other breads for the street peddlers. He does all his baking at night for the vendors to start picking up from midnight onward to take to their different locations. We went to see him just before dinner and bought some freshly baked koulouria. Eaten straight out of the baker's oven, koulouria is even better than when eaten on the street.

1 teaspoon active dry yeast

3 cups unbleached all-purpose flour, plus more for kneading

¾ teaspoon salt

1½ tablespoons extra-virgin olive oil

3 tablespoons sugar

1 cup sesame seeds

2 egg whites, lightly beaten

Not much left to sell. In fact, the lady very kindly gave me one of the tsourekis on the right to taste and refused to take my money.

1   Stir the yeast into ½ cup tepid water, then whisk in ¼ cup flour to make the sponge. Leave in a warm place for 1 hour or until it has doubled in size.

2   When the sponge is ready, sift the remaining flour and the salt into a large mixing bowl and make a well in the center. Add the sponge, 3–4 tablespoons water, the oil, and the sugar to the well and gradually incorporate the flour into the other ingredients. Knead for 10–15 minutes, or until you have a smooth, elastic dough. Leave in a warm place for about 1 hour, or until doubled in size.

3   Punch the dough down and divide into 8 pieces. Lightly flour your working surface and hands and roll each piece into a sausage. Let rest for 10–15 minutes

4   Roll the dough into a longer sausage shape. You will probably have to let the rolls rest one more time to be able to stretch them to 20–25 inches long. It may help to squeeze the dough between your fingers to stretch it out to the necessary length.

5   During the 15 minutes that the dough is resting for the last time, line a large baking sheet with parchment paper. Spread the sesame seeds in a large baking dish and have the egg whites ready in a wide, shallow bowl.

6   Dip the long rolls into the egg white and then roll them in the sesame seeds. Twist 2 together and join the ends to form a ring about 4–5 inches in diameter. Shape the remaining rolls in the same way. Let rise for about half an hour.

7   Preheat the oven to 400 degrees.

8   Bake the galettes in the preheated oven for 15–20 minutes, or until golden and slightly crisp on the outside but still soft inside, like bread. Let cool on a wire rack and serve at room temperature the same day or freeze for later use. Reheat before serving defrosted koulouria.

Neapolitan Pizza

◆

PIZZA NAPOLITANA

WHEN I WENT TO Marseilles in search of street food, I was given a few contacts by a friend who was born and brought up there. The first of her friends I talked to kept telling me that pizza was the main street food in town. I kept thinking, how can pizza be the main street food in Marseilles? I left him, feeling rather dejected by my apparently fruitless meeting, and started walking around, hoping to find something more interesting than pizza. To my amazement, I walked past pizza stall after pizza stall. I could not believe it. What happened to the baguette sandwich? Or pan bagnat? Or crêpes? Not that I don't like pizza, but for it to be the main street food in Marseilles came as a bit of a shock. Mercifully, I found North African breads and savory pastries in the *quartier arabe*, and the high note came when I spotted sheep's heads speared on the same skewers as chickens in an Arab rôtisserie. Unfortunately, the friend I was with did not fancy the idea of sheep's heads, and I never got to taste them cooked "à la Marseillaise."

MAKES 2 8-INCH PIZZAS (SERVES 2–4)

FOR THE DOUGH:

¾ teaspoon active dry yeast

1 cup unbleached all-purpose flour, plus more for kneading

¼ teaspoon salt

1 tablespoon extra-virgin olive oil

a little vegetable oil

FOR THE TOMATO SAUCE:

3 tablespoons extra-virgin olive oil, plus more to drizzle over the
    pizzas

2 cloves garlic, very finely chopped

2 tablespoons finely chopped flat-leaf parsley

1 28-ounce can peeled tomatoes, finely chopped

1 tablespoon dried oregano

salt

3–4 sprigs basil

1 Stir the yeast in ⅓ cup tepid water and leave for 5 minutes.

2 Sift the flour onto the work surface and make a well in the center. Add the salt and olive oil and work the oil into the flour with your fingers. Gradually add the yeast water and knead the dough for about 10 minutes, lightly flouring your hands every now and then, until you have a smooth, malleable dough.

3 Grease a bowl very lightly with a little vegetable oil and place the dough in it. Lightly brush the dough with oil, cover with plastic wrap, and leave for 40–50 minutes, or until doubled in size.

4 To prepare the tomato sauce, put the oil, garlic, and parsley in a saucepan and place over medium-high heat. Sauté for a couple of minutes, then add the tomatoes, oregano, and salt to taste. Cook, uncovered, over medium-high heat for 25–30 minutes, stirring regularly, or until the sauce is very reduced. Taste and adjust the seasoning. Set aside.

5 When the dough is ready, punch it down in the middle and knead for another couple of minutes. Divide into 2 equal pieces and roll each into a ball between the palms of your hands. Cover with plastic wrap and let rest for another 10 minutes.

6 Preheat the oven to its highest setting. Place a baking sheet in the oven so that it will be very hot when you lay the pizzas on it.

7 Lightly flour the work surface. Take a piece of dough, coat lightly with flour, and roll it out until it is about 8 inches diameter, turning it over every now and then. Pinch all around the edges to form a slight rim, then flatten the inside a little more with your hands. Set aside. Roll out the other piece of dough.

8 Remove the hot baking sheet and quickly brush it with a little vegetable oil. Place the pizza crusts on the baking sheet, spread each with half the tomato sauce, and bake in the preheated oven for 8–10 minutes, until it is crisp and golden on the edges. Check after 7–8 minutes—if one edge is a bit darker, just turn the pizza around and allow another 2 minutes to color the other edge. Serve immediately with a drizzle of olive oil if you like.

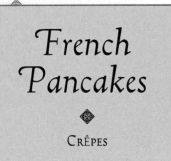

French Pancakes

◆

CRÊPES

THE CRÊPES YOU EAT on the street in France are very large. The vendor cooks them on a big round griddle and turns them over with the help of a spatula, unlike the maître d's in the fancy restaurants, who toss the pan in a showy manner to throw an admittedly much smaller crêpe in the air and catch it effortlessly on the other side. That's a feat I have yet to achieve. In fact, I don't even bother to make crêpes at home. Those made by the street vendors are almost always good, and it is much more fun eating a crêpe walking around a French town than eating it sitting in one's kitchen or dining room. However, here is a recipe for those of you who would like to make your own. The filling can be sweet or savory, depending on your preference. The classical savory fillings are ham and grated cheese, ham and egg, or simply grated cheese. The sweet fillings are either jam or a little granulated sugar.

SERVES 4–6 (ABOUT 10 CRÊPES)

> ½ cup milk
>
> 1 tablespoon unsalted butter
>
> 1 cup and 2 tablespoons unbleached all-purpose flour
>
> ¼ teaspoon fine sea salt
>
> 2 free-range eggs
>
> ½ cup light beer
>
> a little sunflower oil

1 Pour the milk into a small saucepan and place over medium heat. Bring to a boil, then remove from the heat and add the butter.

2 Sift the flour into a mixing bowl, add the salt, and make a well in the center. Break the eggs into the well and whisk into the flour, then gradually add the milk and the beer (if you don't like the idea of using beer, replace it with milk or, for a lighter crêpe, soda water), whisking continuously until you have a smooth batter. Cover and let rest for a couple of hours.

3 Just before the batter is ready, lightly brush a 10- or 12-inch crêpe pan with sunflower oil and place over medium heat. When the pan is very hot, pour in a ladleful of batter all at once and tilt the pan to spread the batter evenly to produce a very thin crêpe. Cook for a minute or so, or until the bottom is lightly golden, then turn over with a spatula (or by tossing the pan if you are good at the turning-over trick). Spread the filling of your choice over one half of the crêpe and fold into a half-moon; if your filling is ham and egg, break the egg over the ham and fold the crêpe over it quickly, making sure you leave the yolk runny. Wait another half minute or so, then remove to a plate and serve immediately. Finish making the rest of the crêpes and serve without delay.

Lone sandwich seller in the medina in Tunis

SANDWICHES

Tunisian "Submarine" ✦ Casse-croûte

Omelet in Flat Tunisian Bread ✦ Mlawi bil-Eggah

Lamb Shawarma ✦ Shawarma Lahmeh

Chicken Shawarma ✦ Shawarma Djaj

Kebabs with Hommus

Jerusalem Mix ✦ Morav Yorushalmi

Spicy Sausages and French Fries ✦ Merguez et Frites

Fried Mussels ✦ Midye Tava

Turkish "Kibbé" ✦ Çig Köfte

Fried Bread ✦ Fricassée

Spicy Fish ✦ Samkeh Harrah

Tomato, Olives, and Anchovy ✦ Pan Bagnat

French Fries ✦ Sandwich Batata

Falafel

Cannellini Bean Salad ✦ Fasulye Piyazi

Grilled Vegetables and Cheese ✦ Panini con Mozzarella e Verdure

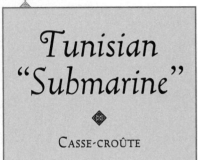

Tunisian "Submarine"

CASSE-CROÛTE

CASSE-CROÛTE LITERALLY MEANS "BREAKING the crust." The French use the word to describe any snack or quick meal, while in Tunisia the word describes a kind of submarine sandwich that is filled to the brim with a combination that varies depending on the customer's request, although the main ingredients are usually tuna, potatoes, and salad. The bread, a large French baguette, is first spread with harissa and mechwiyah before the sandwich maker asks what extras you would like in your sandwich. The salad can be a mixture of tomato, cucumber, and onion or just plain lettuce. There is no need here for exact quantities. Just fill your sandwich with your choice of the ingredients listed below. Even though the Tunisians use only baguettes, you can use other breads, such as ciabatta, buns, or whole wheat rolls.

Putting the finishing touches on the casse-croûte

harissa (page 67)

mechwiyah (page 41)

canned tuna, drained and flaked

boiled potatoes, sliced

lettuce, shredded

tomatoes, chopped small

cucumber, chopped small

onions, thinly sliced

hard-boiled eggs, chopped small

MLAWI SANDWICHES ARE LESS common than the casse-croûte or fricassée and are usually found in the medina, perhaps because they are old-fashioned. The dough, the same as that for Moroccan flat bread, r'ghäyef, is very simple to make, but if you don't like baking, simply use thin pita rounds to make the omelet sandwich. The recipe for the omelet here is Lebanese/Syrian, tastier than the Tunisian version and flavored with more spices.

SERVES 4

Omelet in Flat Tunisian Bread

❖

MLAWI BIL-EGGAH

1 recipe r'ghäyef dough (page 85) or 2 medium
pita bread rounds, opened at the seam to create 4 layers

FOR THE OMELET:

4 eggs

¾ cup finely chopped flat-leaf parsley

1 cup very thinly sliced scallions

1 tablespoon unbleached all-purpose flour

¼ teaspoon ground allspice or 7-spice mixture (page 131)

⅛ teaspoon ground cinnamon

salt

freshly ground black pepper

vegetable oil

harissa (page 67)

1 Divide the dough into 4 balls. Cover with a damp cloth and let rest while you prepare the omelets.

2 Break the eggs into a mixing bowl and beat well. Stir in the parsley, half the scallions, the flour, and 2 tablespoons water. Season with the spices and salt and pepper to taste and blend well.

3 Put enough oil in a medium frying pan to pan-fry the omelets and place over medium-high heat. When the oil is hot, stir the egg mixture again and pour ½ cup in the pan. Spread into a thin round about 6 or 7 inches in diameter, and fry for 1 minute on each side, or until lightly golden all over. Remove and place on a triple layer of paper towels to drain off the excess oil. Make 3 more omelets the same way; you may need to add more oil halfway through. Set aside.

4 To make the breads, lightly grease your hands with vegetable oil and, with your fingers, flatten 1 ball of dough as thinly as you can to form a large square. Fold in half, then in half again, to form a smaller square. Repeat this procedure with the rest of the dough. Brush a large non-stick pan or smooth griddle with a little oil and place it over medium-high heat. When it is hot, flatten a square of dough between your hands and place in the pan or on the griddle. Flatten further with your fingers to about ¼ inch thick and cook for 2–3 minutes on each side, or until the bread is slightly colored. Let cool slightly, then smear with harissa to taste. Repeat with the other 3 squares of dough.

5 Spread each bread with harissa to taste and lay an omelet on each bread, sprinkle with some of the reserved scallions, and roll tightly. Wrap half with a napkin and serve immediately. If you are using pita, smear the rough side with harissa and finish as above.

ABOVE: *Spreading the mlawi with harissa*

BELOW: *Rolling it with an omelet, on left of picture*

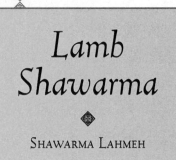

Lamb Shawarma

SHAWARMA LAHMEH

YOU CAN FIND SHAWARMA on every street corner in Lebanon, Syria, and Israel, as well as in many Western countries. Souvlaki is the Greek version, made with pork. The Turkish version, made with lamb or beef, is called doner kebab. Shawarma is a very large, fat "kebab," once made only with lamb but now also with chicken. The meat is sliced into wide, thin pieces, marinated overnight, and threaded onto a long skewer. Between every few pieces there are slices of fat—if chicken is used, the skin is included. The skewer is fixed in front of a vertical grill and left to rotate next to moderate heat for 2–3 hours, or until the meat is cooked through. During cooking, the fat melts down the whole length of the "kebab," basting it and keeping it moist.

Even before the meat is cooked all the way through, the shawarma seller starts slicing the outer, cooked layer to order and piles the thin slivers of meat onto pita bread. On top of the meat go sliced tomatoes, onion, pickles, herbs, and tahini sauce if the meat is lamb or garlic sauce if it is chicken. The bread is rolled tightly over the filling, wrapped partially in paper, and handed to the customer, who may eat it standing by the stall or on the go. Shawarma is not usually prepared at home, but here is a delectable adaptation taught to me by my Lebanese butcher in London. Depending on how much meat you like in your sandwich, the amount given in this recipe will make up to six sandwiches.

MAKES 4–6 SANDWICHES

> 1¾ pounds lamb from the shoulder, thinly sliced (about 3 cups)
>
> 2 medium onions, thinly sliced
>
> juice of 1 lemon, or more to taste
>
> ¼ cup extra-virgin olive oil
>
> ½ teaspoon ground cinnamon
>
> ½ teaspoon ground allspice or 7-spice mixture (see note)
>
> a few sprigs thyme, leaves only
>
> salt
>
> freshly ground black pepper

FOR THE SANDWICHES:

> 2–3 pita bread rounds, about 8 inches in diameter, or 4–6 oval pitas
>
> 4–6 small tomatoes, thinly sliced
>
> ½ medium red onion, very thinly sliced
>
> 4–6 gherkins, thinly sliced lengthwise
>
> ½ teaspoon finely chopped mint
>
> ½ teaspoon finely chopped flat-leaf parsley
>
> tahini sauce (page 71)

1 Put the meat in a large mixing bowl. Add the onions, lemon juice, olive oil, spices, thyme, and salt and pepper to taste and mix well. Let marinate in the refrigerator for 2–4 hours, stirring occasionally.

2 Place a large sauté pan over medium-high heat. When it is very hot, add the meat and sauté for a couple of minutes, or until done to your liking.

3 If you are using round pita bread, tear them open at the seam to have 4 to 6 separate layers. Arrange equal quantities of meat down the middle of each layer. Garnish with equal quantities of tomato, onion, gherkins, and herbs and drizzle on as much tahini sauce as you like. Roll each sandwich quite tight. Wrap the bottom half of the sandwiches with a paper napkin and serve immediately. If you are using oval pita bread, open at the seam to create a large pocket. Spread the bottom half with the tahini sauce and fill each pita with equal amounts of sandwich ingredients. Serve immediately.

Note: 7-spice mixture is a Lebanese blend. The spices and quantities vary from one place to another but the blend usually includes black and white pepper, cinnamon, allspice, cloves, nutmeg, and coriander. It is available in Middle Eastern markets.

Chicken Shawarma

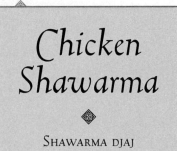

SHAWARMA DJAJ

MIDAN IS A POPULAR food area in Damascus, Syria, and is particularly fun during Ramadan. It was there that I had chicken shawarma with a difference—the chicken was sandwiched inside kibbé balls instead of bread. Even the marinade used for the chicken was different: a blend of tomato paste and crushed garlic seasoned with cayenne, 7-spice mixture, and salt. The vendor rolled the kibbé balls into the fat dripping from the shawarma and stood them against the bottom part of the grill to heat up while he spread garlic mayonnaise and pomegranate molasses over a paper platter. He then arranged a few slices of pickles, tomato, and cucumber along one half and lined the halved kibbé balls on the other. Into these he stuffed a generous amount of chicken shawarma. Because the less common kibbé balls take a long time to prepare and because the vendor refused to divulge his secret, I am sticking to the Lebanese version I know.

MAKES 4 SANDWICHES

 2–3 organic or free-range chicken breasts (about 1 pound)

 ½ cup thinly sliced onion

 juice of 1 lemon

 scant ½ cup extra-virgin olive oil

 ¼ teaspoon ground cinnamon

 ¼ teaspoon ground allspice or 7-spice mixture (page 131)

 ¼ teaspoon finely ground black pepper

 salt

 a few sprigs thyme, leaves only

FOR THE SANDWICHES:

 2 pita bread rounds, about 8 inches in diameter, or 4 oval pitas

 2 small tomatoes, thinly sliced

 1 small red onion, very thinly sliced

 4 gherkins, thinly sliced lengthwise

 2 tablespoons finely chopped mint

 2 tablespoons finely chopped flat-leaf parsley

Cutting chicken shawarma in Midan, Damascus, Syria

1 Put the chicken breasts in a mixing bowl with the onion, lemon juice, olive oil, spices. salt to taste, and thyme and stir well. Let marinate in the refrigerator for 2–4 hours, stirring occasionally.

2 Preheat the oven to 350 degrees.

3 Place the chicken breasts in a roasting pan and bake in the preheated oven for 25–30 minutes, or until done.

4 Remove the chicken breasts from the oven and take off and discard the skin. Shred the chicken into slivers.

5 If you are using round pita bread, tear them open at the seam to have 4 separate layers. Spread as much garlic sauce as you like down the middle of each and arrange equal quantities of chicken over the garlic sauce. Garnish the chicken with equal quantities of tomato, onion, gherkins, and herbs and roll the bread tightly around the filling. Wrap the bottom of the sandwiches with a napkin and serve immediately. If you are using oval pita bread, open at the seam to create a large pocket. Spread the bottom half with the garlic sauce and fill each pita with equal amounts of sandwich ingredients. Serve immediately.

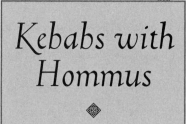

Kebabs with Hommus

THERE IS A VERY successful mini-chain in Lebanon called Kebabji (meaning "kebab maker"), which, not surprisingly, specializes in kebab sandwiches: kefta, shish kebab, or shish tawüq (pages 166, 158, 163). The training of the sandwich makers is quite impressive. They can make up to a dozen sandwiches in one go. First they lay the opened pita rounds in a row, each slightly overlapping the other but leaving the middle free. Each pita is spread with a little hommus down the middle. Then whatever kebabs you have ordered are pulled off the skewer and laid on the hommus, and finally a few slices of pickles are scattered alongside the meat. After that, each sandwich is pulled from underneath the one above, rolled, wrapped in paper, and stuffed inside a Kebabji-branded paper bag. All is done so quickly that it is quite mesmerizing to watch. The only snag to this super efficiency and speed is that you still have to wait for your meat to cook on the charcoal barbecue behind the sandwich counter. Yet it is quite reassuring to see that the meat is cooked to order and not left sitting around, getting dry until the next order.

MAKES 8 SANDWICHES

> 4 medium pita bread rounds, opened at the seam to create 8 layers
> hommus (page 68)
> kebabs (pages 158–63)
> 2 pickled cucumbers or 8 pickled peppers, thinly sliced lengthwise

Lay the pita layers, rough side up, next to each other and spread 2–3 tablespoons hommus down the middle of each. Divide the meat and pickles equally among the layers and roll the bread tightly around the filling. Wrap the bottom half of each sandwich with paper napkins and serve immediately.

Jerusalem Mix

◆

Morav Yorushalmi

JERUSALEM MIX IS SOLD in sandwiches or served on a plate with pita bread and a small mezze of chili and tahini sauces, French fries, and pickles. The stalls stay open until very late at night so people can stop by on their way home after an evening out on the town. I give the authentic recipe here because it is so typical of Israeli street food, but you can make your own mixture of different meats, as long as the texture of the cuts you choose is similar to the ones you are replacing.

MAKES 4 SANDWICHES

1 chicken breast

6–7 chicken hearts

4 chicken livers

3–4 lamb's kidneys

6 ounces rump steak

2 lamb's testicles

2 medium onions, thinly sliced

1 clove garlic, crushed

¼ cup extra-virgin olive oil

½ teaspoon ground turmeric

½ teaspoon curry powder

½ teaspoon ground coriander

½ teaspoon ground sumac

½ teaspoon ground allspice

½ teaspoon ground cumin

¼ teaspoon ground cardamom

⅛ teaspoon ground cloves

salt

freshly ground black pepper

4 pita bread ovals

onion and parsley salad (page 42)

pickled hot chilies

1 Cut the different meats into bite-sized cubes and put in a large mixing bowl. Add the onions, garlic, oil, spices, and salt and pepper to taste and mix well. Let marinate for 30 minutes.

2 Place a large frying pan over high heat. When it is hot, place the meat mixture in the pan. Sauté for about 5 minutes, or until done to your liking.

3 Open the pitas at the seam, halfway down, and fill with equal quantities of meat. Top with onion and parsley salad and serve immediately with pickled hot chilies.

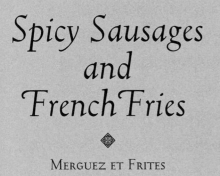

Spicy Sausages and French Fries

◆

MERGUEZ ET FRITES

MERGUEZ (FROM THE ARABIC word *merkaz*) are long, thin, spicy lamb sausages that are originally North African, but have now been completely adopted by the French. I haven't seen this sandwich anywhere in North Africa, but it is quite common in France, sold all over the Quartier Latin in Paris or at beach stalls in the south. It is not necessarily the healthiest sandwich you can eat. If you buy it on the street, I recommend you choose your place quite carefully. I prefer to make it at home using good merguez from my butcher.

MAKES 2 SANDWICHES

vegetable oil for frying

salt

1 pound potatoes, peeled, dried, and cut into sticks for French fries

4 merguez, each about 6 inches long (about ¾ pound)

1 baguette, cut crosswise in half and each half split open lengthwise

1 Pour enough vegetable oil in a large frying pan to deep-fry the potatoes and place over medium-high heat.

2 Salt the cut potatoes to taste. When the oil is hot—dip 1 piece of potato in the oil; if bubbles surround it, the oil is ready—drop in as many potatoes as will fit comfortably in the pan and fry until crisp and golden. Remove and place on several layers of paper towels to soak up the maximum amount of fat.

3 Sauté the merguez in a nonstick pan over medium-high heat for 5–7 minutes, or until they are done. Don't overcook them or they will become dry. Place on paper towels to drain off the fat.

4 Make the sandwiches as soon as the potatoes are ready. Divide the fries equally between the baguette halves, put 2 merguez sausages in each, and wrap the bottom half with a paper napkin. Serve immediately.

THERE ARE TWO WAYS of eating mussels on the street in Turkey, stuffed and steamed (page 64) or threaded onto skewers and fried. In Anadolu Kavagi, a fishing village north of Istanbul on the Asian side, I have seen vendors prepare fresh anchovies the same way. Frying skewered mussels or anchovies is not so easily done in a home kitchen unless you have a very large frying pan to accommodate the skewers. But you can fry them individually, which the Turks also do. I prefer to use batter instead of caking the mussels in flour and dipping them in water as they do in Turkey. The fritters end up much lighter.

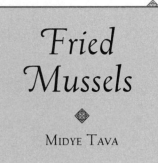

Fried Mussels

❖

MIDYE TAVA

The following batter recipe comes from a place far removed from the Mediterranean, the French Laundry in Napa Valley. During a stay at the Culinary Institute of America in St. Helena, I was given the recipe by Bill Briwa, who had worked at the French Laundry before joining the teaching staff of the CIA.

MAKES 6 SANDWICHES

FOR THE BATTER:

1½ cups unbleached all-purpose flour

just under ⅓ cup cornstarch

1 tablespoon salt

½ tablespoon baking soda

1¼ cups sparkling water

TO FINISH:

vegetable oil for frying

45 large mussels, steamed and shucked (see Note, below), or 36 fresh anchovies

salad garnish (a few lettuce leaves, trimmed scallions, sliced tomato, and a handful of flat-leaf parsley leaves)

tarator (page 71)

lemon wedges

3 baguettes, cut crosswise in half and each half split open lengthwise

1 Combine the batter ingredients and whisk until the mixture is smooth. Cover with a cloth and set aside.

2 Pour enough oil in a large frying pan to deep-fry the mussels and place over medium-high heat. Test the oil by throwing a drop of batter into it; if bubbles surround the batter, the oil is ready. Drop a few mussels in the batter. Stir them to coat evenly, then remove one by one; let the excess batter slide off and drop into the hot oil. Fry for half a minute or so on each side or until golden all over. Remove with a slotted spoon and place on several layers of paper towels. Sprinkle with salt if necessary. It is a good idea to skim the oil clean after each batch so you won't have burned bits of batter clinging to the fritters.

3 To make sandwiches, divide the mussels among the baguette halves, add a salad garnish, and drizzle with tarator. Or serve immediately pricked with toothpicks with the tarator dip and lemon wedges.

Note: If you are using fresh mussels, you need to steam them for 3 minutes before taking them out of their shells and frying them; be sure to discard the mussels that do not open. If you want to use anchovies, make sure they are very fresh; for this you need either a good fishmonger or a place near the sea.

Fried skewered anchovies ready to be slipped into bread in Anadolu Kavagi

Making a fried mussel sandwich

Turkish "Kibbé"

◆

ÇIG KÖFTE

ÇIG KÖFTE IS A regional dish from Sanli Urfa in southeastern Turkey, where it is made at its best. It is a strange dish to find on the streets. A mixture of raw meat and bulgur, it is not the most suitable to be kept in unrefrigerated conditions. Yet it is wheeled around in carts or carried on trays either already rolled into sandwiches or as is, hawked to diners in open-air restaurants for them to buy and add to their mezze. Fortunately, it is sold only in winter. Even then, I did not have the courage to try it on the street. However, it is very tasty when made at home, either to serve as part of a mezze or to use in sandwiches. Just be sure you buy exceptionally fresh meat from a reputable butcher.

MAKES 4 SANDWICHES

4 scallions, trimmed

1 clove garlic

½ cup coarsely chopped flat-leaf parsley

5 ounces finely ground lamb from the leanest part of the leg
    (about ¾ cup)

1½ teaspoons tomato paste

1 teaspoon crushed red pepper flakes, or less to taste

¼ teaspoon ground cloves

¼ teaspoon ground cumin

¼ teaspoon ground cinnamon

¼ teaspoon ground allspice

⅛ teaspoon ground ginger

salt

freshly ground black pepper

⅔ cup fine bulgur

FOR THE SANDWICHES:

> 2 medium pita bread rounds, opened at the seam to create 4 layers
>
> 4–6 lettuce leaves, torn into smallish pieces
>
> 1 tomato, thinly sliced
>
> handful of flat-leaf parsley leaves
>
> 2–4 scallions, trimmed and thinly sliced lengthwise
>
> 1–2 radishes, thinly sliced

1 Put the scallions and garlic in a food processor and process until very finely chopped. Add the parsley and pulse a few times until well blended. Transfer to a mixing bowl. Add the meat, tomato paste, red pepper flakes, spices, and salt and pepper to taste.

2 Rinse the bulgur under cold water, drain well, and add to the meat. Mix with your hands until the meat and bulgur are well blended. Lightly wet your hands and shape the mixture into 8 flat sausage-like shapes, about 6 inches long.

3 Lay the pita layers rough side up. Place 2 "sausages" in the middle of each layer. Scatter equal amounts of the salad ingredients over the meat, sprinkle with a little salt, and roll the bread tightly. Wrap the bottom half of each sandwich with a paper napkin and serve immediately.

Fried Bread

Fricassée

TUNISIANS SPECIALIZE IN GIVING their dishes confusing names. Their tajine has nothing to do with the Moroccan tagines (pages 194–99) and their fricassée, which describes the following sandwich, has nothing to do with the French fricassée. And no Tunisian I have met has been able to explain why.

MAKES 6–8 SANDWICHES

FOR THE DOUGH:

1 teaspoon active dry yeast

2 cups unbleached all-purpose flour

⅛ teaspoon salt

½ egg, beaten

2 teaspoons extra-virgin olive oil

vegetable oil for frying

FOR THE FILLING:

1 tablespoon harissa (page 67), diluted with 1 tablespoon water

1 medium potato, boiled

½ cup flaked canned tuna

¼ cup pitted and halved black olives

2 teaspoons capers

1 Stir the yeast into ⅓ cup warm water and leave for 10 minutes.

2 Sift the flour into a mixing bowl. Add the salt, egg, and oil and work them into the flour. Add the yeast water and knead until you have a smooth dough. You may need a little more water. Let rest for 1½ hours, or until doubled in size.

3 While the dough is rising boil, peel and slice the potato for the filling. Set aside.

4 Punch the dough down and roll it out to just over ½ inch thick. Cut the dough with a 4-inch biscuit cutter or glass—you should end up with 6 to 8 pieces, depending on how thickly you have rolled the dough. Let rise for another 30 minutes.

5 Ten minutes before the dough is ready, pour enough oil in a large frying pan to deep-fry the breads and place over medium heat. When the oil has reached 375 degrees, drop in as many pieces of dough as will fit comfortably in the pan. Remember that they will puff up and expand during cooking. Fry until golden all over, 2–3 minutes on each side. Remove with a slotted spoon and drain on several layers of paper towels. Let cool until warm, cut open the breads, spread with harissa, then fill with equal amounts of sliced potato and the remaining sandwich ingredients. Serve immediately.

ABOVE: *What is left after the dough for fricassée has been rolled and cut out*

RIGHT: *Frying fricassée*

Spicy Fish

SAMKEH HARRAH

USKUDAR, ON THE ASIAN side across from the Dolmabahçe Palace in Istanbul, is known for its boat restaurants, where you can either stop for a fish sandwich or sit down to a meal of grilled mackerel and salad. The fish boats have become a tourist attraction, still fun to visit even though the mackerel is the frozen large Norwegian type and not the smaller, far more delicious local one. Another great place for fish on the street is the mina (fishing port) in Tripoli, Lebanon. A fleet of small fishing boats is moored just below the pavement, and set back from the road is a cluster of gorgeous old houses, sadly falling to ruin. Beyond these is a row of very modest-looking cafés where you can have two of the best sandwiches in Lebanon: samkeh harrah (spicy fish) and akhtabout (octopus). Both are prepared more or less in the same way, except that the sauce for the fish has tahini and that for the octopus doesn't. Here I give a recipe for the spicy fish sandwich that was given to me by Maher Jaber, third-generation owner of Mat'am Jaber (Restaurant Jaber). The fish used in Lebanon is gray mullet, but here I suggest using cod, which is more readily available.

If you want to make the sandwiches with octopus, sauté the cilantro and garlic with all the seasonings as described below and add lemon juice to taste. Once cooled, mix with chopped boiled octopus. Make the sandwiches with the same garnish.

MAKES 6 SANDWICHES

> 2 pounds cod fillet
>
> 3 tablespoons extra-virgin olive oil
>
> 4 cloves garlic, crushed
>
> 1 cup finely chopped cilantro
>
> ½ teaspoon ground coriander
>
> ½ teaspoon ground cumin
>
> ½ teaspoon crushed red pepper flakes
>
> tarator (page 71; see step 4, below)

FOR THE SANDWICHES:

> 12 large slices whole wheat bread, toasted (see note, page 148)
>
> garlic sauce (page 72)
>
> 1 medium tomato, thinly sliced
>
> 1 cup shredded lettuce
>
> salt

1 Preheat the oven to 350 degrees.

2 Lay the cod fillet, skin side down, on a rack in a baking dish. Bake the fish for 25–30 minutes or until it is just done. You do not want to overcook the fish or it will turn rubbery. Let cool. Flake into small pieces, cover, and set aside.

3 Heat the oil in a frying pan and sauté the garlic, cilantro, and ground coriander, stirring all the time, until the aroma rises. Then add the cumin and red pepper flakes, mix well, and remove from the heat. Set aside.

4 Make the tarator with ½ cup water and no garlic and pour into a small saucepan. Place over medium heat and bring to a boil, stirring regularly. When the sauce begins to boil, add the sautéed garlic and cilantro and simmer for about 5 minutes, or until the oil rises to the surface. Remove from the heat and let cool.

5 Drain the liquid from the fish and add to the tarator sauce. Mix well, then taste and adjust the seasoning.

6 Toast the bread slices and spread them with a little garlic sauce. Divide the fish equally among 6 slices, scatter equal amounts of tomato and lettuce over the fish, and sprinkle with a little salt. Lay the rest of the bread slices over the filling and cut each sandwich in half diagonally. Serve immediately.

Note: You can also use the fish as a topping for crostini. Toast 6 slices of brown or other bread and spread each with garlic sauce. Spread a little shredded lettuce over the garlic and cover with equal amounts of the fish mixture. Scatter a small amount of finely diced tomatoes all over and sprinkle with a little sea salt. Serve immediately with lemon wedges.

In Tripoli the sandwiches are made with pita bread. They open the bread at the seams and lay the 2 layers on top of each other, rough side up. A little garlic sauce is spread down the middle, and a generous amount of fish mixture is spooned onto the bread. The sandwich is then folded in half and placed in a hot sandwich press until slightly crisp. Then tomato and lettuce are added and the whole is finished with a sprinkling of salt. The sandwich is wrapped in paper on the bottom half and handed to the customer. If you don't have a sandwich/panini press at home, you can create the same effect by lightly toasting the sandwich in a skillet.

PAN BAGNAT (MEANING "SOAKED bread") is the classic sandwich of the South of France. Although originally a specialty of Nice, it is now available everywhere along the French Riviera and even across the water in Corsica. The recipe below is a classic as far as the ingredients are concerned, although the method is not. You are not really supposed to pound the garlic, anchovies, and olives together. The garlic should be rubbed into the bread and the olives and anchovies coarsely chopped, but I find that the crushed ingredients stay better inside the sandwich and the taste is pretty much unchanged, a little more garlicky perhaps. The filling can be varied endlessly, regardless of how authentic the ingredients. To the basic ingredients given below, you can add whatever takes your fancy, as long as the combination is harmonious and tasty. I sometimes add tuna, other times hard-boiled eggs, and, if I feel like a pungent crunch, I will insert a few slices of red onion.

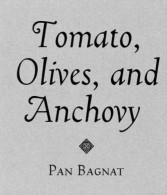

Tomato,
Olives, and
Anchovy

◆

PAN BAGNAT

MAKES 2 SANDWICHES

1 clove garlic

sea salt

½ cup good black olives, pitted

1 2-ounce can anchovy fillets in olive oil (10–12 fillets)

juice of ¼ lemon

2 round loaves French bread, 4 to 5 inches in diameter, with a crust similar to baguette, or 2 pieces of focaccia (page 77), 4 inches sqaure

4 tablespoons extra-virgin olive oil

2 large firm ripe tomatoes, coarsely chopped

2 yellow bell peppers, grilled (see page 32), peeled, and sliced into long strips

freshly ground black pepper

1 Put the garlic and a little salt in a mortar and crush with a pestle until you have a fine paste. Add the olives and drained anchovies and continue pounding until you have a textured purée. Stir in the lemon juice.

2 Slice the top off the bread loaves and hollow them out, leaving enough crumb to absorb the filling. Drizzle 2 tablespoons olive oil inside each loaf and spread half the olive mixture over the bottom of each. Add equal quantities of tomato and grilled peppers and season with black pepper to taste. You will not need any extra salt, as the anchovies are pretty salty. Place the sliced top back on and let sit for about 10 minutes so that the bread soaks up the oil and other juices. If you use focaccia, be careful not to spread the filling all the way to the edges or it will ooze out while you are eating the sandwich.

French Fries

TRAVELING TO TRIPOLI FROM Beirut by bus seems to be everybody's favorite way of getting there. Taxis are too expensive, and driving entails circling endlessly around a heavily congested city to find a parking space. The buses, on the other hand, are very reliable, and the better ones are equipped with air-conditioning (essential in the summer) and television (not necessarily a bonus). And they are very cheap: only $1.00 for more than an hour's ride. They all stop at the "clock" square at the entrance of the city, where you'll find a row of sandwich places on one side and a group of street food vendors on the other, not far from the entrance to the souks.

On a trip back from Aleppo, I finally tried their specialties. We had traveled all day, and because it was Ramadan, we were unable to buy anything decent to eat in Syria. Luckily, we arrived in Tripoli just as the sun was setting, the time for Muslim faithfuls to break their fast. My driver asked for a French fries sandwich and I ordered falafel. My falafel was not so good, too dry and rather stodgy. But his fried potato sandwich looked scrumptious: masses of crisp, hot fries sprinkled with lemon juice and rolled in pita bread spread with garlic sauce.

MAKES 4 SANDWICHES

> vegetable oil for frying
>
> 1 pound potatoes, peeled, dried, and cut into sticks to make French fries
>
> salt
>
> 2 medium pita bread rounds, opened at the seam to create 4 layers
>
> garlic sauce (page 72)
>
> juice of ½ lemon, or more to taste

1 Prepare and deep-fry the potatoes as in the recipe on page 138.

2 Spread the rough side of the pita bread with as much garlic sauce as you like. Divide the fries equally among the pitas. Sprinkle with lemon juice and more salt to taste and roll the bread tightly around the potatoes. Wrap the bottom half of each sandwich in a paper napkin and serve immediately. You can add some cabbage salad (page 38) for a fresher taste.

Falafel

FALAFEL, TOGETHER WITH TABBŪLÉ and hommus, is now part of the global menu. However, these tasty vegetarian patties are originally Egyptian, and in Egypt they are known as ta'miyah. The Egyptian ta'miyah is rather different from the Lebanese/Syrian falafel, softer and starchier. The sandwiches are also made differently. Egyptian pita is smaller and thicker, and when made with coarsely ground whole wheat, it is called aysh baladi. The bread is cut crosswise in half, and the pocket opened and filled with the ta'miyah and garnish. Lebanese/Syrian pita, on the other hand, is large, round, and very thin. It is opened at the seam, and the two layers are placed one on top of the other with the rough side up. The filling is then arranged down the middle and the bread rolled around it. As for the garnish, in Egypt you can have potato chips or French fries, shredded lettuce or tomatoes, radishes or pickles. In Lebanon/Syria the choice is generally herbs, tomatoes, and pickles. Only the tahini sauce is a constant in both countries, although its name differs: tahina in Egypt and tarator in Lebanon.

MAKES 4–6 SANDWICHES

½ cup dried chickpeas, soaked overnight in plenty of water
    with ½ teaspoon baking soda

1 cup peeled split dried fava beans,* soaked overnight
    in plenty of water with 1 teaspoon baking soda

5 large cloves garlic, peeled

1 medium onion, peeled and quartered

1 small leek, washed, trimmed, and cut into 2 or 3 pieces

1 cup fresh cilantro leaves

1 teaspoon ground cumin

1 teaspoon ground allspice or 7-spice mixture (page 131)

¼ teaspoon finely ground black pepper

⅛ teaspoon cayenne pepper

salt

1 teaspoon baking soda

vegetable oil for deep-frying

*You may find it difficult to source peeled, split fava beans. In such a case, replace with an equal amount of chickpeas. The texture of the falafel will be slightly drier but the taste will be just as good.

FOR THE SANDWICHES:

4–6 pita bread rounds, cut in half moons

tarator (page 71), made with chopped parsley

1–2 tomatoes, diced

2 pickled cucumbers, quartered lengthwise

4–6 sweet chili pickles, cut in half lengthwise

2 pickled turnips, thinly sliced

1 Drain the chickpeas and fava beans and rinse under cold water. Put in a blender with the onion, leek, cilantro, spices, and salt to taste; process into a smooth paste. If your blender is too small, process in batches. Transfer to a mixing bowl and add the baking soda. Taste and adjust the seasoning if necessary and let rest for 30 minutes in the refrigerator.

2 Pinch off a handful of the falafel mixture and shape between the palms of your hands into a fat round cake with tapering sides, 2 to 2½ inches in diameter. Place on a plate and continue making the cakes until you have used up the mixture. You should have about 16 falafels, depending on how fat you have made them. But don't make them too fat, or else the falafels will not cook through.

3 Heat enough vegetable oil in a large frying pan to deep-fry the falafels. When the oil is hot—test with the edge of a cake; if the oil bubbles around it, it is ready—drop in as many as will fit comfortably in the pan. Fry until golden, about 2 minutes on each side. Remove with a slotted spoon and drain on several layers of paper towels. Lay another double layer of paper towels on top and pat the falafels to absorb as much oil as you can. Continue frying and draining until all the falafels are cooked. Serve hot or warm with the pita bread, tarator, and an accompaniment of diced tomatoes, pickled cucumbers, sweet chili peppers, and turnips for people to make their own sandwich by stuffing the pita pockets with falafel and their choice of garnish.

Cannellini Bean Salad

Fasulye Piyazi

THIS POPULAR SANDWICH FROM Turkey, which you can buy from any number of street sellers, makes an ideal light meal for vegetarians. Be sure to dress the beans while still hot, as they will absorb the seasoning better.

MAKES 4 SANDWICHES

1 cup cannellini beans, soaked overnight in plenty of water with ½ teaspoon baking soda

salt

1 small onion, thinly sliced

6 cocktail gherkins, sliced into thin half rounds

½ cup finely chopped flat-leaf parsley

¼ cup green or black olives, pitted and halved or quartered

juice of ½ lemon, or more to taste

4 tablespoons extra-virgin olive oil

2 pita bread ovals, half opened at the seam lengthwise

1 Drain and rinse the beans and put in a large saucepan. Cover well with water and place over medium heat. Bring to a boil, reduce the heat to low, and simmer, covered, for 45 minutes or until tender but not mushy. Add salt just before the beans are done. Drain well and transfer to a large mixing bowl.

2 Add the sliced onion, gherkins, parsley, and olives. Pour in the lemon juice and olive oil and toss. Taste and adjust the seasoning if necessary. Let cool before spooning into the pitas. Drizzle with a little more olive oil if you like and sprinkle with a few specks of fleur de sel. Serve immediately.

PANINI ARE AMONGST MY favorite sandwiches. The first time I visited Genoa on my way back from Portofino, I tried every, or what seemed like every, panini bar in the old town to see which had the best sandwiches. Most of the sandwiches were very good and the variety tremendous: different breads, a wide choice of cured meats and cheeses or vegetables, and the option to have the sandwich toasted or not.

Grilled Vegetables and Cheese

◆

PANINI CON MOZZARELLA E VERDURE

MAKES 4 SANDWICHES

1 large eggplant, cut lengthwise into ¼-inch slices

2 medium zucchini, cut lengthwise into ¼-inch slices

extra-virgin olive oil

8 slices good white bread

salt

1 handful fresh basil leaves

8–12 ¼-inch slices mozzarella

1 Preheat the broiler.

2 Brush the eggplant and zucchini slices with a little olive oil on both sides. Broil the zucchini for 3–5 minutes on each side and the eggplant for 8–10 minutes on each side.

3 While the vegetables are broiling, brush the bread slices with a little oil, sprinkle with a little salt, and cover 4 with the basil leaves.

4 When the vegetables are done, remove from under the broiler and let cool.

5 Spread the basil-lined bread slices with equal amounts of eggplant, mozzarella, and zucchini, sprinkling each layer with salt to taste. Cover with the remaining bread and serve. Or if you have a sandwich toaster, toast for 2–3 minutes, or until the bread is golden and crisp. Serve immediately.

BARBECUES

Turkish Kebabs ✦ *Shish Kebabi*

Greek Kebabs ✦ *Souvlakia*

Lebanese Kebabs ✦ *Lahm Meshwi*

Moroccan Kebabs and Pinchitos Morunos

Chicken Kebabs ✦ *Shish Tawüq*

Lebanese Kefta ✦ *Kafta*

Moroccan Kefta ✦ *Kefta*

Swordfish Brochettes ✦ *Qothane del Hüt*

Preparing kebabs in Jame' el Fna, Marrakesh

Turkish Kebabs

◈

SHISH KEBABI

ONE OF THE EARLIEST references to kebabs is found in an eleventh-century Turkish dictionary, which describes men as having "competed against each other in skewering meat." Kebabs were disseminated all over the Middle East and North Africa by the Turks during the Ottoman Empire. Each country, however, has a different way of marinating the meat and sometimes of cutting it. In Greece the chunks of meat are quite large; in Turkey, Lebanon, and Syria they are medium-sized, while in Morocco the meat is cut very small. In Syria the word *kebab* describes minced meat wrapped around skewers and grilled. These long, sausage-like pieces of grilled meat are known as kefta or kofta, depending on where you are. The Greek variation on kefta, keftethes, refers to grilled minced meat patties. In Lebanon kibbé is also wrapped around skewers. And whenever you get to the seaside, grilled fish or fish kebabs will take precedence over meat. But it is a small town in Turkey, Gaziantep, in southern Anatolia, that is renowned for the excellence and variety of its kebabs. Most people think of kebabs as simply grilled meat, but they can also be baked or stewed, although you are not likely to find these more elaborate versions on the street. Kebabs are always served with bread and either plain rice or salad.

This is the master recipe for the following three variations.

SERVES 4

FOR THE MARINADE:

3 cloves garlic, crushed

3 tablespoons extra-virgin olive oil

1 tablespoon tomato paste

½ teaspoon paprika

¼ teaspoon cayenne pepper

¼ teaspoon ground allspice

¼ teaspoon ground cinnamon

¼ teaspoon ground cumin

1–2 tablespoons fresh thyme leaves

salt to taste

freshly ground black pepper to taste

TO FINISH:

1¾ pounds lamb from the leg, skinned, trimmed of most fat, and cut into 1-inch cubes

20–24 cherry tomatoes

1 Put all the marinade ingredients in a large bowl and mix well. Add the meat and toss. Let marinate for at least 2 hours, stirring regularly.

2 Start a charcoal fire or preheat the broiler.

3 Thread the meat onto 7 long skewers and the tomatoes onto an eighth one. Grill over high heat for 3–4 minutes on each side, or until the meat and tomatoes are done to your liking.

Greek Kebabs

◆

SOUVLAKIA

SOUVLAKIA IS ALSO THE name used to describe the Greek version of doner kebab or shawarma (page 130). You can make delicious sandwiches with these kebabs by sliding the grilled meat into pita bread and topping it with tzatziki (page 73). Or you can make bruschetta *à la grecque* by piling the cooked meat onto grilled slices of good bread and drizzling with tzatziki. For the same amount of meat as in the master recipe (page 158), use:

3 tablespoons extra-virgin olive oil

juice of ½ lemon, or more to taste

1½ tablespoons dried oregano

2 cloves garlic, crushed

salt to taste

freshly ground black pepper to taste

16–18 bay leaves

1 Combine all the ingredients except the bay leaves, add the cubed meat, and leave for a couple of hours, turning the meat regularly in the marinade.

2 Thread the meat onto 8 long skewers, inserting a bay leaf between every 2 or 3 pieces. Grill and serve as indicated in the master recipe.

THIS LEBANESE MARINADE IS closer to the Turkish than to the Greek, although it has no tomato paste. For the same amount of meat as in the master recipe (page 158), use:

8 cloves garlic, crushed

2 tablespoons extra-virgin olive oil

juice of 1 lemon, or more to taste

⅛ teaspoon ground cinnamon

½ teaspoon ground allspice or 7-spice mixture (page 131)

pinch cayenne pepper

salt to taste

freshly ground black pepper to taste

14–16 baby onions, peeled

Lebanese Kebabs

❖

LAHM MESHWI

1 Combine all the ingredients except the baby onions, add the cubed meat, and leave for a couple of hours, turning the meat regularly in the marinade.

2 Thread the meat onto 8 long skewers, inserting a baby onion in between every 2 or 3 pieces. Grill as indicated in the master recipe and serve very hot, wrapped in pita bread.

Moroccan Kebabs and Pinchitos Morunos

HERE IS A DRY marinade for Moroccan kebabs. I found a recipe for very similar kebabs in Elisabeth Luard's *Flavors of Andalucia*. The kebabs, Luard tells us, are called pinchitos morunos (Moorish kebabs). They are sold in fairgrounds that are set up during various festivals in Cadiz. According to Luard, "A skewerful (often a fine steel knitting needle which you are honor-bound to return) of tiny pieces of meat, marinated in a mixture of Moorish spices, are deftly turned over a small oblong brazier of glowing coals, each to order, by a 'Moor' in a scarlet fez. The scent of the fire-roasted meat curls up the streets, drawing the crowds to the fairground as seductively as the flashing lights and booming music."

The Moroccan marinade below is somewhat different from the one for pinchitos morunos, which follows. For the same amount of meat as in the master recipe (page 158), use:

> 2 medium onions thinly sliced
>
> ½ cup finely chopped flat-leaf parsley
>
> 1 teaspoon ground cumin
>
> salt to taste
>
> finely ground black pepper to taste

FOR LUARD'S PINCHITOS MORUNOS, use:

> 3 tablespoons extra-virgin olive oil
>
> 1½ teaspoons whole cumin seeds
>
> 1½ teaspoons ground coriander
>
> 1½ teaspoons turmeric
>
> ¾ teaspoon chili powder
>
> salt to taste
>
> freshly ground black pepper to taste

Combine the ingredients for either version, marinate and grill as in the previous recipe.

THIS IS AN EXCELLENT variation on meat kebabs. If you like, you can replace the boned chicken with drumsticks or chicken wings.

SERVES 4–6

FOR THE GARLIC MARINADE:

> 8 large cloves garlic, crushed
>
> 2 tablespoons extra-virgin olive oil
>
> juice of 1 lemon, or more to taste
>
> ½ teaspoon ground allspice or 7-spice mixture (page 131)
>
> ⅛ teaspoon ground cinnamon
>
> pinch cayenne pepper
>
> salt to taste
>
> freshly ground black pepper to taste

TO FINISH:

> 1¾ pounds boneless chicken meat, both white and dark, cut into 1-inch cubes
>
> garlic sauce (page 72)
>
> 1 large pita bread round, opened at the seam, plus more to serve with the kebabs, cabbage salad (page 38)

Chicken Kebabs

◆

SHISH TAWŪQ

1 Combine the marinade ingredients in a large mixing bowl and stir in the chicken. Marinate for at least 2 hours, turning the chicken regularly.

2 Preheat the broiler or start a charcoal fire—the latter being an unbeatable way to grill the meat and the way you will see meat grilled everywhere on the street.

3 Thread an equal number of chicken cubes onto 8–12 long metal skewers. Don't cram them too close or they won't cook evenly. Grill for 5 minutes on each side or until done to your liking. Once you have finished cooking the chicken, lay the skewers on the opened pita bread, rough side up, and serve hot with the garlic sauce, cabbage salad, and more bread.

Lebanese Kefta

◆

KAFTA

I AM ALWAYS UNCERTAIN about eating kefta (seasoned ground meat) on the street. You never know what has gone into the meat. However, there are many butcher-cum-kebab shops where you can buy the meat, have it ground in front of you, and then barbecued to eat then and there. One such place I went to was a camel butcher in Midan, Damascus. The camel's head hanging outside first attracted my attention. It certainly did not look inviting, yet I could not pass up the chance of tasting camel meat. I went in and ordered half a pound of the best cut to be made into kebabs. The butcher suggested that I have it ground, explaining that camel meat was slightly tougher than mutton. The meat did not taste very different—perhaps a little gamy, with a slightly drier texture. The butcher's seasoning consisted simply of salt and pepper, but the recipe below is a little fancier and uses lamb instead of camel.

SERVES 4

2 medium onions, peeled and quartered

½ cup flat-leaf parsley leaves

1¼ pounds ground lamb from the shoulder

½ teaspoon ground cinnamon

½ teaspoon ground allspice or 7-spice mixture (page 131)

salt to taste

freshly ground black pepper to taste

onion and parsley salad (page 42)

4 medium pita bread rounds

1 Preheat the broiler to high or start a charcoal fire.

2 Put the onions and parsley in a food processor and process until finely chopped. Transfer to a mixing bowl, add the ground meat and seasonings, and mix with your hands until well blended. Pinch a little off, sear in a hot pan, and taste. Adjust the seasoning if necessary, then divide the meat into 12 equal portions.

3 Roll each portion of meat into a ball. Put one in the palm of your hand, take a long skewer, preferably a flat one, as the meat will hold better onto it, and start wrapping the meat around the skewer, squeezing it upward, then downward to bind it around the skewer in the shape of a long sausage. Taper the ends and place on a wire rack, ready to grill or broil. Prepare the rest of the meat in the same way.

4 Cook the meat for 2–3 minutes on each side, or until done to your liking. Serve hot on a bed of onion and parsley salad and pita bread.

Moroccan Kefta

◆

Kefta

MOROCCAN KEFTA IS SEASONED quite differently from the Syrian/Lebanese. First of all, it is made with ras el-hanout, a mixture of more than 20 spices, including cardamom, nutmeg, ginger, the aphrodisiac Spanish fly, and dried roses. Also, it has more herbs. It was in the medina in Tangier that I had my best Moroccan kefta to date. The stall was tiny, with hardly any space for diners. The kefta maker was an old man who moved slowly. My guide knew him well, and he encouraged me to join the line. The kefta was exquisite, well worth the wait. Here is the recipe.

SERVES 4–6

1 medium onion, quartered

¼ cup cilantro leaves

¼ cup flat-leaf parsley leaves

8–10 mint leaves

1–2 tablespoons marjoram leaves

2 pounds ground lamb, preferably from the shoulder

1 teaspoon ground cumin

1 teaspoon paprika

½ teaspoon ground allspice

½ teaspoon crushed red pepper flakes

½ teaspoon ras el-hanout (optional), available at Middle Eastern markets

salt

bread

tomato and onion salad (page 37)

1 Preheat the broiler to high or start a charcoal fire.

2 Put the onion and herbs in a food processor and process until very finely chopped. Transfer to a mixing bowl and add the ground lamb, spices, and salt to taste. Mix with your hands until evenly blended.

3 Divide the meat into 24 equal portions. Roll each portion into a ball and wrap it tightly around a long skewer, preferably a flat one, squeezing the meat up and down to form a sausage 4 or 6 inches long. Pinch it quite thin at each end. Prepare the rest of the meat in the same way.

4 Cook the brochettes under the broiler or over a charcoal fire for 2–3 minutes on each side, or until done to your liking. Serve immediately with good bread and the tomato and onion salad.

Swordfish Brochettes

❖

QOTBANE DEL HÜT

ALTHOUGH KEBABS ARE ONE of the most common street foods in the eastern and southern Mediterranean, the variety on the whole is rather limited to either meat, poultry, or variety meats. The treatment of the meats is also limited to the few marinades in the preceding recipes or simply to a plain seasoning of salt and pepper. It is only when you get to the seaside that the choices will start including fish, and even then, it is not very often that you will see grilled fish on the street. I've never understood why except possibly because of the difficulty of keeping fish fresh without refrigeration. I had the following brochettes in a café on the seashore in Rabat, Morocco. Unfortunately, the Moroccans tend to overcook fish and the brochettes were far too dry. In your kitchen, be sure not to broil them too long.

SERVES 4–6

1½ pounds swordfish, cut into 1-inch cubes

1 cup finely chopped flat-leaf parsley

2 cloves garlic, crushed

¼ teaspoon crushed red pepper flakes

2 teaspoons ground cumin

2 teaspoons paprika

salt to taste

tomato and onion salad (page 37)

1 Put the fish cubes in a mixing bowl. Add the parsley, garlic, and seasonings and combine. Let marinate for at least 2 hours.

2 Preheat the broiler to high or start a charcoal fire.

3 Thread the fish cubes onto 8–12 long skewers and place the brochettes under the preheated broiler, as near the heat as you can. Broil for 2–3 minutes on each side or until done to your liking. Be careful, though—fish becomes quite rubbery and tasteless if cooked too long. Serve immediately with the tomato and onion salad.

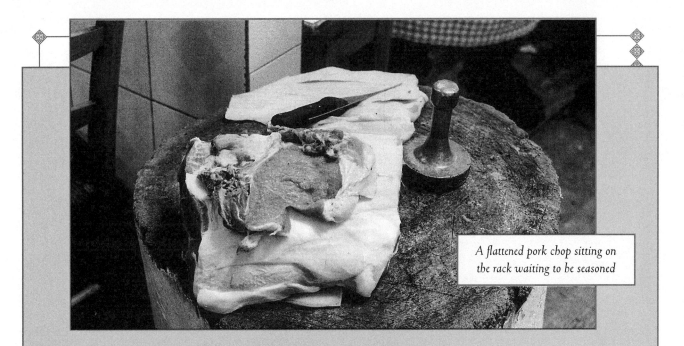

A flattened pork chop sitting on the rack waiting to be seasoned

Grilled Pork Chops

I never liked the idea of eating pork, but not because of any religious prohibition. It's just that when we were children, my mother often gave us pork chops and French fries. I loved the fries, but my mother, like all good Arabs, always overcooked the meat, and I did not like its dry texture. It wasn't until I went to Greece recently that I had a grilled pork chop I really enjoyed. I was strolling through the market in Chania in Crete when I stopped at a small café where the owner was barbecuing a large pork chop. Next to the barbecue was the whole rack of pork laid on a wooden block. It looked very fresh, and the idea of having a pork chop cooked on a charcoal fire was very tempting, even if it wasn't yet lunchtime. I asked for one and watched him cut it off the rack, pound it very flat with a brass implement, then season it with a little oregano, salt, and pepper. He then sandwiched it inside a metal grill and put it over the fire. And he did not overcook it. On the contrary, he left it slightly pink, and I, harking back to my mother's concern about undercooked pork, worried about eating it pink. It was delicious, though, tender and juicy and impeccably seasoned. I will leave it up to you to decide how much seasoning you need for the meat; just remember to go easy on the oregano. Too much and the taste will turn bitter.

Waiting for the tagine in a daily souk near Marrakesh

One-Pot Meals

Baked Lamb with Pasta and Tomatoes ✦ *Yiouvetsi*

Pork and Cannellini Bean Stew ✦ *Hirino me Fasolia*

Lamb and Lettuce Stew ✦ *Arnaki Fricassée me Maroulia*

Baked Stuffed Eggplants ✦ *Melitzanes Papoutsakia*

Octopus and Onion Stew ✦ *Chtapodi Stifado*

Baked Mackerel with Herbs ✦ *Kolioi Lathorigani*

Baked Pasta ✦ *Pasticcio*

Baked Vegetables ✦ *Briami*

Stuffed Tomatoes and Peppers ✦
   Domates Yiemistes me Ryzi

Rice, Lentils, and Vermicelli with Hot Tomato Sauce ✦
   Koshari

Roast Lamb ✦ *Mechoui*

Lamb Stewed with Cumin ✦ *Tangia*

Lamb Tagine with Tomatoes and Potatoes ✦ *L'ham bil Matecha wa B'tata*

Chicken Tagine with Potatoes and Peas ✦ *Djaj bel B'tata wa Jeblana*

Chicken Tagine with Olives and Preserved Lemons ✦ *D'jaj M'chermel*

Lamb Shanks with Chickpeas and Wheat ✦ *Hergma à l'Occidentale*

Couscous ✦ *Kseksü*

Couscous with Seven Vegetables ✦ *Kseksü Bidawi*

Chicken with Moghrabbiyeh ✦ *Moghrabbiyeh ala Dj'ej*

Chicken with Garlic ✦ *Pollo al Ajillo*

Tripe Stew ✦ *Callos*

Paella

ONE OF ATHENS'S GREATEST sites (apart from the Acropolis and other tourist attractions) is the central market, which runs on either side of Athinas Street. It is a bustling place where you can spend hours admiring the marvelous produce and soaking up the atmosphere of a world unchanged by modern progress. If you get hungry at the sight of so much food, you can always stop for a hearty meal at one of the café/restaurants behind the meat section. Street food is always at its best in food markets for two main reasons. First, the market restaurateurs (a rather grand name for the owners of such simple establishments) have constant and immediate access to fresh foods. Second, they are cooking for people who, by the nature of their trade, know a thing or two about good food and expect to be served it.

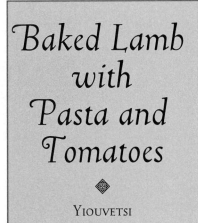

Baked Lamb with Pasta and Tomatoes

YIOUVETSI

SERVES 4

2 tablespoons extra-virgin olive oil

1 14-ounce can peeled tomatoes, finely chopped

6 cloves garlic

1 tablespoon dried oregano

salt

freshly ground black pepper

4 lamb shanks (about 3 pounds)

2 cups orzo or spaghetti broken into 2-inch pieces

1 cup grated Parmesan cheese

1 Preheat the oven to 375 degrees.

2 Pour the olive oil in an oven-to-table baking dish measuring 9 × 13 inches and about 1½ inches deep. Add the tomatoes, garlic, and oregano and stir in 1 cup water. Season with salt and pepper to taste and add the lamb. Bake on the middle shelf of the preheated oven for 1 hour, turning the shanks in the sauce every 15 minutes. The sauce should be very reduced at the end but not dry.

3 Add 2 cups water to the sauce. Stir in the orzo or broken spaghetti and bake for another 20–30 minutes, stirring regularly, or until the sauce is absorbed into the pasta and the pasta is done to your liking. Sprinkle the grated Parmesan all over the pasta. Taste and adjust the seasoning if necessary and serve immediately.

THIS GREEK STEW IS also very much part of the menu in the Turkish esnaf lokantasi, although in Turkey it would never be cooked with pork, only with lamb or beef. We have a similar version in Lebanon, but we never eat it on the street or even in restaurants—the stew is primarily home-cooked.

SERVES 4–6

Pork and Cannellini Bean Stew

◆

HIRINO ME FASOLIA

¼ cup vegetable oil

2 medium onions, thinly sliced

2½ pounds pork, cut into chunks

1¼ cups dried cannellini beans, soaked overnight in plenty of water with 1 teaspoon baking soda

5 tablespoons tomato paste

¼ cup chopped flat-leaf parsley

salt

freshly ground black pepper

1 Put the oil and onions in a flameproof casserole and place over medium heat. Fry, stirring occasionally, until the onions are lightly golden. Add the meat and stir for a few minutes, until it has lost its pink color. Pour in 3 cups water, bring to a boil, and reduce the heat to low. Simmer, covered, for 45 minutes.

2 Drain and rinse the beans and add them to the meat. Stir in the tomato paste and simmer, covered, for another 45 minutes, or until the beans are tender. Add the chopped parsley and salt and pepper to taste and simmer for another 5 minutes. By now the sauce should be really thick; if it is not, uncover the pan, increase the heat to high, and boil, stirring regularly, until thickened. Serve very hot with good bread.

Lamb and Lettuce Stew

ARNAKI FRICASSÉE
ME MAROULIA

FRICASSÉE IS A ANOTHER staple of the market café/restaurants in Greece. In these establishments it often contains less lettuce and the sauce will be quite runny. This dish is ideal for informal dinner parties. You can prepare it well ahead of time and stop at step 2. When you are ready to serve the fricassée, simply reheat the meat and sauce before proceeding with steps 3 and 4. Here the word *fricassée*, a French term to describe meat cooked in white sauce, is used more or less correctly, unlike in the recipe for Tunisian fricassée (page 144).

SERVES 4

3 tablespoons extra-virgin olive oil

3 medium onions, thinly sliced

4 lamb shanks (about 3 pounds)

½ cup chopped dill, plus a little more for the garnish

salt

freshly ground black pepper

1 head romaine lettuce, shredded into thin strips (about 4 cups)

2 eggs

juice of 1½ lemons, or more to taste

plain cooked rice or noodles

1 Put the oil and sliced onions in a large saucepan and fry over medium heat until soft and transparent. Add the shanks and brown all over. Add 2 cups water and bring to a boil. Stir in the dill, season with salt and pepper to taste, and reduce the heat to medium-low. Cover the pan and simmer, stirring occasionally, for 1 hour, or until the meat is tender.

2 Add the shredded lettuce and simmer, covered, for another 10–15 minutes, or until the lettuce is completely wilted.

3 Beat the eggs in a large mixing bowl, add the lemon juice, and blend well before gradually adding a ladle of hot broth from the fricassée pan.

4 Remove the fricassée from the heat and transfer the shanks to a serving platter. Slowly pour the egg and lemon mixture into the sauce, stirring all the time—you will notice the sauce becoming lighter in color. Return to very low heat and, still stirring, cook for a minute or so for the sauce to thicken slightly—don't let it boil or it will curdle. Pour the sauce over the shanks. Serve hot, garnished with fresh dill and accompanied by rice, noodles, or simply good bread.

A selection of dishes in a café in Izmir, Turkey.

Baked Stuffed Eggplants

Melitzanes Papoutsakia

HERE YOU CAN EITHER fry the eggplants or bake them before stuffing. The final dish will be less oily if you bake them. You can also vary the meat filling by using cheese, either feta or myzithra (page 230), mixed with a little fried onion and chopped parsley. It was in Crete that I tried the eggplant filled with cheese—a delightful and lighter vegetarian alternative that doesn't require béchamel sauce.

SERVES 4

5 tablespoons extra-virgin olive oil

2 medium eggplants (about ½ pound each), cut in half lengthwise

salt

freshly ground black pepper

2 medium onions, finely chopped

10 ounces ground lamb from the shoulder, (about 1½ cups)

1 14-ounce can peeled tomatoes, finely chopped

¼ cup finely chopped flat-leaf parsley

FOR THE BÉCHAMEL SAUCE:

2 tablespoons unsalted butter

2 tablespoons all-purpose flour

1¼ cups whole milk

1 egg yolk

TO FINISH:

2–3 tablespoons grated Parmesan cheese

1 Preheat the oven to 350 degrees. Grease with 1 tablespoon olive oil a baking dish large enough to hold the 4 eggplant halves.

2 Scoop out a little of the eggplant flesh, chop coarsely, and set aside.

3 Brush the eggplant halves inside and out with 2 tablespoons olive oil and season lightly with salt and pepper. Place the eggplants in the prepared dish and bake in the preheated oven for 40 minutes, or until just soft.

4 Prepare the stuffing. Put the remaining 3 tablespoons olive oil and the chopped onions in a frying pan and fry until the onions are soft and transparent. Add the chopped eggplant and ground meat and fry, stirring continuously and mashing the meat to break up the lumps, until browned. Add the chopped tomatoes and parsley (reserve a little for the final garnish) and season with salt and pepper to taste. Simmer, covered, for 15 minutes, or until the sauce is reduced but not completely dry.

5 While the stuffing is cooking, prepare the béchamel. Melt the butter in a saucepan and whisk in the flour. Slowly add the milk, whisking all the time, and bring to a boil, stirring occasionally. Remove from the heat and leave until warm, then whisk in the egg yolk.

6 Remove the eggplant from the oven and spoon an equal portion of meat filling into each half. Cover the filling with the béchamel and sprinkle with the Parmesan. Return to the oven and bake for another 30–40 minutes, or until the eggplants are very soft. Serve very hot with good bread.

Octopus and Onion Stew

◆

CHTAPODI STIFADO

THIS UPMARKET VERSION OF another typical street dish was given to me by Theodore Kyriakou, chef-owner of The Real Greek restaurant in London. Theodore recommends using frozen octopus, which he says is already tenderized by the freezing process. He also recommends not washing the octopus so that it retains the flavor of the sea. Once you have defrosted it, simply drain the excess water and use.

SERVES 4–6

1 cinnamon stick, about 1 inch

1 whole clove

1 teaspoon coriander seeds

1 teaspoon black peppercorns

¼ cup extra-virgin olive oil

1 frozen whole octopus (about 3 pounds), defrosted and cut into
    1-inch chunks

2 bay leaves

salt

½ cup good red wine

1½ pounds baby onions or shallots, peeled

3 tablespoons tomato paste

2 tablespoons red wine vinegar

¼ cup finely chopped flat-leaf parsley

Octopus for sale in Athens's central market

1 Finely grind the spices in a mortar with a pestle. Combine them in a large flameproof casserole with the oil. Place over medium heat and stir for 2–3 minutes, until the oil is hot and you can smell the spices.

2 Add the octopus, bay leaves, and salt to taste. Cover the pan and cook for 15 minutes, by which time the octopus should be immersed in its own juices. Add the red wine and onions and continue cooking for another 45 minutes, or until the octopus is very tender and the onions are falling apart. Remove from the heat, stir in the tomato paste, vinegar, and parsley, and let cool. Serve warm or at room temperature with good bread.

Baked Mackerel with Herbs

KOLIOI LATHORIGANI

HERE IS A VERY simple and excellent way to prepare mackerel, an often maligned fish. The mackerel found in Greece have slightly different markings than the Atlantic mackerel often found in American and British fish markets. Both can be used with great success.

SERVES 6

½ cup extra-virgin olive oil

juice of 2 lemons, or more to taste

4 cloves garlic, very finely chopped

½ cup finely chopped flat-leaf parsley

1 tablespoon dried oregano

salt

freshly ground black pepper

6 mackerel (about 1 pound each), rinsed, patted dry, and rubbed with
    salt inside and out

1 Preheat the oven to 350 degrees. Grease with a little olive oil a large baking dish that will comfortably hold the fish side by side. Lay the fish in the baking dish.

A pot of fricassée balanced over a tray of kolioi lathorigani

2 Pour the oil into a mixing bowl and add the lemon juice, garlic, and herbs. Season with salt and pepper to taste and pour all over the fish. Bake in the preheated oven for 25–30 minutes, or until the fish is just done. You do not want to overcook the fish, as it will turn rubbery. Remove from the oven and baste with the cooking juices. Let rest for a couple of minutes, then serve hot or warm with roast potatoes or a salad.

RENA SALAMAN, AUTHOR OF *Greek Food*, is very contemptuous of this dish. "Not Greek at all," she tells me. Theodore Kyriakou (see page 180) disagrees with her. For him pasticcio is firmly anchored in the Greek repertoire, even if it is originally Italian. It is Theodore who taught me to make it in the unusual way I describe below. Pasticcio is normally made with ground meat and topped with a heavy béchamel sauce. Like Rena, I do not like the classic version, but I was won over by Theodore's. He sometimes makes his with ham and sometimes without. The recipe here is for the lighter, vegetarian version. If you want to use ham, grind a few slices and spread the ground ham between the two layers of pasta, then finish and bake as directed below.

Baked Pasta

◆

PASTICCIO

SERVES 4–6

6 tablespoons unsalted butter

¼ cup all-purpose flour

3 cups whole milk

⅛ teaspoon grated nutmeg

salt

freshly ground white pepper

1 cup grated kefalotiri or Parmesan cheese

2 egg yolks, beaten

1 pound penne or 1 pound Greek macaroni no. 2

I Melt 4 tablespoons butter in a saucepan and whisk in the flour. When the flour is completely incorporated, gradually pour in the milk, whisking constantly. Keep whisking until the milk comes to a boil, simmer for a couple of minutes, then remove from the heat. Stir in the nutmeg, salt and pepper to taste, and ⅓ of the cheese. Let the sauce cool until warm, then stir in the beaten egg yolks. Set aside.

2 Bring a large pot of water to a boil. Add salt and the pasta and cook for 2 minutes less than the package instructions say. You want the pasta to be very al dente, as it will continue cooking in the oven.

3 Preheat the oven to 375 degrees. Grease a 2-inch-deep baking dish measuring 9 × 13 inches with a little butter.

4 Drain the pasta and toss with the remaining 2 tablespoons butter. Spread half the pasta over the bottom of the baking dish, pour half the béchamel over it, and sprinkle with half the remaining cheese. Cover with the rest of the pasta and pour in the rest of the béchamel, distributing it evenly. Sprinkle the rest of the cheese all over and bake in the middle of the preheated oven for 20–30 minutes, or until golden. Serve warm or at room temperature with a crisp green salad.

I HAD THE BEST version of this dish in a delightful taverna in Athens, Stoa Tou Vangelis, set in a courtyard off Euripides Street, very near the central market. The restaurant serves the best one-pot meals in town. You can use different vegetables from those I list below, depending on what is in season.

SERVES 4 AS A MAIN COURSE OR 8 AS A SIDE DISH

3 medium potatoes, cut into 1-inch-thick wedges

1 yellow bell pepper, seeded, cored, and sliced

4 medium zucchini, sliced on the slant into medium-thin rounds

2 cloves garlic, thinly sliced

1 small onion, thinly sliced

1 14-ounce can peeled tomatoes, coarsely chopped

¼ cup finely chopped flat-leaf parsley

2 teaspoons dried oregano

⅓ cup extra-virgin olive oil

salt to taste

freshly ground black pepper to taste

1 Preheat the oven to 350 degrees.

2 Place all the vegetables and seasonings in a large mixing bowl and mix well. Dip a finger in the tomatoes to taste and adjust the seasoning if necessary.

3 Transfer to a baking dish and spread into a tightly packed layer. Pour ¼ cup water into the dish. Bake in the preheated oven for 1 hour 45 minutes, turning the vegetables at regular intervals. Serve hot, warm, or at room temperature.

Stuffed Tomatoes and Peppers

◆

DOMATES YIEMISTES ME RYZI

THE FILLING BELOW WORKS well with a number of other vegetables, such as zucchini flowers, zucchini, and vine leaves. If you use other vegetables, simply peel and chop a couple of tomatoes to replace the tomato pulp below. You can stand potato wedges between the stuffed vegetables to make sure they stay upright while cooking. It was in Temenia, a small village nestled in a valley in the spectacular mountains south of Chania, that I had my favorite Greek meal. I nearly drove past the Oikoteneiakh (or ikoyenyaki, meaning "family") café, wondering if I should trust its sign advertising authentic Cretan cooking. But I was hungry, and the simplicity of the place was appealing. There was no menu. Instead, I was taken by the pretty daughter of the owner to an immaculate kitchen at the back of the house, complete with old-fashioned range and ceramic sink. She showed me what her mother had cooked that day: stuffed tomatoes, vine leaves, zucchini and zucchini flowers, all in the same pot, and in a separate baking dish, eggplant "little shoes" (melitzanes papoutsakia), a cute name to describe baked stuffed eggplant (page 178), which she had filled with cheese instead of meat. The stuffed vegetables were better than I could have imagined, with plenty of dill in the rice and each grain separate and cooked just right. And to think that I nearly drove past.

SERVES 4–6 AS A MAIN COURSE

8 large tomatoes

4 red or green bell peppers

¾ cup short-grain rice

2 large onions, very finely chopped

½ cup finely chopped dill

¼ cup finely chopped flat-leaf parsley

½ cup extra-virgin olive oil

salt

freshly ground black pepper

1 Cleanly slice the tops off the tomatoes and peppers and discard the seeds from the pepper tops, as well as the seeds and ribs from the insides. Reserve the tops. Scoop out the inside of the tomatoes and chop finely. Set aside.

2 Preheat the oven to 350 degrees.

3 Rinse and drain the rice and put in a large mixing bowl. Add the chopped tomato pulp, onions, herbs, and half the olive oil; season with salt and pepper to taste.

4 Fill the tomato and pepper shells three-quarters full with the rice mixture. Cover with the reserved tops and spread the remaining ¼ cup oil in a baking dish large enough to hold the vegetables, tightly packed. Arrange the tomatoes and peppers in the dish and bake in the preheated oven for about 1½ hours. Serve warm or at room temperature.

Rice, Lentils, and Vermicelli with Hot Tomato Sauce

❖

KOSHARI

SOME YEARS AGO I spent a couple of months in Egypt, on a friend's mango farm just outside Cairo. We went regularly into the city to explore the Islamic sites and always stopped for lunch at one of the food stalls that line the streets. We had fül müdammas, ta'miyah (falafel), and koshari, which was my favorite. I loved standing by a hand-painted wooden cart to tuck into a steaming bowl of rice, lentils, and pasta topped with a fiery tomato sauce and caramelized onion. It was much more enjoyable than munching on a sandwich. Traditionally, the lentils, rice, and pasta are cooked separately and spooned in layers in the bowl. I find this process too tiresome and cook everything in the same pan, although in stages—I am not straying too far from tradition, as nowadays the rice is cooked with a certain amount of lentils and vermicelli. The final result might not be as fluffy nor have such a good color contrast, but the taste is just as good and you don't have to wash so many pans. The quantities I give below are rather large, but koshari keeps well and is equally delicious eaten at room temperature. The Turks have a somewhat similar version with rice and chickpeas, but it is nowhere near as exciting as the Egyptian one.

SERVES 8

FOR THE TOMATO SAUCE:

3 tablespoons extra-virgin olive oil

½ cup very finely chopped onion

4 cloves garlic, crushed

1 14-ounce can peeled tomatoes, coarsely chopped

¼ teaspoon finely ground black pepper

¼ teaspoon crushed red pepper flakes, or more to taste

8 tablespoons extra-virgin olive oil

1½ cups sliced onions

½ cup vermicelli broken into 1-inch pieces

1¼ cups brown lentils

1¼ cups basmati rice

salt

1 To make the tomato sauce, put the oil and chopped onion in a saucepan and fry over medium heat until golden. Stir in the garlic and fry for a couple more minutes, then add the tomatoes and spices. Increase the heat to medium-high and let bubble for 10–20 minutes, or until thickened. Process the sauce through a food mill or in a food processor until smooth and keep warm.

2 While the tomato sauce is cooking, start preparing the koshari. Put the oil in a frying pan and place over medium heat. Add the onions and fry, stirring occasionally, until they are golden brown and caramelized. Remove with a slotted spoon and spread on paper towels to drain off the excess oil. Add the vermicelli to the oil and sauté until browned. Set aside.

3 Put the lentils in a saucepan with 5 cups water. Bring to a boil, reduce the heat, and simmer, covered, for 15–30 minutes, depending on the type of lentils you are using. They should be quite tender by the time you add the rice.

4 Rinse the rice under cold water and add to the lentils. Simmer for 10 minutes, then stir in the vermicelli and the oil from the pan; add salt to taste. Wrap the lid of the pan with a clean kitchen towel, place the lid back on the pan, and remove the pan from the heat. Let sit for 10 minutes, or until the vermicelli is tender and the liquid is fully absorbed. Stir in half the caramelized onions and reserve the other half for garnish. Use a fork to stir the rice so that you fluff it up at the same time. Transfer the koshari to a serving dish, ladle the tomato sauce all over, and scatter the remaining caramelized onions over the sauce. Serve hot.

Roast Lamb

◆

MECHOUI

ONE OF MY FAVORITE sights on the streets of Morocco is whole roasted lambs resting on large slabs with their golden skin glistening in the sun. The lambs are baked early in the morning in large, round, clay pit ovens that can hold several lambs at once. Once done, the roasts are taken out, one at a time. The lamb is placed on a large counter facing the street, and people gather to eat their chosen cuts, sold by the weight, off pieces of paper with a little salt and cumin. Often customers take the meat home for an impromptu meal or buy several lambs, wrapped in black bin bags, for celebration meals. When Moroccans make mechoui at home in the city, they roast a quarter lamb (neck, shoulder, and ribs), but I am reducing the cut even further to just a shoulder. There is a Turkish, or, to be more accurate, Anatolian, version of mechoui, firin kebab, in which the lamb is cut up into large roasts, arranged in very large round copper dishes, and baked all night in a slow-burning wood-fired oven. The cooked meat is sold by the weight and served on pide bread with a jug of frothy ayran (page 255).

SERVES 4

Untying the mechoui. . .

and coming to the end of the lamb, Marrakesh

1 4½-pound shoulder of lamb

4 tablespoons (½ stick) unsalted butter, softened

2 tablespoons salt

1 tablespoon ground cumin

I Preheat the oven to 350 degrees.

2 Rub the shoulder of lamb with the softened butter and put on a rack in a baking dish. Cook in the preheated oven for 2 to 2½ hours, or until the meat is very tender and the skin is crisp and completely browned. While the meat is roasting, baste it every 15 minutes with a little water. Once it is done, remove from the oven and let rest for about 15 minutes. Combine the salt and cumin in a small bowl and serve with the meat, which should be falling off the bone.

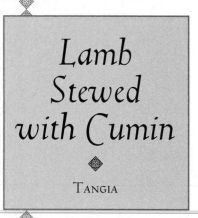

Lamb Stewed with Cumin

TANGIA

TANGIA, A SPECIALTY OF Marrakesh, is the name of the tall earthenware jars as well as the meat stewed in them. The same is true of tagine, which describes both the earthenware dish with a conical lid and the tagine (Moroccan stew) that is cooked in it. The tangia jars are set in the hot ashes of the hammam (Turkish bath) fire houses and left in the care of the men who tend the fires. They know when to transfer the cooked tangia from the hot ashes to the cooler ones so that it stays warm until it is picked up. Long ago tangia was exclusively prepared by men who made it on Thursday night, away from their wives, to take the next day on their illicit amorous picnics, or so I am told.

The recipe below was given to me by Boujemaa Mars, head chef at one of Marrakesh's most stylish hotels, the Mamounia. You might think, as I did, that stewing meat without any liquid cannot work, but lamb releases a lot of liquid during slow cooking. The preserved lemon is essential for the sauce, even though only a small quantity is called for. If you cannot find any in the stores, make your own. Cut unwaxed lemons into quarters, and spread a teaspoon of sea salt over the cut surfaces. Pack the lemons tightly in a hermetically sealed jar and leave for 3–4 weeks. The preserved lemons used in tangia are at least 6 months old.

SERVES 4

½ cup extra-virgin olive oil

1 large clove garlic, finely chopped

pinch saffron threads

1 teaspoon finely ground white pepper

1 teaspoon ground cumin

¼ teaspoon ground ginger

1 teaspoon grated nutmeg

salt

2½ pounds lamb meat from the rump, skinned and trimmed of fat, then cut into chunks

¼ preserved lemon, preferably an old one, rind only

Put the oil, chopped garlic, spices, and a little salt in a heavy flameproof casserole. Stir well, then add the meat. Turn it in the seasoned oil and add the preserved lemon rind. Cover and place over low heat. Simmer for 1 hour 15 minutes, stirring from time to time, or until the meat is very tender and the sauce thickened. Taste and adjust the seasoning if necessary. If the sauce is still runny, increase the heat to high and boil for a few minutes to reduce it. Serve very hot with good bread.

Khadija's tangia cooking in the ashes of a hammam in Marrakesh

Tagines and a kitten for sale

THIS IS ANOTHER TYPICAL street tagine that in Morocco is made with fresh tomatoes. However, I normally use canned ones, preferably an Italian brand, unless I can get very ripe tomatoes. I doubt if any street cook uses real saffron. They use either the fake stuff, safflower (which traders try to palm off onto unsuspecting tourists as real saffron), or turmeric. Any of these will give you the color but not the subtle, exotic taste of real saffron. Do be careful, though, not to use too much or the sauce will turn bitter.

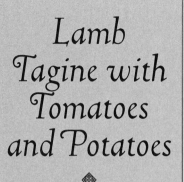

Lamb Tagine with Tomatoes and Potatoes

◆

L'HAM BIL MATECHA
WA B'TATA

SERVES 4

¼ cup extra-virgin olive oil

¾ teaspoon ground ginger

good pinch saffron threads

2½ pounds lamb from the rump, cut into chunks

3 28-ounce cans peeled tomatoes, drained and coarsely chopped

salt

freshly ground black pepper

1 pound potatoes, cut into medium chunks

½ cup finely chopped flat-leaf parsley, plus a little more for the garnish

1 Put the oil and spices in a large saucepan and mix together. Add the meat, turn it a few times in the spiced oil, and let marinate.

2 Add the tomatoes and salt and pepper to taste and barely cover with water, between ½ and 1 cup, depending on how juicy the tomatoes are. Place over medium-high heat and bring to a boil. Cook, covered, for 45 minutes to 1 hour, turning the meat regularly in the sauce until the sauce is quite reduced. Add the potatoes and parsley, reduce the heat to medium-low, and simmer for another 20–30 minutes, or until the meat and potatoes are done and the sauce very thick. Serve hot with good bread.

Chicken Tagine with Potatoes and Peas

◆

DJAJ BEL B'TATA WA JEBLANA

IF YOU WALK THROUGH the medina around midmorning, you will be able to watch the street tagines being made. First, terra-cotta braziers, on which the tagines will cook, are filled with glowing charcoal. Then a little oil is poured into the tagine dishes—on the street it will be vegetable, not olive oil—after which a handful of sliced onion is neatly piled in the middle of the dish. The onions are seasoned with different spices, usually cumin, paprika, pepper, and turmeric or safflower instead of saffron, and then topped with meat, either lamb or chicken. The conical lid is placed on the dish, and the tagine put on the fire. When the meat is half cooked, the vendor will uncover the tagine to add his choice of vegetables, which is more often than not sliced potatoes. In the summer tomatoes or peas are also added, again neatly arranged to cover the meat. The tagine is covered again and left to simmer until the customers start trooping in for lunch. By the end of your stay in Morocco, you won't need this or any other recipe book to teach you how to make a tagine. Watching these men and their precise method of cooking will be enough for you to go back to your kitchen and make your own. You can prepare this tagine with chicken, as below, or with lamb, in which case use 2 pounds boned lamb from the rump or shoulder.

SERVES 4–6

1 medium chicken, cut into 8 pieces

2 medium onions, thinly sliced

2 cloves garlic, finely chopped

¼ cup extra-virgin olive oil

pinch saffron threads

½ teaspoon ground cumin

½ teaspoon ground ginger

½ teaspoon finely ground black pepper

1 teaspoon paprika

salt to taste

1 cup finely chopped flat-leaf parsley

1 cup finely chopped cilantro, plus a little more for the garnish

4 cups medium-diced potatoes

2 cups fresh or frozen green peas

1 Put the chicken pieces, onions, garlic, oil, and seasonings in a large flameproof casserole, barely cover with water (about 2 cups), and place over medium-high heat. Bring to a boil and cook, covered, for 30 minutes.

2 Add the herbs and potatoes and cook, covered, for another 15 minutes, stirring occasionally, until the potatoes are nearly done. Then add the peas, lower the heat, and simmer for 5 more minutes. If the sauce is still runny, uncover the pan and boil hard until thickened. Taste and adjust the seasoning if necessary, then transfer to a preheated serving dish and serve very hot with good bread.

Chicken Tagine with Olives and Preserved Lemons

◆

D'JAJ M'CHERMEL

JAME' EL FNA IS the ultimate place for street food in Morocco. Before it became the evening gathering place in Marrakesh, it was a national bus stop. As in all terminals, there was a large group of street vendors stationed there to cater to the multitude of travelers in need of nourishment or refreshment. When the CTM (Compagnie de Transports Marocaine) moved to its present location at Bab Doukkala, the vendors stayed behind in Jame' el Fna and eventually became a tourist attraction. The food may not be the best available, but it is great fun to walk around the square and watch the cooks serve the crowds. The following tagine is always on their menu, but prepared differently. On the street the chickens are boiled separately from the sauce and look as if they were dyed bright yellow (probably because of the turmeric added to the boiling water). The sauce is also much simpler and made without herbs.

SERVES 4–6

1 clove garlic, finely chopped

1 teaspoon ground ginger

½ teaspoon ground cumin

½ teaspoon paprika

pinch saffron threads

¼ teaspoon finely ground white pepper

salt

1 free-range chicken (about 3 pounds)

2 medium onions, thinly sliced

1 cup finely chopped flat-leaf parsley

1 cup finely chopped cilantro

1 cinnamon stick

2 tablespoons extra-virgin olive oil

1½ tablespoons unsalted butter

juice of ½ lemon, or more to taste

1 large preserved lemon, rind only, cut lengthwise into strips (see page 192)

1¼ cups green or purple olives, pitted

1 Put the garlic, spices, and a little salt in a large flameproof casserole and stir. Add the chicken and rub it well, inside and out, with the spice mixture.

2 Add the onions, herbs, and cinnamon stick and half cover with water (about 3 cups). Bring to a boil over medium-high heat, then add the oil and butter. Cover and cook for 45 minutes, or until the chicken is cooked and the broth has become very concentrated. If the sauce is still quite thin, boil over high heat until thickened.

3 Discard the cinnamon stick, then add the lemon juice, preserved lemon rind, and olives. Reduce the heat to medium-low and simmer for another 10–15 minutes. Transfer the chicken to a serving dish. Taste the sauce and adjust the seasoning if necessary, then pour it all over and around the chicken. Serve very hot with good bread.

Lamb Shanks with Chickpeas and Wheat

◆

HERGMA À L'OCCIDENTALE

THE VERSION OF HERGMA that I give here is different from the classic one, in which calves' feet or sheep trotters are used instead of lamb shanks. Hergma is traditionally served for breakfast, but I find it better suited for lunch or dinner. The early-morning sight of huge enamelware dishes filled with greasy trotters and chickpeas is a turnoff even for someone very keen on variety meats. I was never able to bring myself to try it on the street. Fortunately, a friend of mine agreed to make it for me in her home and share this perfectly luscious recipe.

SERVES 6–8

4 lamb shanks (about 3–4 pounds)

1½ cups dried chickpeas, soaked overnight in plenty of water with 1 teaspoon baking soda

1 cup hard wheat, soaked overnight

6 tablespoons extra-virgin olive oil

4 cloves garlic

2 tablespoons ground cumin

¼ teaspoon red pepper flakes

2 tablespoons paprika

salt

1 Put the shanks in a large flameproof casserole. Rinse and drain the chickpeas and add to the meat along with the wheat, oil, garlic, cumin, and chilies. Pour in 2½ quarts water and place over medium-high heat. Bring to a boil, lower the heat to medium-low, and simmer, covered, for 2½ hours, stirring occasionally, or until the meat, chickpeas, and wheat are tender. By then the broth should be reduced to an unctuous sauce. If the sauce is still runny, uncover the pot and boil hard for a few minutes or until reduced.

2 Add the paprika and salt. Taste and adjust the seasoning if necessary. Serve hot with good bread and a refreshing salad.

Couscous

◈

KSEKSÜ

THERE IS NO COMPARISON between the steamed couscous that people use in Morocco and other North African countries and the precooked "instant" one that most people use in the West. The former is finer and has a slight crunch even when you reheat it, while the precooked is rather mushy. Most people in Europe and the United States expect couscous to be served as a side dish with tagines, but in North Africa couscous is always served with its own special accompaniments (a vegetable and meat broth, a fish stew, or chicken with onion and raisins), never as a side dish.

SERVES 4–6

2½ cups fine unprocessed couscous (not "instant")

salt

1 tablespoon extra-virgin olive oil

2 tablespoons butter, melted

1 Put the couscous in a shallow mixing bowl. Dissolve 1 teaspoon salt in ⅔ cup water and sprinkle the salted water over the couscous, stirring the grains with your fingers and breaking up any lumps. When the couscous has soaked up all the water, stir in the oil.

2 Put the couscous in the top part of a couscoussière or a steamer lined with cheesecloth (if the holes are too big) and set over the bottom part filled with either boiling water or the broth to be served with the couscous (see following recipe). Ideally, no steam should escape from the bottom pan, so if necessary, wrap a strip of cloth around the edge of the pan before setting in the top. Steam the couscous, covered, for 20 minutes.

3 Transfer the couscous to a bowl and sprinkle, little by little, with another ⅔ cup water, this time using a wooden spoon, as the grains will be too hot for your hands. Add the melted butter and stir well. Let sit, covered with a clean kitchen cloth, for 15 minutes to fluff up.

4 Return the couscous to the top part of the couscoussière and set over the pan of boiling liquid. Steam, uncovered, for a further 10–15 minutes or the last 10–15 minutes of the cooking time of the broth. Tip the couscous into a large serving bowl, and arrange into a mound. Garnish with the following recipe and serve hot.

Couscous with Seven Vegetables

Kseksü Bidawi

A VERY VERSATILE BROTH that you can prepare with or without meat. You can also replace the meat with chicken. Whichever way you choose to make it, it will be good. I rather like the delicate, clean taste of the meatless version. You can vary your choice of vegetables according to what is in season: pumpkin, artichoke hearts, peas, and sweet potatoes, to name a few, are all good substitutes for any of the vegetables listed below.

SERVES 4–6

⅓ cup dried chickpeas, soaked overnight in plenty of water with
 ½ teaspoon baking soda

good pinch saffron threads

2 medium onions, quartered

1 14-ounce can peeled tomatoes, finely chopped

1½ teaspoons finely ground black pepper

2 pounds boned lamb, preferably from the shoulder

3 tablespoons extra-virgin olive oil

2 tablespoons unsalted butter

2½ cups uncooked couscous (see previous recipe)

heart of ½ small cabbage, cut lengthwise into 4 wedges

2 medium carrots, cut crosswise in half, quartered lengthwise, and
 cored

1 medium zucchini, cut crosswise in half and quartered lengthwise

2 medium turnips, peeled and quartered

1 cup fresh or frozen fava beans

¼ cup finely chopped cilantro

¼ cup finely chopped flat-leaf parsley, plus a little more for the garnish

⅓ cup seedless raisins

salt

chili powder (optional)

1 Drain and rinse the chickpeas and place in the bottom half of a couscoussière or steamer, along with the saffron, onions, and tomatoes. Add 2 quarts water and the pepper and bring to a boil over medium heat. Then add the meat, olive oil, and butter; cover and simmer for 30 minutes. Steam, then prepare the couscous following the instructions in the previous recipe.

2 Add the cabbage to the pan and cook, covered, for a further 15 minutes. Then add the rest of the vegetables, together with the herbs, raisins, and salt to taste. Put the couscous on to steam, uncovered, for the second time, 10–15 minutes, or until the vegetables are ready. Transfer the couscous to a serving dish and arrange into a pyramid. Taste the broth and adjust the seasoning if necessary, then arrange the meat and vegetables on top of the couscous. Sprinkle with a little broth and garnish with a little parsley. Serve immediately with more broth on the side, which you can spike with a little chili powder if you like your couscous spicy.

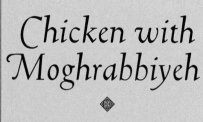

Chicken with Moghrabbiyeh

◆

MOGHRABBIYEH ALA DJ'EJ

MOGHRABBIYEH, WHICH MEANS "NORTH African" in Arabic, is the Lebanese version of couscous, although the grain is much bigger, more like m'hamssa, the large-grain couscous. You can buy it freshly made, when it is at its best, or dried, in which case you need to soak it before steaming. The only place I have seen moghrabbiyeh sold on the street is in the souks of Tripoli. One stall belonged to a charming man with a huge beard. He stood behind a very large griddle on which he sautéed the moghrabbiyeh together with boiled onions and chickpeas. He then rolled the grain in a double layer of pita bread to serve as a sandwich—a most unusual way of serving it. When I asked if his moghrabbiyeh was fresh, he explained that he made his own in a large factory outside the town and that during Ramadan he stopped selling it to eat on the street because everyone was fasting. Instead, he sold the steamed grain, together with the required amount of boiled onions, chickpeas, and spices, for people to take home and finish to their taste. During that month his stall is heaving with people, all wanting to buy moghrabbiyeh, obviously a favorite for breaking the fast.

SERVES 4–6

5 tablespoons unsalted butter

16 baby onions, peeled

1 medium chicken (about 3 pounds)

⅔ cup dried chickpeas, soaked overnight in plenty of water with
    ½ teaspoon baking soda

3 cinnamon sticks

1 teaspoon ground caraway

1½ teaspoons ground allspice or 7-spice mixture (page 131)

½ teaspoon finely ground black pepper

1 pound dried moghrabbiyeh

salt

½ teaspoon ground cinnamon

1 Melt 2 tablespoons butter in a large flameproof casserole and sauté the onions until lightly golden. Remove to a plate and set aside.

2 Put the chicken in the casserole and brown it on all sides. Add the drained and rinsed chickpeas and 5 cups water and bring to a boil. Just as the water is about to boil, skim the surface clean, then add the cinnamon sticks, caraway, allspice, and pepper. Reduce the heat to medium and boil gently, covered, for 45 minutes to 1 hour, or until the chickpeas are tender. Add the baby onions and boil for another 15 minutes.

3 While the chicken is cooking, put the dried moghrabbiyeh in a bowl and cover it with boiling water. Stir well so that the pellets do not stick, and leave for 15 minutes. Drain and stir in the remaining 3 tablespoons butter. Put the moghrabbiyeh in a steamer and steam, covered, for 20 minutes.

4 When the chicken and chickpeas are ready, add salt to taste and let sit for a few minutes.

5 Place the chicken on a board. Peel off and discard the skin and remove the flesh from the bones in big chunks. Keep warm.

6 Tip the moghrabbiyeh into a large frying pan. With a slotted spoon, remove the onions and chickpeas from the stock and add to the moghrabbiyeh. Stir in the ground cinnamon and about 1 cup stock, or more if you like your moghrabbiyeh to be really juicy. Place over medium-high heat and sauté for about 5 minutes. Taste and adjust the seasoning if necessary, then transfer to a preheated serving platter. Arrange the chicken all over the moghrabbiyeh and serve hot with more broth on the side.

Note: If you want to make sandwiches, as they do in Tripoli, open a round pita bread at the seam, put the 2 layers one on top of the other, rough side up, and spoon as much moghrabbiyeh as you like down the middle. Roll the bread tightly around the filling, wrap the bottom half of the sandwich with a napkin, and serve immediately. This is definitely not a sandwich for those watching their figure and, as far as I am concerned, not even a particularly successful combination. Simply too starchy.

THIS CLASSIC TAPA, WHEN served as a main course, needs no other accompaniment apart from a green salad and good bread to mop up the rich sauce. Cooking poultry with so much garlic is as much a Spanish tradition as it is French. In Spain the bird is cut up in small pieces and cooked on top of the stove, while in France it is roasted whole in the oven with the unpeeled garlic cloves. Roasting the chicken or, even better, free-range poussin will produce a more elegant presentation, although the meat will be less infused with the taste of garlic.

Chicken with Garlic

POLLO AL AJILLO

SERVES 4

¼ cup extra-virgin olive oil

1 medium chicken (about 3 pounds), cut into 12–16 pieces

salt

freshly ground black pepper

2 heads garlic, separated into cloves (about 20 large) but not peeled

2–3 sprigs rosemary

⅓ cup dry sherry, or 2 tablespoons lemon juice

1 Put the oil in a large sauté pan and place over medium-high heat. While the oil is heating up, season the chicken pieces with salt and pepper to taste. Add the chicken to the pan together with the garlic and rosemary. Fry for 10 minutes, turn the chicken pieces and garlic, and fry for another 10 minutes.

2 Deglaze the pan with the sherry or lemon juice (for a fresher taste) and reduce the heat to medium-low. Cook for another 10 minutes, turning the chicken halfway through, and serve very hot.

Tripe Stew

◆
CALLOS

CALLOS IS ANOTHER CLASSIC tapa that's best eaten in the market tapas bars, where you can be sure of the freshness of the meat. There are many variations on the following recipe. In Andalucia they add garbanzos (chickpeas) to the stew, while in Barcelona I sampled it with head meat added to the tripe. The recipe below is a refined version given to me by Isidre, of Ca Isidre in Barcelona, one of the best restaurants in the city and a favorite of King Juan Carlos, who is reputed to be a *fine bouche*.

SERVES 4–6

6 tablespoons extra-virgin olive oil

1 large onion, finely chopped

1 head garlic, separated into cloves and peeled

1 ham bone

5 ounces jabugo or serrano ham, sliced into thin strips or diced into small cubes, depending on how you buy it

5 ounces thin chorizo, sausage sliced medium thick

1 bouquet garni (thyme and bay leaf)

2 ripe tomatoes, peeled, seeded, and finely chopped

½ teaspoon crushed red pepper flakes, or to taste

2 teaspoons Spanish paprika

2¼ pounds cooked ox tripe, half honeycomb and half regular, cut into pieces about 1½ inches square

2–3 tablespoons all-purpose flour

½ cup white wine

1 Put the oil in a large flameproof casserole and place over medium heat. When the oil is hot, add the chopped onion and garlic and cook, stirring occasionally, until golden.

2 Add the ham bone, ham, chorizo, and bouquet garni and sauté for another minute. Add the tomatoes, red pepper flakes, and paprika and simmer for 5 minutes.

3 Add the tripe and sprinkle with the flour. Stir well and add the white wine. Let it bubble for a minute or two, then add 3 cups water. Reduce the heat to low and simmer, covered, for 2–3 hours, depending on how low your heat is. Stir occasionally, especially toward the end of cooking. The sauce should not reduce so much as thicken. If the tripe starts to stick, take it off the heat if it is done or add a little water. Serve very hot with good bread. When the tripe cools, the sauce will turn to jelly. To reheat, place the pan over very low heat and add a little water.

Paella

EVEN THOUGH PAELLA IS an outdoor dish, it does not really qualify as street food in Spain. However, it does outside Spain, particularly in the southwest of France. You will not find it on the street there year-round, but it does make an appearance during the *fêtes du village* or *ferias*. People come from all over the country to participate in the village festivities or attend bullfights. During that time paella stalls are advertised as one of the main attractions, and you will see people walking around with paper or aluminum containers filled with the hearty rice mixture. The paella sold at these makeshift stalls is not as well garnished as the one below.

SERVES 4–6

6–8 large mussels, scrubbed clean

¼ cup extra-virgin olive oil

6 large fresh shrimp

14 ounces squid, gutted, scraped clean, and sliced into rings

1 small free-range chicken, cut into 12 pieces

1 14-ounce can peeled tomatoes, drained and finely chopped

good pinch saffron threads

½ teaspoon Spanish paprika

salt

freshly ground black pepper

2 cups Calasparra or other medium-grain rice

⅔ cup frozen petits pois, thawed in boiling water and drained

1 Pour enough water in a saucepan to cover the bottom by about an inch and add the mussels. Place over high heat and boil for a couple of minutes, or until the mussels have opened and are barely done. Strain and remove and discard the empty half-shells. Set aside.

2 Put the oil in a 15- or 16-inch paella pan and place over medium-high heat. When the oil is hot, add the shrimp and fry for 1 minute on each side. Remove to a plate.

3 In the same pan, sauté the squid for a couple of minutes. Remove to the same plate as the shrimp and set aside.

4 Add the chicken pieces to the pan and fry for about 7–10 minutes on each side, or until browned and almost done. Add the chopped tomatoes.

5 While the chicken is cooking, measure 1 quart water and stir the saffron into it, along with the paprika and salt and pepper to taste. Pour over the chicken, then stir in the rice, distributing it evenly over the bottom. Bring to a boil and let it bubble for 10–15 minutes, or until the rice has absorbed almost all the liquid. During that time, turn the pan around for the heat to reach all sides equally. Reduce the heat to medium-low and simmer for 5 minutes, then garnish with the peas, the shrimp and squid with any juices on their plate, and the mussels. Simmer for another 5 minutes, remove from the heat, and cover loosely with foil. Let sit for 3–5 minutes and serve hot.

A sweet shop in the medina in Marrakesh

Sweets and Desserts

CHESTNUT PUDDING ✦ *Castagnaccio*

WATERMELON PUDDING ✦ *Gelo di Melone*

SUGAR SYRUP ✦ *Qatr*

MILK PUDDING ✦ *M'hallabiyeh*

DRIED FRUIT AND NUT COMPOTE ✦ *Khoshaf*

WALNUT PANCAKES ✦ *Qatayef bil-Joz*

ARABIC CLOTTED CREAM ✦ *Qashtah*

ALMOND TRIANGLES ✦ *Samsa*

SEMOLINA CAKE ✦ *Basbüssa*

KAIROUAN PASTRIES ✦ *Maqrüd*

CREAM PIE ✦ *Bougatsa*

SWEET CHEESE PIES ✦ *Kallitsünia*

CLOTTED CREAM FRITTERS ✦ *Kellage*

LEBANESE SHORTBREAD ✦ *Ghraybeh*

MOROCCAN SHORTBREAD ✦ *Ghreyba*

Anise Cookies ✦ *Brigidini*

Sesame Cookies ✦ *Baraziq*

Sicilian Sesame Candy ✦ *Cubbàita di Giuggiulena*

Instant Granita

Sicilian Almond Ice Cream ✦
   Granita di Mandorle

Mango Ice Cream ✦ *Büza ala Manga*

Pistachio Nut Ice Cream ✦
   Büza ala Festuq Halabi

Milk Ice Cream ✦ *Büza ala Haleeb*

Chestnut Pudding

CASTAGNACCIO

THIS IS A LIGURIAN specialty that is also found in neighboring Tuscany, as well as other parts of Italy. Castagnaccio is an ancient sweet that used to be, and still is in some places, cooked in wood-fired ovens or on flat griddles. It is especially relished by schoolchildren as an after-school snack, while adults enjoy it in cafés and friggitorie with a glass of light sparkling white wine.

SERVES 4

1 tablespoon raisins

1 cup chestnut flour

salt

½ tablespoon pine nuts

¼ teaspoon fennel seeds

extra-virgin olive oil

1 Soak the raisins in tepid water to cover for 15 minutes. Drain and dry on a clean kitchen cloth.

2 Preheat the oven to 375 degrees. Grease a 9-inch round baking pan with a little olive oil.

3 Sift the chestnut flour into a large mixing bowl. Add a pinch of salt and ⅔ cup water and stir with a whisk until you have a smooth mixture with the consistency of batter.

4 Pour the chestnut mixture into the prepared pan and spread evenly. Scatter the raisins, pine nuts, and fennel seeds over the top. Drizzle with a little olive oil and bake in the preheated oven for 20 minutes, or until the surface is crisp. Serve hot or at room temperature.

Watermelon Pudding

GELO DI MELONE

THE BEST TIME TO make gelo di melone is at the height of summer, when watermelons are very sweet. In fact, it is always prepared in mid-August for the Virgin's Assumption, when jasmine is still in full bloom for making jasmine water. You soak a small handful of jasmine flowers in water and leave for a few hours. If you do not have access to jasmine plants, use a few drops of jasmine or even rose essence. The traditional gelo di melone is pretty dense, but I use less cornstarch than recommended in conventional recipes for a softer texture and a stronger taste of fruit. I also prefer to make mine without the usual garnishes of candied zuccata (a kind of long pale zucchini) and chocolate chips.

SERVES 8

4–5 pounds watermelon flesh

⅓ cup sugar, or more if the watermelon is not very sweet

⅔ full cup cornstarch

3 tablespoons jasmine water (optional)

¼ cup candied zuccata, diced into small cubes (optional)

1½ tablespoons dark chocolate chips (optional)

ground cinnamon

¼ cup pistachio nuts, coarsely ground

I Remove and discard the seeds from the watermelon flesh. Purée the flesh in a food processor or blender. Pass through a fine sieve, collecting the juice in a large mixing bowl, preferably one with a spout. Press on the pulp with the back of a small ladle to drain the juice quickly. You should end up with about 1½ quarts watermelon juice. Add the sugar and cornstarch and whisk until the sugar is diluted and the cornstarch completely blended. Taste and add more sugar if necessary.

2 Pour into a saucepan and place over medium heat. Bring to a boil, stirring constantly. When the mixture starts to bubble, let it boil, still stirring, for a couple of minutes. Remove from the heat and add the jasmine water or rose essence if you are using either.

3 If you are using the zuccata and chocolate chips, divide them equally among 8 individual bowls.

4 When the pudding is lukewarm, divide it equally among the bowls. Refrigerate and serve cold, sprinkled with a little cinnamon and ground pistachios.

SUGAR SYRUP VARIES SLIGHTLY, depending on where you are. The following recipe is Lebanese/Syrian. In Turkey, Tunisia, and Greece it is made without any fragrant flavorings, although in Greece a little honey is added.

MAKES 1½ CUPS

> 2 cups sugar
> ¾ cup water
> 1½ teaspoons lemon juice
> 4 teaspoons rose water
> 4 teaspoons orange blossom water

Sugar Syrup

QATR

Put the sugar, water, and lemon juice in a saucepan and place over medium heat. Bring to a boil, stirring occasionally, and let bubble for 3 minutes. Stir in the rose and orange blossom waters, let bubble for a few seconds more, then remove from the heat. Let cool before using in the recipes that call for it. The syrup will keep in the refrigerator for at least a week.

Milk Pudding

◆

M'HALLABIYEH

M'HALLABIYEH IS GENERALLY SOLD in individual glass or plastic bowls in sweet or ice cream stores in Lebanon and Syria. In some places like the ice cream parlors in souk Hamidiyeh in Damascus, the bowls are piled high like a stack of cards on the counter by the window. Occasionally, especially during Ramadan, you will find m'hallabiyeh peddled by ambulant street vendors, who will have the bowls of pudding neatly arranged inside a glass cabinet that they wheel around on a wooden cart. You can make m'hallabiyeh with either cornstarch or ground rice. There is quite a difference in texture between the two—cornstarch is finer. As for the taste of rose or orange blossom water, those of you who are not used to fragrant flavorings may think they taste like perfume. You can adjust the quantities to your liking. Mastic, the other flavoring, is the resin of a tree native to Chios, in Greece, which gives an exotic and mysterious taste to sweets and ice cream; it is also occasionally used in savory dishes. You can omit it if you cannot find it. Mastic has a very long shelf life, so it is a good idea to buy it when you find it to keep in your larder. In Israel they make a water-based version called Malabi, which is not as good as this version.

SERVES 4

A display of m'hallabiyeh in plastic bowls
in an ice-cream parlor in Damascus

3 cups milk

3 heaping tablespoons cornstarch or ground rice

½ cup sugar

scant ¼ teaspoon ground mastic (optional), available in Middle
   Eastern markets

1½ teaspoons orange flower water

1½ teaspoons rose water

½ cup blanched almonds or coarsely ground pistachio nuts

I Put the milk and cornstarch or ground rice in a saucepan, place over high heat, and bring to a boil, stirring constantly. Reduce the heat to low, add the sugar, and continue stirring for another 5–7 minutes, or until the liquid is thickened.

2 Add the orange flower and rose waters and simmer, still stirring, for a couple more minutes. Remove from the heat, pour into a large shallow bowl or 4 individual ones, depending on how you want to serve it, and let cool before garnishing with almonds or pistachios. Serve cold.

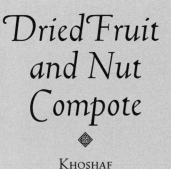

Dried Fruit and Nut Compote

KHOSHAF

KHOSHAF IS AN EXQUISITE COMPOTE of soaked rather than stewed dried fruit. It is found, with slight variations, throughout the Levant and probably originates in Persia, as the name indicates—khosh-ab meaning "good water" in Persian. There used to be a stall in downtown Beirut, right by a nineteenth-century fountain, that was famous for its cold puddings and iced drinks. We knew it as just the "fountain" (birkeh in Arabic) and always stopped there for refreshment when we went to the souks. Their khoshaf was one of the best in town. Sadly, the stall, like everything else in the town center, was destroyed during the civil war, and even though the whole area is being rebuilt now, the birkeh is gone and with it their delicious khoshaf. If the following classic recipe is not quite as perfect as the one I used to have at the birkeh, it is still pretty delightful.

SERVES 6–8

1 cup seedless raisins

1 cup dried pitted apricots, halved

⅓ cup halved blanched almonds

⅓ cup pistachio nuts

⅓ cup walnuts

½ cup pine nuts

½ cup sugar

3 tablespoons orange blossom water

1 Rinse the raisins and dried apricot halves under cold water. Place in a bowl, cover with 1 quart cold water, and let soak for 2–4 hours.

2 Put the nuts in a bowl, cover with boiling water, and let soak for 45 minutes. This will soften them and freshen their taste.

3 Transfer the fruit and its macerating liquid to a serving bowl. Add the sugar and orange blossom water and stir until the sugar is dissolved. Rinse and drain the nuts and add to the fruit. Mix well. Serve immediately or refrigerate.

ONE OF THE FIRST things I do whenever I am in Damascus is go to the souks, in particular to souk Madhat Pasha. There I have special friends who make some of the best pancakes I've ever eaten on the street. Lebanese-Syrian pancakes are smooth on one side and full of holes on the other, a bit like English muffins. They come in two sizes: a dainty 2 inches wide and a regular 4 inches. I love watching my friends make the pancakes: stirring the batter by hand, pouring it into a funny kind of funneled implement, and then dispensing it in spurts onto the hot griddle. While one person makes the pancakes, another fills them with cheese, walnuts, or clotted cream and fries them. They are then dropped into a large pan of sugar syrup. The Moroccans have similar pancakes called beghrir, although theirs are prepared with milk. They make them large to have for breakfast with butter and sugar or honey.

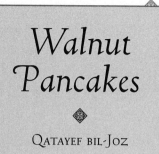

Walnut Pancakes

◆

QATAYEF BIL-JOZ

MAKES 12 SMALL PANCAKES TO SERVE 4–6

FOR THE PANCAKE BATTER:

½ teaspoon active dry yeast

¾ cup unbleached all-purpose flour

pinch salt

FOR THE WALNUT FILLING:

scant ⅔ cup ground walnuts

1 tablespoon sugar

¼ teaspoon ground cinnamon

1 tablespoon orange blossom water

FOR THE CREAM FILLING:

¾ cup Arabic clotted cream (page 224)

vegetable oil for frying

sugar syrup (page 217)

1 Stir the yeast into ½ cup plus 2 tablespoons water and let rest for 10 minutes. Add the flour and salt and whisk until you have a smooth batter. Cover with a clean kitchen towel and leave for 1 hour or until the batter has risen and its surface is bubbly.

2 Meanwhile, make the filling by combining the walnuts, sugar, cinnamon, and orange blossom water. Set aside.

3 Shortly before the batter is ready, grease a shallow frying pan with a little vegetable oil and place over medium heat. When the pan is very hot, measure a heaped tablespoon of batter and pour it into the pan, to make a disk about 2¾ inches in diameter and ¼ inch thick. It is best to spread the batter as you are pouring it into the pan because it is too thick to spread by tilting the pan. Cook on one side for 2–3 minutes, or until the bottom is barely colored and the top is bubbly and dry. Remove to a plate and finish frying the rest of the batter in the same way. Let the pancakes cool.

4 One at a time, lay the pancakes in your hand, smooth side down. Spread 1 tablespoon walnut or cream filling in a line down the middle, leaving the edges clear. Fold the pancake in a half-moon, aligning the edges, and with your fingers, pinch tightly shut—you do not want them to open during frying. Place each filled pancake on a platter and continue filling the rest.

5 Pour the sugar syrup into a shallow bowl.

6 Pour enough vegetable oil into a large frying pan to deep-fry the filled pancakes and place over medium heat. Test the oil by dipping the corner of a pancake in it; if bubbles surround it, the oil is ready. Slide in as many pancakes as will fit comfortably in the pan and fry for 2–3 minutes on each side, or until golden all over. Remove with a slotted spoon and drop into the sugar syrup. Turn in the syrup until well coated and remove to a serving platter. Serve warm or at room temperature the same day. They are really best eaten soon after they are made, as they quickly become soggy.

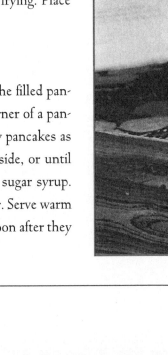

*Making qatayef during Ramadan
outside a sweet shop in Tripoli*

Arabic Clotted Cream

◆

QASHTAH

ALL THE TIME I lived in Lebanon, I never saw, nor even knew how, qashtah was made. It wasn't until a very recent visit that I first saw it being made in Tripoli. The large basement dairy was filled with huge round, very shallow pans of milk. Each pan was placed over a single gas flame positioned at the very edge, so that as the milk bubbled in one place, the skin shifted away to the sides. The skin was then skimmed off and left to drain in plastic colanders. Once it lost all its excess liquid, it was packed and sent to the various sweet stores. Sadly, the milk they used was powdered, and according to the cream makers, hardly anyone uses real milk nowadays. Gone are the days of the unpasteurized qashtah of my youth, which in some places was made with sheep's milk. There are two ways of preparing qashtah: a homemade version as below similar to the traditional method, and a quick version that I call artificial qashtah, which was devised by a friend. She boils milk with the soft inside of white bread. She simmers 2¾ cups half-and-half with 2 slices of white bread, crust removed and the white torn in tiny pieces, for 10 minutes. Once the mixture has cooled, it becomes very much like clotted cream. Qashtah is normally used as a component in other desserts but is sometimes served on its own, drizzled with honey.

MAKES JUST OVER ½ CUP

> 4 cups milk
> 1¼ cup heavy cream

I Put the milk and cream in a wide, shallow, round pan and place over low heat. Use the widest possible pan to maximize the amount of skin formed. Bring to a boil, then reduce the heat to very low and leave simmering for 1½–2 hours.

2 Cover the pan and leave undisturbed for 6–8 hours, then put in the refrigerator and leave for the same amount of time.

3 Skim off the thick skin and put in a bowl to use with the recipes calling for qashtah. Discard the leftover liquid.

TRADITIONALLY, THESE PASTRIES ARE made with warqa or malsūqa (see page 23), also known as brik pastry, but you can use filo if you have a problem finding warqa. The size of filo sheets varies according to brand. The Greek or Turkish brands are generally larger and better; just cut them into long 5-inch-wide strips that you then double up and brush with melted butter before filling and folding to form a triangle.

Almond Triangles

◆

SAMSA

MAKES ABOUT 24

1⅔ cups blanched almonds, lightly toasted in a nonstick pan

¼ cup confectioners' sugar

½ teaspoon orange zest

1 egg white, lightly beaten

2 tablespoons rose water

12 sheets brik pastry or filo, available in Middle Eastern markets

sugar syrup (page 217), made without rose water or orange blossom water

vegetable oil for deep-frying

¼ cup sesame seeds, lightly toasted in a nonstick pan

1 Grind the toasted almonds in a food processor until very fine, then transfer to a mixing bowl. Add the sugar, orange zest, egg white, and rose water; blend well.

2 Take 1 sheet of brik pastry and cut it in half. Fold the round bit over to form a long rectangle, then put 2–3 teaspoons of the almond mixture at the top of the strip of pastry. Fold the top corner over the filling to form a triangle and continue folding as you would fold a flag until the filling is completely encased. Tuck in the end, place on a plate, and continue filling and shaping the triangles until you finish both filling and pastry.

3 Pour the sugar syrup into a shallow bowl.

4 Pour enough vegetable oil into a large frying pan to deep-fry the pastries and place over medium-high heat. To test the oil, dip the corner of a pastry in it; if bubbles surround it, the oil is hot enough. Drop in about 4 pastries but don't crowd the pan. Fry for a couple of minutes on each side or until golden brown all over. Remove with a slotted spoon and drop into the syrup. Turn in the syrup a couple of times, then remove to a serving dish. Once you have made all the samsas, sprinkle them with toasted sesame seeds. Serve at room temperature or keep hermetically sealed to serve later. They should keep for 2–3 days.

Semolina Cake

✦

BASBÜSSA

VARIATIONS ON THESE CAKES are found everywhere in the eastern Mediterranean, but Egypt is where they are most likely to be wheeled through the streets. The sticky cakes are kept in glass cabinets or under plastic to stop the flies from swarming around them. You can buy them wrapped in paper to eat on the run, or you can eat them there and then on a plate. I suggest you choose the latter option, or you might have sugar syrup trickling down your fingers.

SERVES 4

1½ cups semolina flour (regular grade, not fine)

scant ¼ cup sugar

6 tablespoons unsalted butter, softened

scant 1½ cups yogurt

¼ teaspoon baking soda

1 teaspoon tahini

⅓ cup blanched almonds

2¼ cups sugar syrup (page 217)

1 Put the semolina, sugar, and softened butter in a mixing bowl and work together with your hands until well blended. Add the yogurt and baking soda and mix well until you have a firm batter.

2 Grease an 8 × 12 × 1½-inch baking dish with the tahini and spread the batter evenly in the dish. Flatten it gently with the back of a spoon, cover with a clean kitchen towel, and let rest for 3 hours.

3 Preheat the oven to 400 degrees.

4 Cut the uncooked cake into 2-inch squares and press one blanched almond in the middle of each. Bake in the preheated oven for 20–30 minutes, or until golden.

5 Remove from the oven and pour the cooled syrup all over. Let the cake stand for 30 minutes to soak up the syrup. If you think the amount of syrup is excessive, reduce the quantity to your taste. Bear in mind that the cake will take time to absorb the syrup, and although it may look as if it is swimming in the syrup to start, it will fully absorb it within the half hour.

Kairouan Pastries

Maqrūd

TRADITIONALLY, THESE PASTRIES ARE made with a special stamp that apparently is available only in Kairouan, the place of origin of maqrūd. I was promised the stamp by a Tunisian friend, but it never appeared and I ended up testing the recipe without it. I merely flattened the filled dough with my fingers. Mine were not as well shaped as those made with the stamp, but the taste was pretty much the same as those I ate in Tunisia. So yours may not look perfect either, but they should taste delicious.

MAKES 45–50

3 cups fine semolina flour

¼ teaspoon sea salt

pinch saffron threads, crushed to a fine powder

pinch baking soda

¼ cup extra-virgin oil

FOR THE FILLING:

1½ cups pitted dates

2 tablespoons extra-virgin olive oil

¼ teaspoon ground cinnamon

zest of 1 orange

TO FINISH:

sugar syrup (page 217), made with an additional 1 cup water, ⅓ cup
    honey, and no rose water or orange blossom water

vegetable oil for deep-frying

1 Put the semolina in a large mixing bowl. Add the salt, saffron, and baking soda. Make a well in the middle. Add the oil and 1 cup warm water to the well and knead until you have a smooth, malleable dough. Cover with plastic wrap and let rest for 15 minutes.

2 To make the filling, put the dates in a food processor and process until coarsely chopped. Add the oil, cinnamon, and orange zest. Process until reduced to a smooth paste.

3 Divide the date paste into 12 pieces and roll each into a sausage about ¾ inch thick. Cover with plastic wrap and set aside.

4 Pinch off a piece of dough the size of an orange and roll it out into a long oval about ½ inch thick. Lay 1 date roll in the middle of one half of the dough and roll the dough around the date filling to form a thick sausage. Flatten the pastry to about ½ inch thick with the special maqrüd stamp if you have it or with your fingers if you don't. You can also use the smallest side of a grater. Trim the ends. With a straight-edged knife, cut the pastry on the slant into medium diamonds. Lay them on an oiled baking sheet and finish making the rest of the pastries in the same way.

5 Pour the sugar syrup into a shallow bowl.

6 Heat enough vegetable oil in a large frying pan to deep-fry the pastries. To test the heat of the oil, dip a corner of a pastry into it; if bubbles surround it, the oil is ready. Drop as many pastries as will fit comfortably in the pan and fry for 2–3 minutes on each side, or until golden all over. Remove with a slotted spoon and drop into the syrup. Turn a few times in the syrup and remove to a serving platter. Finish frying and coating the pastries in syrup and let cool. Serve at room temperature. Maqrüd can be stored for about a week if kept hermetically sealed.

Kairouan pastries

Cream Pie

BOUGATSA

YOU CAN MAKE BOUGATSA in several different ways: in individual pies or in one large pie and with a cheese filling or a cream one. According to a Greek friend of mine, the best bougatsa is made by Jordanes in Chania, Crete. Theirs is always made into large pies and filled with cheese, myzithra. They serve the pie hot, cut into individual portions, which are then cut further into small bite-sized pieces. You are asked if you want your bougatsa sprinkled with sugar or left plain, in which case it will not be sweet at all. On the table there is ground cinnamon for you to use. Jordanes' bougatsa is very different, and by far better, than any I have tried in Athens or anywhere else in Crete. Unfortunately, the recipe below is not theirs—they wouldn't part with their secret. This one is made with cream, but if you prefer it with cheese, use 1½ cups curd or qarish cheese (page 96) and sprinkle the baked pie with sugar.

SERVES 4

A plate of bougatsa at Jordanes in Chania, Crete

FOR THE CREAM:

    2 cups milk

    ¼ teaspoon vanilla extract (or 1 vanilla bean)

    4 tablespoons (½ stick) unsalted butter

    ⅓ cup fine semolina flour

    ⅓ cup sugar

    1 egg plus 1 egg yolk

TO FINISH:

    12 sheets filo pastry

    4 tablespoons (½ stick) unsalted butter, melted

    confectioners' sugar and ground cinnamon for the garnish

1 Bring the milk to a boil with the vanilla extract or bean. In a separate saucepan, melt the butter over medium heat and add the semolina. Stir for 1 minute.

2 Strain the milk over the semolina, stirring continuously. Add the sugar and continue stirring for 4–5 minutes, or until the mixture is thickened. Remove from the heat and let cool, stirring every now and then to prevent the formation of a skin.

3 When the mixture is cool, beat the egg and yolk together and stir it in.

4 Preheat the oven to 400 degrees. Brush an 8-inch-square baking dish with a little melted butter.

5 Cut the sheets of filo to fit the baking dish and lay 6 strips, brushing each with melted butter, over the bottom. Spread the cream over the pastry and cover with the remaining sheets, again brushing each with butter. Keep the filo covered with a slightly damp kitchen towel at all times so it does not dry out.

6 Bake in the preheated oven for about 25 minutes, or until the pastry is crisp and golden. Cut into 4 squares and serve hot or warm, sprinkled with confectioners' sugar and a little cinnamon.

Sweet Cheese Pies

◆

KALLITSÜNIA

KALLITSÜNIA IS A SPECIALTY from Crete and, like bougatsa, comes in different shapes and sizes. The pies can be filled with spinach, spinach and cheese, or simply cheese. The cheese filling can be sweet or savory, but I prefer the former, which in any case is not too sugary. If you can't find myzithra, you can make qarish (page 96) or use curd cheese. Either will be good as long as the cheese is quite dry.

MAKES 20–25

½ teaspoon active dry yeast

½ cup warm milk

8 tablespoons (1 stick) unsalted butter, softened

½ cup sugar

2½ cups unbleached all-purpose flour

2 tablespoons orange juice

⅓ cup extra-virgin olive oil

FOR THE FILLING:

3 cups myzithra or curd cheese

1 egg

6 tablespoons sugar

ground cinnamon for the garnish

1 Stir the yeast into the milk and let stand for 10 minutes.

2 Using a wooden spoon, blend the butter and sugar together in a large mixing bowl, then sift in the flour. Add the yeast milk, orange juice, and olive oil and knead until you have a smooth dough. Cover the bowl and let rise for 1 hour.

3 Meanwhile, make the filling by mixing the cheese with the egg and sugar. Set aside.

4 Preheat the oven to 425 degrees. Line 2 large baking sheets with parchment.

5 Divide the dough into 2 or 3 pieces and roll out the first one to ½-inch thickness. Cut out as many disks as you can using a 4-inch biscuit cutter. With the tips of your fingers, flatten the edge of each disk and fold it in at regular intervals to produce a fluted, slightly raised edge. Place on the lined baking sheet and flatten the dough a little more inside the edges. Repeat with the other disks of dough.

6 Spread 1½–2 tablespoons cheese on each disk. Sprinkle with a little cinnamon and bake in the preheated oven for 20–25 minutes, or until lightly golden. Serve at room temperature. These are best eaten on the day they are made.

Clotted Cream Fritters

◆
KELLAGE

KELLAGE IS THE RAMADAN sweet par excellence in Lebanon. During that entire month of Muslim fast, sweet makers set up a separate stand outside their shops with a deep-frying pan and large trays of kellage ready for frying. Throughout the night, people troop to their favorite kellage maker to either buy industrial quantities for home or to have one or two on their way to or from their evening entertainment. It is fascinating to watch the kellage being dropped into the oil, where it sinks out of sight for a while and then slowly resurfaces as it cooks, a bit like fish rising to gobble up flies. You can have kellage un-fried, but the texture is not so good. Kellage is also the name of the sheets of pastry used to make it, which are large, round, and wafer thin.

MAKES 8

> 8 round sheets kellage pastry, or 8-brik pastry, available at Middle Eastern markets
>
> a small bowl of milk
>
> 1 cup Arabic clotted cream (page 224)
>
> sugar syrup (page 217)
>
> vegetable oil for deep-frying

1 Lay 1 kellage sheet on a work surface and brush it with milk. Fold in the sides of the circle to make a rectangle measuring about 6 × 8 inches, brushing the folds with more milk if they are too dry.

2 Place 1 heaping tablespoon of clotted cream in the middle, spreading it slightly, then fold over the long sides first, then the shorter ones to make a filled rectangle measuring about 2½ × 4 inches. Prepare and fill the other sheets in the same way. Set aside.

3 Pour the sugar syrup into a shallow bowl.

4 Pour enough vegetable oil into a large frying pan to deep-fry the rectangles and place over medium heat. To test the heat of the oil, dip the tip of a pastry into the oil; if bubbles surround it, the oil is hot enough. Drop in as many pastries as will fit comfortably in the pan and fry until lightly golden on both sides. Remove with a slotted spoon and drop into the sugar syrup. Turn over a couple of times, then remove to a serving platter. Finish frying and coating the rest of the kellage in the same way. Serve immediately.

Lebanese Shortbread

GHRAYBEH

I WAS GIVEN THIS recipe by a compatriot, Bashir al-Shorbaji, whom I came across in the souks in Tripoli. I noticed him wheeling a cart laden with ghraybeh wrapped in plastic bags. Not the most aesthetic way to present these delectable cookies but a good solution to keep them from softening. Bashir was very keen to promote his ghraybeh as the best in the world, but then, Lebanese people are prone to exaggeration. His ghraybeh were good, although nowhere nearly as good as those I had in Essaouira (see following recipe).

MAKES 22

12 tablespoons (1½ stick) unsalted butter, softened

⅓ cup sugar

1¾ cups unbleached all-purpose flour

pinch baking soda

1 Preheat the oven to 350 degrees. Line a baking sheet with parchment.

2 Using a wooden spoon, blend the butter and sugar together in a large mixing bowl. Add the flour and baking soda and knead until you have a smooth dough. Divide into 22 pieces and shape each into a thick oval cookie with a rounded top.

3 Bake in the preheated oven for about 20 minutes, or until barely colored. Let cool, then serve or store in an airtight container. The cookies will keep for at least a week.

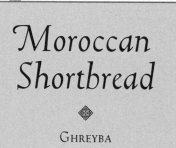

Moroccan Shortbread

❖

GHREYBA

HERE IS AN EXCELLENT recipe for ghreyba, given to me by a Berber woman in Essaouira. She sat beside a kaftan shop with a tray of ghreyba in front of her, placidly waiting for passersby to buy her cookies. I did not like the look of her cookies. They were not very prettily shaped, and the tray was not only bashed up but also not so clean. Still, there was something about her that inspired confidence. So I bought a cookie and walked on. My instinct proved right and the shortbread was scrumptious. I walked back. She was still there, sitting quite immutable. I bought another cookie, and in the next 15 minutes I went back and forth several times, each time thinking it would be the last. The recipe she provided doesn't quite create the crumbly texture I remember, but it's not far off.

MAKES 30–35

½ pound (2 sticks) unsalted butter, softened

1 cup sugar

½ teaspoon mastic (page 218), available in Middle Eastern markets

2 small egg yolks

3¼ cups unbleached all-purpose flour, plus more for kneading

2 ounces (just under ½ cup) blanched whole almonds (optional)

I Preheat the oven to 350 degrees. Grease a baking sheet with a little of the butter.

2 Put the sugar and mastic in a mixing bowl and make a well in the center. Add the egg yolks and incorporate into the sugar with the tips of your fingers. Add the butter and blend well. Then gradually add the flour and knead the dough until smooth and firm. This should take about 5 minutes. Add a little more flour if you think the dough is too soft. Let rest in a cool place for 10 minutes.

3 Pinch off a piece of dough and roll it into a ball the size of a walnut. Flatten it on your palm, leaving the top quite rounded to shape a cookie measuring about 2 inches in diameter. Press an almond, if you are using them, in the middle and place on the greased baking sheet. Finish shaping the cookies and bake in the preheated oven for 15–20 minutes, or until barely colored. Let cool before serving or storing in an airtight container, where they will keep for one week or so.

THIS IS A TYPICAL Tuscan cookie that is usually sold at country fairs. It is also found all year round in some towns. According to Giuliano Bugialli, author of *The Fine Art of Italian Cooking*, the villagers of Lamporecchio are famous for making the best brigidini. They follow the fairs from town to town to set up stalls where they make their celebrated brigidini, which is a spectacle in itself. The pastry is rolled into a walnut-sized ball and placed inside a preheated mold (stiaccia), rather similar to a waffle iron except that it is round and the pattern inside can vary from star shapes to dots to small squares. The mold is then closed over the pastry to flatten it and, at the same time, stamp it on both sides, after which it is placed over an open fire to cook the cookie inside.

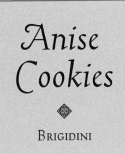

Anise Cookies

❖

BRIGIDINI

MAKES 12–14

½ cup sugar

2 eggs

pinch salt

1 tablespoon ground anise seeds

2 cups unbleached all-purpose flour, plus more for kneading

1 Put the sugar, eggs, salt, and ground anise seeds in a large mixing bowl. Using a wooden spoon, mix together until well blended.

2 Preheat the oven to 375 degrees; line a baking sheet with parchment paper.

3 Sift in the flour and knead for a few minutes until you have a smooth, firm dough. Roll out the dough to a ¼-inch thickness and, with a 5-inch biscuit cutter, cut out as many disks as you can. Prick each with a fork to form the pattern of your choice and transfer to the prepared baking sheet. Repeat with the remaining dough, making sure to use up the scraps, and bake for 10–15 minutes, or until done and barely colored. Serve warm or at room temperature. If you have a stiaccia, use as described above. The cookies will keep for a week in a hermetically sealed container.

Sesame Cookies

◆

BARAZIQ

BARAZIQ ARE A SYRIAN specialty, but you will also find them in most shops in Lebanon. On the street they are sold only during Ramadan, when they are loaded onto wooden carts together with Ramadan and date breads. The size of those sold on the street is much larger than the dainty ones you buy in sweet shops. You can make yours either size, depending on your preference, but a word of warning—they are much easier to handle when they are made small.

MAKES 18–20 SMALL COOKIES

FOR THE COOKIES:

> 4 tablespoons sugar
>
> 4 tablespoons (½ stick) unsalted butter
>
> 1 medium egg
>
> ½ teaspoon white wine vinegar
>
> 1 cup unbleached all-purpose flour, plus more for kneading
>
> pinch salt
>
> ⅓ teaspoon baking powder

FOR THE GARNISH:

> 1 egg white, lightly beaten
>
> ½ cup quartered pistachio nuts
>
> ½ cup sesame seeds, toasted in a nonstick pan until lightly golden

1 Put the sugar and softened butter in a mixing bowl and work together with a wooden spoon until completely blended. Add the rest of the ingredients and blend with your hands until you have a soft dough. If the dough is too soft to work with immediately, refrigerate it for 1 hour. Divide the dough into 18–20 pieces to make small baraziq or 6 pieces to make the larger size.

2 Preheat the oven to 350 degrees. Line a large baking sheet with parchment paper.

3 Shape each ball of dough with your hands until you have quite a thin disk, about 2½ inches wide, and place on a large platter. When you have shaped all the disks, dip each in the egg white, then in the pistachios on one side and the toasted sesame seeds on the other. Make sure you coat them well with the seeds. Arrange on the lined baking sheet with the pistachio side down.

4 Bake for 25–35 minutes, or until the cookies are golden brown. Let cool before serving. Baraziq will keep for up to 2 weeks in a hermetically sealed container.

Sicilian Sesame Candy

❖

CUBBÀITA DI GIUGGIULENA

ONE OF MY FAVORITE treats when I was a child was when my father took us for Sunday lunch to a riverside restaurant in Zahleh, a small town in the Beqaa valley famous for its restaurants. To reach the restaurant, we had to walk over a small bridge lined with peddlers who sold all kinds of nuts, candy, and sweets. We always stopped on the way back to buy various nut and sesame candies, which we ate on the drive back home. The recipe below varies slightly from the Arab version, which is made with sugar only and is therefore more brittle. The Greeks, like the Sicilians, also use honey in their sesame candy, which makes for a more chewy texture. Be sure, though, to use good honey, as it will make a difference in the taste. If you want, you can replace the sesame seeds with almonds, hazelnuts, or peanuts.

MAKES 16–20 CANDIES

> 2 cups sesame seeds
>
> ¼ cup sugar
>
> ¾ cup very good honey
>
> ¾ teaspoon lemon zest
>
> scant ¼ teaspoon ground cinnamon

I Grease a large baking sheet with a little vegetable oil.

2 Combine the ingredients in a saucepan and place over medium heat. Stir continuously until the sesame seeds turn golden, about 20 minutes. Pour the mixture out onto the oiled baking sheet, and using an oiled spatula, spread to a ½-inch thickness. Let cool, then cut into medium diamonds or sticks. Serve at room temperature or store in a hermetically sealed container. If the weather is really hot, keep in the refrigerator.

Instant Granita

It was not so long ago that ice was sold on the street in massive blocks wheeled on wooden carts. During the day the blocks were covered with thick blankets so that the ice would not melt in the sun. Now that refrigeration is commonly available to rich and poor alike, it is rare to find ice on the street except in Sicily, where it serves to make instant granita. The seller uses a special implement, the grattarola, to shave the ice off the block and straight into the glasses. He then pours your choice of syrup over the ice, and there you are, an instant granita. Perhaps not as delicate nor as smooth as the real ones sold in cafés and bars, but very refreshing nonetheless, and a lot cheaper.

To make your own, put a few ice cubes in a clean kitchen towel. Twist the towel tightly around the ice and smash it against a work surface or beat it with a rolling pin. When the ice is crushed very fine, spoon it into tall glasses, pour in fresh fruit juice sweetened to taste or a syrup such as lemon, anise, mint, grenadine, or orzata (almond milk, page 248), and serve with a long spoon. You can, if you like, pep up your granita with a small handful of presoaked pine nuts and a sprig of mint.

Sicilian Almond Ice Cream

◆

GRANITA DI MANDORLE

SICILIANS OFTEN HAVE THEIR ice cream sandwiched inside a brioche—a strange but fun way of serving it and just as good, if not better, as inside a cone. Once you have made the brioche (see note below), cut each open across the middle without detaching the two halves and fill the inside with as much ice cream as is manageable. Serve as if it were a sandwich. You will have to eat it double-quick or else you will look like a toddler who has had a few mouthfuls of ice cream. You can vary the nuts here by using pistachios, hazelnuts, or any other you prefer.

MAKES 5–6 CUPS

3 tablespoons cornstarch

1 quart whole milk

1¼ cups sugar

1½ cups blanched almonds, soaked in boiling water for 20 minutes,
    then dried and ground very fine (about 1 cup)

1 Using a whisk, dissolve the cornstarch in about ½ cup milk and set aside. Put the rest of the milk in a saucepan. Place over medium heat and bring to a boil. Remove from the heat and whisk in the cornstarch mixture. Add the sugar and return to the heat, whisking until the milk is back to boiling. Remove from the heat and set aside. Stir occasionally to dissolve the skin.

2 Once the milk has cooled completely, stir in the ground almonds and either freeze in an ice cream maker following the manufacturer's instructions or put in a freezer container and freeze, whisking the mixture every hour or so for about 6 hours, or until the ice cream is the right consistency. Serve plain or inside brioches.

Note: To make Sicilian ice cream sandwiches, prepare the Easter bread recipe on page 110, but omit the spices and either make the dough plain or add the zest of 1 lemon. Divide the dough into 6 equal parts and shape each into a round, flat bun measuring about 3 inches in diameter. Bake for 10–15 minutes and cool, then split and fill with ice cream.

YOU CAN USE THE following recipe as a master recipe for any fruit ice creams of your choice. Simply replace the mango with an equal amount of any other fruit that takes your fancy—prickly pears, mulberries, figs, strawberries, watermelon, or peaches—but be sure to adjust the amount of sugar according to the sweetness of the fruit.

MAKES 1 QUART

1¼ cups milk

⅔ cup sugar

3 medium to large mangoes

1 cup crème fraîche

1 Pour the milk in a saucepan and place over medium heat. Bring to a boil, keeping an eye on the milk so that it does not boil over. Pour the milk into a mixing bowl, preferably with a spout, and stir in the sugar until dissolved. Let cool.

2 Peel the mangoes and take the flesh off the seed. Process the flesh in a food processor until you have a smooth purée. You should end up with about 2 cups mango purée. Add to the milk along with the crème fraîche and stir until completely blended. Pour into an ice cream maker and freeze following the manufacturer's instructions. If you don't have an ice cream maker, put the mixture in a freezer container and freeze, whisking the mixture every hour or so for about 6 hours, or until the ice cream is the right consistency.

Mango Ice Cream

◆

BŪZA ALA MANGA

Pistachio Nut Ice Cream

Būza ala Festuq Halabi

AN ARAB VARIATION ON Sicilian almond ice cream. Whereas in Sicily they serve ice cream sandwiched in a brioche, in Lebanon and Syria they serve it in a rectangular cookie container. The ice cream vendor will stuff as much ice cream as he can into the cookie, filling it almost to bursting, and pile more on top. You can vary the nuts by using pine nuts, almonds, or hazelnuts. Prepare them in the same way as the pistachios.

MAKES 1 QUART

2¾ cups whole milk

¾ cup sugar

1 cup raw pistachio nuts, soaked (and peeled if you have the patience)

1½ cups crème fraîche

2 tablespoons rose water

1 Pour the milk into a saucepan and place over medium heat. Bring to a boil, then remove from the heat and strain into a mixing bowl. Add the sugar and stir until completely dissolved. Let cool.

2 Put the peeled pistachios in a food processor and process until ground medium fine. Add the nuts to the milk and stir in the cream and rose water. Blend until the cream is fully incorporated. If you have an ice cream maker, follow the manufacturer's instructions to freeze the mixture. If not, put the mixture in a freezer container and freeze, whisking the mixture every hour or so for about 6 hours, or until the ice cream is the right consistency.

THE RECIPE BELOW IS Lebanese, but I have had a very similar ice cream in Crete, where it is called kaymaki (a word that indicates the use of mastic [page 218] in the preparation), and in Turkey, where it is called dondurma. The combination of salep and mastic gives the ice cream a luscious, chewy texture that prolongs the pleasure of savoring it. You can vary on the rose water flavoring by using vanilla.

MAKES 5 CUPS

Milk Ice Cream

◆

BŪZA ALA HALEEB

4 cups whole milk

¾ cup sugar

½ teaspoon ground mastic, available in Middle Eastern markets

1 tablespoon salep powder (page 255), available in Middle Eastern markets

1¼ cups crème fraîche

2 tablespoons rose water

2 tablespoons finely chopped pistachio nuts for the garnish

1 Put the milk in a saucepan and place over medium heat. Bring to a boil, then strain into a mixing bowl and stir in the sugar. Let stand until warm, then pour 2 tablespoons over the ground mastic and stir until well blended. Set aside.

2 Pour the milk into a clean saucepan and place over moderately high heat. Bring to a boil, stirring constantly, then add the salep little by little—don't add the powder too quickly or else it will not dilute properly but will form lumps. Keep stirring over the heat for a few minutes, then pour into a mixing bowl and add the diluted mastic, crème fraîche, and rose water. Blend well and let cool.

3 If you have an ice cream maker, follow the manufacturer's instructions to freeze the mixture. If not, put the mixture in a freezer container and freeze, whisking the mixture every hour or so for about 6 hours, or until the ice cream is the right consistency. Sprinkle with the chopped pistachio nuts before serving.

DRINKS

Almond Milk ✦ *H'leeb del Loz*

Pomegranate Juice

Fresh Lemonade

Carrot Juice

Licorice Drink ✦ *'Assir 'Erq el-Süss*

Bulgur Drink ✦ *Boza*

Tamarind Drink ✦ *Tamer Hindi*

Salep ✦ *Sahlab*

Yogurt Drink ✦ *Ayran*

Mint Tea ✦ *Atay bel Na'na'*

An old lady stopping for a drink of water in an ancient doorway; everywhere you go in Cairo, you'll find jars of water for people to drink from, although nowadays most jars are modern metal ones.

Almond Milk

◆

H'LEEB DEL LOZ

DIFFERENT VERSIONS OF THIS drink are available throughout the Mediterranean. In Italy it is called latte di mandorle or orzata, and the almond milk is simply sweetened. In Spain it is called horchata, and cinnamon is added to flavor the drink. The Moroccans use orange blossom water, while the Israelis add mastic (page 218). You can buy almond milk ready-made, but the homemade version is very simple and so much better. Do take the trouble, though, to soak the almonds before pulverizing them, or the liquid will not be as smooth or milky.

SERVES 4

2 cups blanched almonds

⅓ cup sugar, or to taste

1 tablespoon orange blossom water

1 Soak the almonds in boiling water for 30 minutes. Drain well and put in a food processor. Add the sugar and process until you have a very fine paste. Transfer to a mixing bowl, preferably one with a spout, and pour in 2⅓ cups water. Stir until the sugar is completely dissolved and leave to infuse in the refrigerator for 30 minutes, or until you are ready to serve the drink.

2 Strain through a very fine sieve into a jug (if you don't have a fine sieve, line a colander with cheesecloth) and press on the almond pulp to extract as much liquid as you can. Discard the almond pulp and stir the orange blossom water into the drink. Taste and adjust the sweetness if necessary. Serve chilled. The almond milk will keep for a day or two at the most, well covered in the refrigerator.

THE IDEA OF EXTRACTING juice from pomegranates might initially sound incongruous, especially when you think of how long it takes to remove the seeds. But you can squeeze pomegranates as you do oranges. One drawback, though, is the slightly bitter taste imparted by the pith. As an alternative, you can cut the fruit in half, turn it over a bowl, holding the cut side loosely against your palm, and lightly tap the skin with the back of a knife. The seeds will fall out, and you can process them through a juicer to produce a drink without any hint of bitterness. The color of the juice will be an exquisite red or a pearly pink, depending on the type of pomegranate you use.

Pomegranate Juice

MAKES 1–1½ QUARTS

>   5 large juicy sweet pomegranates (about 4¼ pounds), slightly chilled
>   1½ tablespoons orange blossom water, or to taste

Extract the pomegranate juice as described above and pour into a jug. Stir in the orange blossom water and serve immediately. If you are not serving the juice immediately, cover it well so that it does not oxidize.

Fresh Lemonade

ONCE YOU HAVE HAD this freshly made lemonade, you will never want to drink the artificial beverage again. In Turkey it is flavored with added lemon zest. The zest is pounded with sugar, wrapped in cheesecloth, and dropped into the lemonade to infuse for a couple of hours before being discarded and the lemonade served.

MAKES 1 QUART

juice of 4 lemons

¼ cup sugar, or to taste

Pour the lemon juice into a large pitcher. Add 3–4 cups water, depending on how sour you like your lemonade, and stir in the sugar. Let the sugar dissolve completely before adding ice cubes. Taste and adjust the sweetness if necessary and serve immediately.

Carrot Juice

BECAUSE OF ITS HEALTHFUL qualities, carrot juice is often sold by the bottle for people to take to hospital patients in Lebanon and Egypt. If the vendor does not have the plastic caps anymore, he will use a piece of carrot as a stopper. Rather attractive, but perhaps not the safest way to transport the supposedly sealed bottle.

MAKES ABOUT ¾ QUART

2½ pounds carrots, slightly chilled

4 teaspoons orange blossom water

Process the carrots through a juicer. The amount given should yield about 3¼ cups juice. Transfer to a jug or individual glasses and add the orange blossom water. Stir well and serve immediately. If you want to store the juice, keep it well covered so that it does not oxidize.

Licorice drink is a great favorite during Ramadan, when it is sold on the street either by the glass or packed into plastic bags. The way to prepare it is rather complicated but worth explaining here just in case you want to try it. The dried licorice root needs to be first pulverized. Boiling water mixed with a little baking soda is added gradually and

Licorice Drink

◈

'Assir 'Erq el-Süss

rubbed into the pulverized licorice, after which the licorice is left to soak for 2 hours. The street vendor who explained the process to me rubs the boiling water into the licorice by hand, but I'd recommend using a wooden spoon or other implement. The wet licorice is then carefully wrapped in a cloth without being squeezed, shaped into a cushion, and laid on a tray. Some trays have holes in the middle and are placed over a container, while others have a kind of spout and are placed on a slant with the spout over the container. Cold water is then drizzled onto the licorice cushion, and the drink seeps through the licorice cushion and into the container. You can achieve the same effect using a colander or coffee filter. The

proportions to make the drink are as follows: for 2 pounds ground licorice, you will first need 3 cups hot water and 1 teaspoon baking soda, then 5 quarts cold water to drizzle over the licorice cushion. By the way, you can buy licorice root already ground in Middle Eastern stores.

A precarious and very common way of packaging licorice drink; the Arabic writing above the bags reads "the work, daily—the service, nightly."

Sprinkling the glasses of boza with cinnamon

THIS CURIOUS TURKISH CONCOCTION is a typical winter drink that is made with bulgur and rice and left to ferment before being served with roasted chickpeas. It is somewhat of an acquired taste, although worth trying, especially at the amazingly unchanged 1920s Vefa Bozacisi in Istanbul, where they still have the glass in which Ataturk drank boza. The color of homemade boza is not as white as that of the commercial one. Also the taste is not as unusual; on the contrary it is more palatable and makes you feel very healthy, especially if you make it less sweet, as in the recipe below.

Bulgur Drink

❖

BOZA

MAKES JUST OVER A QUART (TO SERVE 6–8)

- ⅔ cup fine bulgur
- 1 heaping tablespoon short-grain white rice
- ½ cup sugar
- ½ teaspoon active dry yeast
- 1 teaspoon ground cinnamon

1 Put the bulgur and rice in a large saucepan, add 2 quarts water, and place over medium-high heat. Bring to a boil, lower the heat, cover, and simmer for 1½ hours. Strain through a fine sieve, pressing down on the pulp to extract as much liquid as possible, and return to the heat. Stir in the sugar and simmer for another 2–3 minutes, stirring continuously, until the sugar is completely dissolved.

2 Let stand until tepid. Spoon a little of the mixture into a bowl and stir in the yeast. Transfer the rest to a large pitcher. When the yeast liquid starts rising, stir it into the drink in the pitcher and cover with a clean kitchen towel. Leave at room temperature to ferment overnight or about 8 hours if you are preparing the drink in the morning. The boza will be ready when bubbles form on the surface. Serve chilled or at room temperature sprinkled with a little cinnamon.

Tamarind Drink

◆

TAMER HINDI

WHENEVER I BUY ANYTHING to drink on the street, I always wonder whether I should really drink out of the vendors' glasses, which are only rinsed in water between customers, but to be honest, the thought has never stopped me from enjoying the different exciting drinks that are available throughout the Mediterranean. The following is a very sweet drink, kept in massive glass jars packed with ice or carried on the vendor's back in elaborate metal containers. It provides a welcome refreshment at the height of the summer heat in Jerusalem or Cairo.

MAKES ABOUT 3 CUPS

½ pound tamarind paste

1 cup sugar

juice of 1 lemon

Soak the tamarind paste in 4 cups water for at least 10 hours. Then dissolve the paste in the water with your hands or in a blender. Pass through a fine sieve, pressing on it with the back of a ladle, and transfer the liquid to a heavy-based saucepan. Stir in the sugar and place over low heat. Simmer, stirring occasionally, for 30 minutes, or until thickened, then add the lemon juice and continue simmering for another 20 minutes. Pour into a sterilized bottle and seal the bottle only when cooled completely. To make the drink, use 1 tablespoon syrup for each cup of ice water, or adjust to your liking.

Tamarind drink vendor in Cairo

SALEP IS A FINE powder extracted from a variety of dried orchid tubers. It is used as a thickening agent in Arabic, Greek, and Turkish ice cream or boiled with milk to produce a thick, warming winter drink. You will find it in Turkey (usually drunk with simit), Syria, Lebanon, Israel, and Egypt. In Israel and Egypt the drink is garnished with nuts, raisins, and desiccated coconut, while in Lebanon and Syria the garnish is a sprinkling of ground cinnamon. A similar drink was common in France in the seventeenth century.

SERVES 4

> 4 cups whole milk
>
> ½ teaspoon ground mastic (page 218), available in Middle Eastern markets
>
> 1 tablespoon salep powder, available in Middle Eastern markets
>
> 6 tablespoons sugar
>
> ground cinnamon for the garnish

Pour the milk in a saucepan and place over medium heat. As the milk warms up, remove a little and mix it with the mastic. Bring the rest of the milk to a boil, then add the salep little by little so that it does not form lumps. Keep stirring over the heat for about 5 minutes, then add the sugar and stir for another 3 minutes. Stir in the mastic mixture and ladle into soup bowls. Sprinkle with the cinnamon and serve hot as is or with simit (page 116).

Salep

SAHLAB

A DELICIOUSLY REFRESHING DRINK that is at its best when made with sheep's or goat's milk yogurt.

MAKES 1 QUART

> 2 cups sheep's or goat's milk yogurt
>
> salt

Put the yogurt in a blender and add 2 cups chilled water and salt to taste. Blend until lightly frothy. Pour into 4 glasses and serve with or without ice cubes. This will keep a couple of days in the refrigerator.

Yogurt Drink

AYRAN

Mint Tea

◆

ATAY BEL NA'NA'

THERE ARE MANY TYPICAL sights on the streets of Morocco: wooden carts with huge pots of fiery snail soup; corn grilled right on the pavement; stacks of unshelled hard-boiled eggs; or mounds of unshelled peanuts wheeled through the narrow streets of the medina. But no sight is more typical than that of young boys carrying trays with silver-plated teapots filled with mint tea and surrounded by elaborately decorated glasses. The tea is not carried around with the hope of finding takers on the street; rather, it is taken to the merchants for them to have or to offer to clients. Thus, you will hardly ever need to buy a cup of tea in Morocco. Simply walk into a shop and start looking at what they have. In no time at all you will have a burning glass of cloyingly sweet mint tea in your hand. In Tunisia you will have the added bonus of finding pine nuts at the bottom of your cup.

SERVES 4

2 teaspoons green tea leaves

3 tablespoons sugar

1½ cups fresh mint

2 tablespoons pine nuts (optional)

First heat your teapot with boiling water, then add the tea leaves. Add about 2¾ cups boiling water and stir in the sugar. Bruise the mint a little, then add to the pot. Push the mint down with a spoon and let the tea infuse for a couple of minutes. Serve in traditional tea glasses or regular small glasses, adding ½ tablespoon pine nuts to each glass if desired.

A little mint tea to finish off a mechoui lunch, Marrakesh

SELECTED BIBLIOGRAPHY

BALKANS

Mirodan, Valadimir. *The Balkan Cookbook*. London: Lezzard Publishing, 1987.

Kaneva-Johnson, Maria. *The Melting Pot, Balkan Food & Cookery*. London: Prospect Books, 1995.

EGYPT

Abdennour, Samia. *Egyptian Cooking*. Cairo: The American University in Cairo Press, 1984.

Aït Mohamed, Salima. *La Cuisine Egyptienne*. Paris: Temps Gourmands Editions, 1997.

Darby, William J., Paul Ghaliongui & Louis Grivetti. *The Gift of Osiris*. San Diego: Academic Press, 1971.

FRANCE

Escudier, Jean-Noël. *La Véritable Cuisine Provençale et Niçoise*. Toulon, France: Les Editions Provencia-Toulon, 1964.

Lheureux, Simone. *La Cuisine du Soleil entre Provence et Languedoc*. Nîmes, France: Editions Lacour, 1986.

Saint-Ange, Mme E. *La Bonne Cuisine*. Paris: Larousse, 1995.

GREECE

Alexiadou, Vepha. *Greek Pastries and Desserts.* Thessaloniki, Greece: self-published, 1991.

Kochilas, Diane. *The Food and Wine of Greece*. New York: St. Martin's Press, 1990.

Kremezi, Aglaia. *The Foods of Greece*. New York: Stewart, Tabori & Chang, 1999.

Psilakis, Maria. *La Cuisine Crétoise*. Greece: Karmanor, 1996.

Salaman, Rena. *Greek Food*. London: HarperCollins, 1993.

————.*Greek Island Cookery*. London: Ebury Press, 1987.

Souli, Sofia. *Grèce, Cuisine & Vins*. Editions Toubis, 1997.

ISRAEL

Abu-Ghosh, Nawal. *The Arab-Israeli Cuisine*. Jerusalem: Keter Publishing House, 1996.

Tower of David Museum. *Eating in Jerusalem*. Tel Aviv: Modan, 1992.

Valero, Rina. *Delights of Jerusalem*. Brai-Brak, Israel: Nahar Publishing House and Steimatzky, 1985.

Ganor, Avi, and Ron Maiberg. *Taste of Israel*. New York: Rizzoli, 1990.

ITALY

Accame, Franco, Silvio Torre, and Virgilio Pronzati. *Il Grande Libro della Cucina Ligure*. Italy: De Ferrari Editore, 1997.

D'Alba, Tommaso. *La Cucina Siciliana di Derivazione Araba*. Palermo, Italy: self-published, 1980.

Anonymous. *Millericette*. Italy: Avallardi, 1998.

Bugialli, Giuliano. *The Fine Art of Italian Cooking*. New York: Times Books, 1977.

Lo Monte, Mimmetta. *Classic Sicilian Cooking*. New York: Simon and Schuster, 1990.

Medici, Lorenza de'. *The Heritage of Italian Cooking*. New York: Random House, 1995.

Pradelli, Alessandro Molinari. *La Cucina Ligure*. Rome: Newton & Compton Editori, 1996.

Randazzo, Giuseppina. *La Cucina Siciliana*. Palermo, Italy: Reprint S.A.S., 1992.

Salda, Anna Gosetti della. *Le Ricette Regionali Italiane*. Italy, Solares, 1980

Simeti, Mary Taylor. *Pomp and Sustenance: Twenty-five Centuries of Sicilian Food*. New York: Henry Holt & Co., 1991.

Lanza, Anna Tasca. *The Heart of Sicily*. New York: Cassell, 1993.

———.*The Flavors of Sicily*. New York: Clarkson Potter/ Crown Publishers, 1996.

LEBANON/SYRIA

Corey, Helen. *The Art of Syrian Cookery*. New York: Doubleday & Co, 1962.

Helou, Anissa. *Lebanese Cuisine*. New York: St. Martin's Press, 1995.

Khayat, Marie Karam, and Margaret Clark Keatinge. *Food from the Arab World*. Beirut: Khayat, 1959.

Mouzannar, Ibrahim. *La Cuisine Libanaise*. Beirut: Librairie du Liban, 1981.

MOROCCO

Benani Smires, Latifa. *La Cuisine Marocaine*. Morocco: n.p., n.d.

Ginaudeau-Franc, Zette. *Les Secrets des Cuisines en Terre Marocaine*. Paris: Tallandier,1991.

Helou, Anissa. *Café Morocco*. New York: Contemporary Books, 1999.

SPAIN

Andrews, Colman. *Catalan Cuisine*. London: Grub Street, 1997.

Domingo, Xavier, and Pierre Hussenot. *Le Goût de l'Espagne*. Paris: Flammarion, 1992.

Luard, Elisabeth. *The Flavours of Andalucia*. Glasgow: Collins & Brown, 1991.

Mendel, Janet. *Traditional Spanish Cooking*. Reading, England: Garnet, 1996.

Sevilla, Maria José. *Life and Food in the Basque Country*. London: Weidenfeld & Nicholson, 1989.

TUNISIA

Kaak, Zeinab. *La Sofra*. Tunis: Cérès Éditions, 1995.

Kouki, Mohamed. *Cuisine et Patisserie Tunisiennes*. Tunis: Dar el-Türath el-Tünssi, 1997.

———.*La Cuisine Tunisienne d'Ommok Sannafa*. Tunis: Presses de l'Imprimerie Wafa, 1998.

TURKEY

Algar, Ayla. *Classical Turkish Cooking*. New York: HarperCollins, 1991.

Ertürk, Ilyas. *Turkish Kitchen Today*. Istanbul: Istanbul Mastabaasi, 1967.

Halici, Nevin. *Turkish Cookbook*. London: Dorling Kindersley, 1989.

————.*Classical Turkish Cuisine*. Istanbul: Gategourmet, 1999.

GENERAL

Larousse Gastronomique. Paris: Larousse, 1938.

Aharoni, Israel. *La Cuisine des Rues*. Paris: Minerva, 1999.

Alford, Jeffrey, and Naomi Duguid. *Flatbreads and Flavors*. New York: William Morrow and Company, Inc., 1995.

Andrews, Colman. *Flavors of the Riviera*. New York: Bantam Books, 1996.

Boxer, Arabella. *Mediterranean Cookbook*. London: Penguin, 1983.

Davidson, Alan. *Oxford Companion to Food*. Oxford, England: Oxford University Press, 2000.

————.*Mediterranean Seafood*. London: Penguin, 1981.

Evans, Judith, and Evan Evans. *The Book of Bread*. New York: Harper & Row, 1982.

Goldstein, Joyce. *Mediterranean: The Beautiful Cookbook*. San Francisco: Harper San Francisco, 1994.

Mallos, Tess. *The Complete Middle East Cookbook*. New York: McGraw-Hill, 1979.

O'Shea, Bernadette. *Pizza Defined*. Bantry, Ireland: Estragon Press, 1997.

Perl, Lila. *Rice, Spice and Bitter Oranges*. Cleveland: The World Publishing Company, 1967.

Roden, Claudia. *A New Book of Middle Eastern Food*. New York: Penguin, 1986.

Wolfert, Paula. *Mediterranean Cooking*. New York: HarperCollins, 1996.

INDEX

Page numbers in *italics* refer to illustrations.

Acorns, boiled, 46
Almond:
    Ice Cream, Sicilian, 242
    Milk, 248
    Triangles, 225–26
Anchovy(ies):
    fried, skewered, 139–40, *140*
    Tomato, Olives and (sandwiches), 149–50
Anise Cookies, 237
Apricots, in Dried Fruit and Nut Compote, 220
Arancini (or *Arancine*):
    in Bianco, 58
    al Ragù, 56–58
Argan oil, 37
Arnaki Fricassée me Maroulia, 176–77
Artichoke(s):
    grilled, 47–48
    Pie, 102–4, *103*
'Assir 'Erq el-Süss, 251
Atay bel Na'na', 256, *257*
Ayran, 255

Babouch, 14–15
Baraziq, 238–39
Barbecues, xxiv–xxv, 157–69

Chicken Kebabs, 163
Kebabs, Greek, 160
Kebabs, Lebanese, 161
Kebabs, Moroccan, and *Pinchitos Morunos*, 162
Kebabs, Turkish, 158–59
Kefta, Lebanese, 164–65
Kefta, Moroccan, 166–67
pork chops, grilled, 169
Swordfish Brochettes, 168
Basbüssa, 226–27
Bean(s). *See* Cannellini bean(s); Chickpea(s);
    Fava bean(s)
Beef:
    Ragù, 56–57
    rump steak, in Jerusalem Mix, 136–37
Beyssara, *10*, 11
Boiled snacks, 46–47
Borekas Tapükhay Adama, 97–98
Boreks, Potato, 97–98
Bougatsa, 230, 230–31
Boza, 252, 253
Breads, xxii–xxiii, 75–123
    Easter, 110–11, *111*, *119*
    Flat, Moroccan, 85–86
    Flat, Tunisian, Omelet in, 127–28, *129*
    Focaccia, Lemon and Olive Oil, 77–78
    Focaccia, Sicilian, 79–80, *80*

Breads (cont.)

    Fried, Tunisian, 144–45, *145*

    Fried, Yemeni, 83–84

    Meat, Turkish, 90–91

    Moroccan, 81–82

    Pancakes, French, 122–23

    Pizza, Neapolitan, 120–21

    Ramadan, with Dates, 114–15

    Sesame Galettes, Greek, 118–19

    Sesame Galettes, Turkish, 116–17, *117*

    Thursday, 112–13

    Thyme, *88*, 88–89

    see also Pastries (savory)

Briami, 185

Brigidini, 237

Brochettes:

    Swordfish, 168

    see also Kebabs

Bulgur:

    Drink, *252*, 253

    "Kibbé," Turkish, 142–43

Büza:

    ala Festuq Halabi, 244

    ala Haleeb, 245

    ala Manga, 243

Cabbage:

    Couscous with Seven Vegetables, 202–3

    White, Salad, 38

Cacik, 73

Cake, Semolina, 226–27

Calamari, Fried, 55, *55*

Callos, 208–9

Calmares e Pescados Fritos, 55, *55*

Candy, Sesame, Sicilian, 240–41

Cannellini bean(s):

    and Pork Stew, 175

    with Saffron, 36

    Salad (sandwiches), 154

    Tagine with Parsley, Tunisian, 23–24

Carrot(s):

    Couscous with Seven Vegetables, 202–3

    Juice, 250

    Vegetable Fritters, 52–53, *53*

Casse-croûte, 126, *126*

Castagnaccio, 215

Cauliflower, Fried, 51

Cazzilli, 59–60

Chakchüka, 39

Cheese:

    Artichoke Pie, 102–4, *103*

    Baked Pasta, 183–84

    Feta, Salad, 33

    Grilled Vegetables and (sandwiches), 155

    Pies, Sweet, 232–33, *233*

    Rice Pie, 106–7

    Saj Borek with Spinach and, *92*, 92–93

    Spinach Rolls, 99–100

    Swiss Chard Pie, 104–5

    Triangles (Greek), 101

    Triangles (Lebanese), 96

    Vegetable Loaf, 21–22

    White Rice Croquettes, 58

Chermüla, 44–45

Chestnut(s):

    grilled, 48

    Pudding, 215

Chicken, xviii

    with Garlic, 207

    Jerusalem Mix, 136–37

Kebabs, 163

livers, in Jerusalem Mix, 136–37

with Moghrabbiyeh, 204–6

Paella, 210–11

Shawarma, 132–34, *133*

Tagine with Olives and Preserved Lemons, 198–99

Tagine with Parsley, Tunisian, 23–24

Tagine with Potatoes and Peas, 196–97

Chickpea(s):

Chicken with Moghrabbiyeh, 204–6

Couscous with Seven Vegetables, 202–3

Falafel, 152–53

Fritters, *53*, 54

Hommus, 68

Lamb Shanks with Wheat and, 200

and Lamb Soup, 6–7

Snack, *25*, 25–26

Soup, 8–9

Chili(es):

Cilantro Chutney, Yemeni, 69

Paste, Hot, 67

Shrimp, 43

Chtapodi Stifado, 180–81

Chutney, Cilantro, Yemeni, 69

Çig Köfte, 142–43

Cilantro Chutney, Yemeni, 69

Çingene Pilavi, 33

Cipolle Ripieni, 30

Clotted cream:

Arabic, 224

Fritters, 234–35

Cod, in Spicy Fish (sandwiches), 146–48

Compote, Dried Fruit and Nut, 220

Cookies:

Anise, 237

Sesame, 238–39

Shortbread, Lebanese, 235

Shortbread, Moroccan, 236

Corn, grilled, 48

Couscous, 201

Moghrabbiyeh, Chicken with, 204–6

with Seven Vegetables, 202–3

Cream:

Clotted, Arabic, 224

Clotted, Fritters, 234–35

Pie, *230*, 230–31

Crêpes, 122–23

Croquettes:

Potato, 59–60

"Red" Rice, 56–58

White Rice, 58

Crostini, Spicy Fish as topping for, 148

Cubbàita di Giuggiulena, 240–41

Cucumbers, in Yogurt Dip, 73

Dates:

Kairouan Pastries, 228–29, *229*

Ramadan Bread with, 114–15

Desserts. *See* Sweets and desserts

Dips:

Hazelnut, 70

Hommus, 68

Tahini, 71

Yogurt, 73

Djaj bel B'tata wa Jeblana, 196–97

D'jaj M'chermel, 198–99

Domates Yiemistes me Ryzi, 186–87

Doughnuts, Moroccan, 108–9

Dressing, Mayonnaise, 38

Dried Fruit and Nut Compote, 220
Drinks, xxv, 247–57
    Almond Milk, 248
    Bulgur, *252*, *253*
    Carrot Juice, 250
    Lemonade, Fresh, 250
    Licorice, 251
    Mint Tea, 256, *257*
    Pomegranate Juice, 249
    Salep, 255
    Tamarind, 254
    Yogurt, 255

Easter Bread, 110–11, *111*, *119*
Eggplant(s):
    Baked Stuffed, 178–79
    Fans, Fried, 51
    Fried Vegetables à la Tunisienne, 60–61
    Grilled Vegetables and Cheese (sandwiches), 155
    Salad, Moroccan, 40
    Vegetable Fritters, 52–53, *53*
Eggs:
    hard-boiled, *16–17*, 46
    Omelet in Flat Tunisian Bread, 127–28, *129*
    Potato Omelet, Spanish, 19
    Spinach Omelet, Italian, 20
    "Submarine," Tunisian, 126
    Tagine with Parsley, Tunisian, 23–24
    Vegetable Loaf, 21–22
Egyptian fare, xviii–xix, xxii, 46, 48
    bibliography for, 258
    Fava Bean Salad, 34–35
    Rice, Lentils, and Vermicelli with Hot Tomato
        Sauce, 188–89

Semolina Cake, 226–27
Etli Ekmek, 90–91

Falafel, 152–53
Farinata, *25*, 25–26
Fassüliah K'dra, 36
Fasulye Piyazi, 154
Fatayer bil-Qarish, 96
Fatayer bil-Sabanegh, 94–95
Fava bean(s):
    Boiled, with Spiced Salt, 49–50
    Couscous with Seven Vegetables, 202–3
    Falafel, 152–53
    Salad, 34–35
    Soup, *10*, 11
Feta cheese:
    Cheese Triangles, 101
    Saj Borek with Spinach and, *92*, 92–93
    Salad, 33
    Spinach Rolls, 99–100
Filo pastry:
    Almond Triangles, 225–26
    Artichoke Pie, 102–4, *103*
    Cheese Triangles, 101
    Cream Pie, *230*, 230–31
    Onion Pie, 107
    Rice Pie, 106–7
    Spinach Rolls, 99–100
    Swiss Chard Pie, 104–5
Fish:
    anchovies, fried, skewered, 139–40, *140*
    Anchovy, Tomato, and Olives (sandwiches), 149–50
    Fried, Italian, 55
    Fried, Moroccan, 44–45

Mackerel with Herbs, Baked, 182–83
Spicy (sandwiches), 146–48
Swordfish Brochettes, 168
tuna, in Fried Bread, 144–45, *145*
tuna, in Tunisian "Submarine," 126
see also Seafood
Flat bread:
Moroccan, 85–86
Tunisian, Omelet in, 127–28, *129*
Focaccia:
Lemon and Olive Oil, 77–78
Sicilian, 79–80, *80*
Focaccia con Limone e Olio, 77–78
French fare, xvi–xvii
bibliography for, 258
Pancakes, 122–23
Sausages, Spicy, and French Fries (sandwiches),
138
Tomato, Olives, and Anchovy (sandwiches),
149–50
French fries:
Sandwich Batata, 151
Spicy Sausages and (sandwiches), 138
Fricassée (Greek), *182*
Arnaki, me Maroulia, 144–45
Fricassée (Tunisian), 144–45, *145, 182*
Fried:
Bread, Tunisian, 144–45, *145*
Bread, Yemeni, 83–84
Calamari and Other Fish, 55, *55*
Cauliflower, 51
Eggplant Fans, 51
Fish, Moroccan, 44–45
Mussels (sandwiches), 139–40, *140–41*
Vegetables à la Tunisienne, 60–61

see also Croquettes; Fritters
Frittata di Spinaci, 20
Frittelle di Verdure, 52–53, *53*
Fritters:
Chickpea, *53,* 54
Clotted Cream, 234–35
Vegetable, 52–53, *53*
Fül Maslüq, 49–50
Fül Müdammas, 34–35

Galettes:
Sesame, Greek, 118–19
Sesame, Turkish, 116–17, *117*
Gambas Pil-Pil, 43
Garlic:
Chicken with, 207
Marinade, 163
Sauce, 72
Gelo di Melone, 216–17
Genoese fare:
Artichoke Pie, 102–4, *103*
Chickpea Snack, *25,* 25–26
Rice Pie, 106–7
Stuffed Vegetables, 27–32
Swiss Chard Pie, 104–5
Vegetable Fritters, 52–53, *53*
Vegetable Loaf, 21–22
Vegetables, Grilled, and Cheese (sandwiches),
155
Ghlala, 14–15
Ghraybeh, 235
Ghreyba, 236
Granita, Instant, 241
Granita di Mandorle, 242
Greek fare, xvii, xxv, 48

Greek fare *(cont.)*
    bibliography for, 258
    Cheese Pies, Sweet, 232–33, *233*
    Cheese Triangles, 101
    Cream Pie, *230*, 230–31
    Easter Bread, 110–11, *111*, *119*
    Eggplants, Baked Stuffed, 178–79
    Kebabs, 160
    Lamb and Lettuce Stew, 176–77
    Lamb with Pasta and Tomatoes, Baked,
        173–74
    Mackerel with Herbs, Baked, 182–83
    Octopus and Onion Stew, 180–81
    Pasta, Baked, 183–84
    Pork and Cannellini Bean Stew, 175
    Sesame Galettes, 118–19
    Spinach Rolls, 99–100
    Tomatoes and Peppers, Stuffed, 186–87
    Vegetables, Baked, 185
    Yogurt Dip, 73
Green beans, in Vegetable Loaf, 21–22
Grilled snacks, 46, 47–48

Harira, 6–7
Harissa, 67
Hazelnut Dip, 70
Hergma à l'Occidentale, 200
Hirino me Fasolia, 175
H'leeb del Loz, 248
Hommus, 68
    Kebabs with (sandwiches), 135
Hommus bi-Tahineh, 68
Hot Chili Paste, 67
Hüt bel Chermüla, 44–45

Ice cream:
    Almond, Sicilian, 242
    Mango, 243
    Milk, 245
    Pistachio Nut, 244
Ingredients, 2
Intestines, grilled, 48
Iskembe Çorbasi, 12–13
Israeli fare, xxvi, 46
    bibliography for, 258
    Cilantro Chutney, Yemeni, 69
    Jerusalem Mix, 136–37
    Lamb Shawarma, 130–31
    Potato Boreks, 97–98
Italian fare, xvi–xvii, xxiii–xxiv, 46–48
    Almond Ice Cream, Sicilian, 242
    Anise Cookies, 237
    Artichoke Pie, 102–4, *103*
    bibliography for, 259
    Calamari and Other Fish, Fried, 55, *55*
    Cauliflower, Fried, 51
    Chestnut Pudding, 215
    Chickpea Fritters, *53*, 54
    Chickpea Snack, *25*, 25–26
    Eggplant Fans, Fried, 51
    Focaccia, Sicilian, 79–80, *80*
    Granita, Instant, 241
    Lemon and Olive Oil Focaccia, 77–78
    Onion Pie, 107
    Pizza, Neapolitan, 120–21
    Potato Croquettes, 59–60
    Rice Croquettes, "Red," 56–58
    Rice Croquettes, White, 58
    Rice Pie, 106–7

Sesame Candy, Sicilian, 240–41
Spinach Omelet, 20
Stuffed Vegetables, 27–32
Swiss Chard Pie, 104–5
Vegetable Fritters, 52–53, *53*
Vegetable Loaf, 21–22
Vegetables, Grilled, and Cheese (sandwiches), 155
Watermelon Pudding, 216–17

Kafta, 164–65
Kairouan Pastries, 228–29, *229*
Kallitsünia, 232–33, *233*
Kalustyan's, 2
Kebabs, *156–57*
    Chicken, 163
    Greek, 160
    with Hommus (sandwiches), 135
    Lebanese, 161
    Moroccan, and *Pinchitos Morunos*, 162
    Swordfish Brochettes, 168
    Turkish, 158–59
Kefta:
    Lebanese, 164–65
    Moroccan, 166–67
Kefta, 166–67
Keftagi, 60–61
Kellage, 234–35
Khobz al-Khamiss, 112–13
Khobz Ramadan, 114–15
Khoshaf, 220
"Kibbé," Turkish, 142–43
Kolioi Lathorigani, 182, *182*
Koshari, 188–89

Koulouria, 118–19
Kseksü, 201
Kseksü Bidawi, 202–3
K'sra, 81–82

Lablabi, 8–9
Lahm Meshwi, 161
Lamb, xviii
    and Chickpea Soup, 6–7
    Couscous with Seven Vegetables, 202–3
    Kebabs, Greek, 160
    Kebabs, Lebanese, 161
    Kebabs, Moroccan, and *Pinchitos Morunos*, 162
    Kebabs, Turkish, 158–59
    Kefta, Lebanese, 164–65
    Kefta, Moroccan, 166–67
    "Kibbé," Turkish, 142–43
    kidneys and testicles, in Jerusalem Mix, 136–37
    and Lettuce Stew, 176–77
    Meat Bread, Turkish, 90–91
    with Pasta and Tomatoes, Baked, 173–74
    Roast, *190*, 190–91, *191*
    Sausages, Spicy, and French Fries (sandwiches), 138
    Shanks with Chickpeas and Wheat, 200
    Shawarma, 130–31
    Soup, 14–15
    Stewed with Cumin, 192–93, *193*
    Stuffed Eggplants, Baked, 178–79
    Tagine with Tomatoes and Potatoes, 195
Lebanese fare, xxiv–xxv
    bibliography for, 259
    Cheese Triangles, 96

Lebanese fare *(cont.)*
    Chicken with Moghrabbiyeh, 204–6
    Clotted Cream, Arabic, 224
    Clotted Cream Fritters, 234–35
    Dried Fruit and Nut Compote, 220
    Falafel, 152–53
    Fish, Spicy (sandwiches), 146–48
    French Fries (sandwiches), 151
    Garlic Sauce, 72
    Kebabs, 161
    Kebabs with Hommus (sandwiches), 135
    Kefta, 164–65
    Lamb Shawarma, 130–31
    Mango Ice Cream, 243
    Milk Ice Cream, 245
    Milk Pudding, *218*, 218–19
    Omelet, 127–28, *129*
    Pistachio Nut Ice Cream, 244
    Ramadan Bread with Dates, 114–15
    Salep, 255
    Sesame Cookies, 238–39
    Shortbread, 235
    Spinach Triangles, 94–95
    Sugar Syrup, 217
    Tahini Dip, 71
    Thursday Bread, 112–13
    Thyme Bread, *88*, 88–89
    Walnut Pancakes, 221–22, *223*
    White Cabbage Salad, 38
    Yogurt Dip, 73
Lemon(s):
    and Olive Oil Focaccia, 77–78
    Preserved, Chicken Tagine with Olives and,
        198–99
Lemonade, Fresh, 250

Lentils, Rice, and Vermicelli with Hot Tomato Sauce,
    188–89
Lettuce and Lamb Stew, 176–77
L'ham bil Matecha wa B'tata, 195
Licorice Drink, 251

Mackerel with Herbs, Baked, 182–83
Main courses. *See* Barbecues; One-pot meals
Manaqish bil-Za'tar, *88*, 88–89
Mango Ice Cream, 243
Maqrūd, 228–29, *229*
Marinades:
    Garlic, 163
    Greek, 160
    Lebanese, 161
    Moroccan, 162
    Turkish, 158–59
Mayonnaise Dressing, 38
Meat Bread, Turkish, 90–91
Mechoui, 190–91
Mechwiyah, 41
Melanzane a Quaglia, 51
Melitzanes Papoutsakia, 178–79
Merguez et Frites, 138
M'hallabiyeh, *218*, 218–19
Midye Dolmasi, 64–66, *65*
Midye Tava, 139–40, *140–41*
Milk:
    Almond, 248
    Ice Cream, 245
    Pudding, *218*, 218–19
Mint Tea, 256, *257*
Mlawi bil-Eggah, 127–28, *129*
M'lawwah, 83–84
Moghrabbiyeh, *205*

Chicken with, 204–6
Moghrabbiyeh ala Dj'ej, 204–6
Morav Yorushalmi, 136–37
Moroccan fare, xvii–xviii, xxii, xxv, xxvi, 46, 48
    Almond Milk, 248
    bibliography for, 259
    Bread, 81–82
    Cannellini Beans with Saffron, 36
    Chicken Tagine with Olives and Preserved
        Lemons, 198–99
    Chicken Tagine with Potatoes and Peas, 196–97
    Chickpea and Lamb Soup, 6–7
    Couscous, 201
    Couscous with Seven Vegetables, 202–3
    Doughnuts, 108–9
    Eggplant Salad, 40
    Fava Bean Soup, *10*, 11
    Fish, Fried, 44–45
    Flat Bread, 85–86
    Kebabs and *Pinchitos Morunos*, 162
    Kefta, 166–67
    Lamb Roast, *190*, 190–91, *191*
    Lamb Shanks with Chickpeas and Wheat, 200
    Lamb Stewed with Cumin, 192–93, *193*
    Lamb Tagine with Tomatoes and Potatoes, 195
    Mint Tea, 256, *257*
    Pepper, Grilled, and Tomato Salad, 39
    Potato Cakes, 59
    Shortbread, 236
    Snail Soup, 14–15
    Swordfish Brochettes, 168
    Tomato and Onion Salad, 37
Mozzarella, Grilled Vegetables and (sandwiches),
    155
Mushrooms. *See* Porcini

Mussels:
    Fried (sandwiches), 139–40, *140–41*
    Paella, 210–11
    Stuffed, 64–66, *65*

Neapolitan Pizza, 120–21
Nut(s):
    and Dried Fruit Compote, 220
    see also specific nuts

Octopus:
    boiled, 46–47, *47*
    and Onion Stew, 180–81
Olive Oil and Lemon Focaccia, 77–78
Olives:
    Chicken Tagine with Preserved Lemons and,
        198–99
    Fried Bread, 144–45, *145*
    Tomato, and Anchovy (sandwiches), 149–50
Omelets:
    in Flat Tunisian Bread, 127–28, *129*
    Potato, Spanish, 19
    Spinach, Italian, 20
One-pot meals, xxv, 171–211
    Chicken Tagine with Olives and Preserved
        Lemons, 198–99
    Chicken Tagine with Potatoes and Peas,
        196–97
    Chicken with Garlic, 207
    Chicken with Moghrabbiyeh, 204–6
    Couscous, 201
    Couscous with Seven Vegetables, 202–3
    Eggplants, Baked Stuffed, 178–79
    Lamb and Lettuce Stew, 176–77
    Lamb Roast, *190*, 190–91, *191*

One-pot meals *(cont.)*
    Lamb Shanks with Chickpeas and Wheat, 200
    Lamb Stewed with Cumin, 192–93, *193*
    Lamb Tagine with Tomatoes and Potatoes, 195
    Lamb with Pasta and Tomatoes, Baked,
        173–74
    Mackerel with Herbs, Baked, 182–83
    Octopus and Onion Stew, 180–81
    Paella, 210–11
    Pasta, Baked, 183–84
    Pork and Cannellini Bean Stew, 175
    Rice, Lentils, and Vermicelli with Hot Tomato
        Sauce, 188–89
    Tomatoes and Peppers, Stuffed, 186–87
    Tripe Stew, 208–9
    Vegetables, Baked, 185
Onion(s):
    Couscous with Seven Vegetables, 202–3
    Moroccan Flat Bread, 85–86
    and Octopus Stew, 180–81
    and Parsley Salad, 42
    Pie, 107
    Stuffed, 30
    and Tomato Salad, 37
Oriental Pastry and Grocery Co., 2

Paella, 210–11
Panini con Mozzarella e Verdure, 155
Pan Bagnat, 149–50
Pancakes:
    French, 122–23
    Walnut, 221–22, *223*
Panelle (panisse or *panissa)*, *53*, 54
Parmesan cheese:
    Artichoke Pie, 102–4, *103*

Rice Pie, 106–7
    Vegetable Loaf, 21–22
Parsley:
    Moroccan Flat Bread, 85–86
    Omelet in Flat Tunisian Bread, 127–28, *129*
    and Onion Salad, 42
    Tagine with, Tunisian, 23–24
Pasta:
    Baked, 183–84
    Lamb with Tomatoes and, Baked, 173–74
    Vermicelli, Rice, and Lentils with Hot Tomato
        Sauce, 188–89
Pasticcio, 183–84
Pastries (savory):
    Cheese Triangles (Greek), 101
    Cheese Triangles (Lebanese), 96
    Doughnuts, Moroccan, 108–9
    Potato Boreks, 97–98
    Saj Borek with Spinach and Cheese, *92*, 92–93
    Spinach Rolls, 99–100
    Spinach Triangles, 94–95
    see also Pies (savory)
Pastries (sweet):
    Almond Triangles, 225–26
    Cheese Pies, Sweet, 232–33, *233*
    Clotted Cream Fritters, 234–35
    Cream Pie, *230*, 230–31
    Kairouan, 228–29, *229*
Peas, Chicken Tagine with Potatoes and, 196–97
Pepper(s):
    Baked Vegetables, 185
    Fried Vegetables à la Tunisienne, 60–61
    Grilled, and Tomato Salad, Moroccan, 39
    Grilled, and Tomato Salad, Tunisian, 41
    Stuffed, Grilled, 32

Stuffed Tomatoes and, 186–87
Vegetable Fritters, 52–53, *53*
Pepperoni, Ripieni di, 32
Pescados e Calmares Fritos, 55, *55*
Pies (savory):
    Artichoke, 102–4, *103*
    Onion, 107
    Rice, 106–7
    Swiss Chard Pie, 104–5
Pies (sweet):
    Cheese, 232–33, *233*
    Cream, *230,* 230–31
Pinchitos Morunos, 162
Pistachio Nut Ice Cream, 244
Pizza:
    Neapolitan, 120–21
    see also Focaccia
Pizza Napolitana, 120–21
Pollo al Ajillo, 207
Polpettone, 21–22, *53*
Pomegranate Juice, 249
Pomodori Ripieni, 31
Porcini:
    Artichoke Pie, 102–4, *103*
    Vegetable Loaf, 21–22
Pork:
    and Cannellini Bean Stew, 175
    chops, grilled, 169
Potato(es):
    Baked Vegetables, 185
    Boreks, 97–98
    Cakes (Moroccan), 59
    Chicken Tagine with Peas and, 196–97
    Croquettes (Sicilian), 59–60
    French Fries (sandwiches), 151

French Fries, Spicy Sausages and (sandwiches),
    138
Fried Bread, 144–45, *145*
Fried Vegetables à la Tunisienne, 60–61
Lamb Tagine with Tomatoes and, 195
Omelet, Spanish, 19
Stuffing (for Italian Stuffed Vegetables), 28
"Submarine," Tunisian, 126
Vegetable Loaf, 21–22
Prickly pears, xxvi
Puddings:
    Chestnut, 215
    Milk, *218,* 218–19
    Watermelon, 216–17

Qarish, 96
Qashtah, 224
Qatayef bil-Joz, 221–22, *223*
Qatr, 217
Qotbane del Hüt, 168

Ragù, 56–57
Raisins, in Dried Fruit and Nut Compote, 220
Ramadan, xxii
Ramadan Bread with Dates, 114–15
"Red" Rice Croquettes, 56–58
R'ghäyef, 85–86
Rice:
    Croquettes, "Red," 56–58
    Croquettes, White, 58
    Lentils, and Vermicelli with Hot Tomato Sauce,
        188–89
    Paella, 210–11
    Pie, 106–7
    Stuffed Tomatoes and Peppers, 186–87

Ricotta cheese:
    Artichoke Pie, 102–4, *103*
    Rice Pie, 106–7
    Swiss Chard Pie, 104–5
    Vegetable Loaf, 21–22
Ripieni, 27–32
    Cipolle, 30
    di Pepperoni, 32
    Pomodori, 31
    Zucchini, 29
Riso, Torta di, 106–7

Saç Boregi, 92, 92–93
Saffron, Cannellini Beans with, 36
Sahadi's, 2
Sahlab, 255
Saj Borek with Spinach and Cheese, *92,* 92–93
Salads:
    Cannellini Bean (sandwiches), 154
    Eggplant, Moroccan, 40
    Fava Bean, 34–35
    Feta Cheese, 33
    Onion and Parsley, 42
    Pepper, Grilled, and Tomato, Moroccan, 39
    Pepper, Grilled, and Tomato, Tunisian, 41
    Tomato and Onion, 37
    White Cabbage, 38
Salatat Baqdüness wa Bassal, 42
Salatet Malfüf Abyad, 38
Salep, 255
Salt, 2
Samkeh Harrah, 146–48
Samsa, 225–26
Sandwich Batata, 151
Sandwiches, xxii–xxiv, 125–55

Cannellini Bean Salad, 154
Chicken Shawarma, 132–34, *133*
Falafel, 152–53
Feta Cheese Salad, 33
Fish, Spicy, 146–48
French Fries, 151
Fried Bread, 144–45, *145*
Jerusalem Mix, 136–37
Kebabs with Hommus, 135
"Kibbé," Turkish, 142–43
Lamb Shawarma, 130–31
Mussels, Fried, 139–40, *140–41*
Omelet in Flat Tunisian Bread, 127–28, *129*
Sausages, Spicy, and French Fries, 138
"Submarine," Tunisian, 126, *126*
Tomato, Olives, and Anchovy, 149–50
Vegetables, Grilled, and Cheese, 155
see also Spreads
Sauces:
    Chermüla, 44–45
    Garlic, 72
    Ragù, 56–57
    Tomato, 120–21
    Tomato, Hot, 188–89
Sausages, Spicy, and French Fries (sandwiches), 138
Scallions, in Omelet in Flat Tunisian Bread,
    127–28, *129*
Seafood:
    Mussels, Fried (sandwiches), 139–40, *140–41*
    Mussels, Stuffed, 64–66, *65*
    octopus, boiled, 46–47, *47*
    Octopus and Onion Stew, 180–81
    Paella, 210–11
    Shrimp, Chili, 43
    Snail Soup, 14–15

see also Fish

Semolina:
    Cake, 226–27
    Kairouan Pastries, 228–29, 229

Sesame:
    Candy, Sicilian, 240–41
    Cookies, 238–39
    Galettes, Greek, 118–19
    Galettes, Turkish, 116–17, 117

Sfincione, 79–80, 80

Sfinge, 108–9

Shawarma:
    Chicken, 132–34, 133
    Lamb, 130–31

Shawarma Djaj, 132–34, 133

Shawarma Lahmeh, 130–31

Shellfish. See Seafood

Shish Kebabi, 158–59

Shish Tawüq, 163

Shlada Matecha, 37

Shortbread:
    Lebanese, 235
    Moroccan, 236

Shrimp:
    Chili, 43
    Paella, 210–11

Sicilian fare, xvii, xxvi, 46, 47–48
    Almond Ice Cream, 242
    Cauliflower, Fried, 51
    Chickpea Fritters, 54
    Focaccia, 79–80, 80
    Potato Croquettes, 59–60
    Rice Croquettes, "Red," 56–58
    Rice Croquettes, White, 58
    Sesame Candy, 240–41

Simit, 116–17, 117

Snacks, salads, and dips, 17–73
    boiled and grilled snacks, 46–48
    Calamari and Other Fish, Fried, 55, 55
    Cannellini Beans with Saffron, 36
    Cauliflower, Fried, 51
    Chickpea Fritters, 53, 54
    Chickpea Snack, 25, 25–26
    Chili Paste, Hot, 67
    Cilantro Chutney, Yemeni, 69
    Eggplant Fans, Fried, 51
    Eggplant Salad, Moroccan, 40
    Fava Beans, Boiled, with Spiced Salt, 49–50
    Fava Bean Salad, 34–35
    Feta Cheese Salad, 33
    Fish, Fried, Moroccan, 44–45
    Garlic Sauce, 72
    Hazelnut Dip, 70
    Hommus, 68
    Mussels, Stuffed, 64–66, 65
    Onion and Parsley Salad, 42
    Pepper, Grilled, and Tomato Salad, Moroccan, 39
    Pepper, Grilled, and Tomato Salad, Tunisian, 41
    Potato Croquettes, 59–60
    Potato Omelet, Spanish, 19
    Rice Croquettes, "Red," 56–58
    Rice Croquettes, White, 58
    Shrimp, Chili, 43
    Spinach Omelet, Italian, 20
    Stuffed Vegetables, Italian, 27–32
    Tagine with Parsley, Tunisian, 23–24
    Tahini Dip, 71
    Tomato and Onion Salad, 37
    Vegetable Fritters, 52–53, 53

Snacks, salads, and dips (cont.)
    Vegetable Loaf, 21–22
    Vegetables, Fried, à la Tunisienne, 60–61
    White Cabbage Salad, 38
    Yogurt Dip, 73
Snail Soup, 14–15
Soffrito, 28
Soups, xxv, 5–15
    Chickpea, 8–9
    Chickpea and Lamb, 6–7
    Fava Bean, 10, 11
    Snail (or Lamb), 14–15
    Tripe, 4–5, 12–13
Souvlakia, 160
Spanakopitta, 99–100
Spanish fare, xvi–xvii, xxiv, xxv
    bibliography for, 259
    Calamari and Other Fish, Fried, 55, 55
    Chicken with Garlic, 207
    Paella, 210–11
    Potato Omelet, 19
    Shrimp, Chili, 43
    Tripe Stew, 208–9
Spinach:
    Omelet, Italian, 20
    Rolls, 99–100
    Saj Borek with Cheese and, 92, 92–93
    Triangles, 94–95
Spreads:
    Chili Paste, Hot, 67
    Cilantro Chutney, Yemeni, 69
    Pepper, Grilled, and Tomato Salad, Tunisian, 41
Squid, in Paella, 210–11
Starters. See Breads; Pastries (savory); Sandwiches;
    Snacks, salads, and dips; Soups

Steak, in Jerusalem Mix, 136–37
Stews:
    Lamb, with Cumin, 192–93, 193
    Lamb and Lettuce, 176–77
    Octopus and Onion, 180–81
    Pork and Cannellini Bean, 175
    Tripe, 208–9
Stuffed:
    Eggplants, Baked, 178–79
    Mussels, 64–66, 65
    Onions, 30
    Peppers, Grilled, 32
    Tomatoes, 31
    Tomatoes and Peppers, 186–87
    Vegetables, Italian, 27–32
    Zucchini, 29
Stuffing, 28
"Submarine," Tunisian, 126, 126
Sugar, 2
    Syrup, 217
Sweet potatoes, baked, 48
Sweets and desserts, xxv, 213–45
    Almond Ice Cream, Sicilian, 242
    Almond Triangles, 225–26
    Anise Cookies, 237
    Cheese Pies, Sweet, 232–33, 233
    Chestnut Pudding, 215
    Clotted Cream, Arabic, 224
    Clotted Cream Fritters, 234–35
    Cream Pie, 230, 230–31
    Dried Fruit and Nut Compote, 220
    Granita, Instant, 241
    Kairouan Pastries, 228–29, 229
    Mango Ice Cream, 243
    Milk Ice Cream, 245

Milk Pudding, *218*, 218–19
Pistachio Nut Ice Cream, 244
Semolina Cake, 226–27
Sesame Candy, Sicilian, 240–41
Sesame Cookies, 238–39
Shortbread, Lebanese, 235
Shortbread, Moroccan, 236
Sugar Syrup, 217
Walnut Pancakes, 221–22, *223*
Watermelon Pudding, 216–17
Swiss Chard Pie, 104–5
Swordfish Brochettes, 168
Syrian fare, xviii, xxii–xxiii
    bibliography for, 259
    Chicken Shawarma, 132–34, *133*
    Fava Beans, Boiled, with Spiced Salt, 49–50
    French Fries (sandwiches), 151
    Hommus, 68
    Lamb Shawarma, 130–31
    Milk Pudding, *218*, 218–19
    Omelet, 127–28, *129*
    Pistachio Nut Ice Cream, 244
    Salep, 255
    Sesame Cookies, 238–39
    Sugar Syrup, 217
    Walnut Pancakes, 221–22, *223*
    Yogurt Dip, 73
Syrup, Sugar, 217

Tagines, *194*
    Chicken, with Olives and Preserved Lemons,
      198–99
    Chicken, with Potatoes and Peas, 196–97
    Lamb, with Tomatoes and Potatoes, 195
    with Parsley, Tunisian, 23–24

Tahini:
    Dip, 71
    Hommus, 68
Tajine Ma'danüs, 23–24
Tamarind Drink, 254
Tamer Hindi, 254
Tangia, 192–93, *193*
Tapas:
    Calamari and Other Fish, Fried, 55, *55*
    Chicken with Garlic, 207
    Potato Omelet, Spanish, 19
    Shrimp, Chili, 43
    Tripe Stew, 208–9
Tarator:
    Lebanese, 71
    Turkish, 70
Tea, Mint, 256, *257*
Thüm, 72
Thursday Bread, 112–13
Thyme Bread, *88*, 88–89
Tomato(es), 2
    Couscous with Seven Vegetables, 202–3
    Fried Vegetables à la Tunisienne, 60–61
    and Grilled Pepper Salad, Moroccan, 39
    and Grilled Pepper Salad, Tunisian, 41
    Lamb Tagine with Potatoes and, 195
    Lamb with Pasta and, Baked, 173–74
    Olives, and Anchovy (sandwiches), 149–50
    and Onion Salad, 37
    Ragù, 56–57
    Sauce, 120–21
    Sauce, Hot, Rice, Lentils, and Vermicelli with,
      188–89
    Stuffed, 31
    Stuffed Peppers and, 186–87

Torta:
> di Bietola, 104–5
> di Cipolle, 107
> Pasqualina, 102–4, *103*
> di Riso, 106–7

Tortilla de Patatas, 19

Triangles:
> Almond, 225–26
> Cheese (Greek), 101
> Cheese (Lebanese), 96
> Spinach, 94–95

Tripe:
> Soup, 4–5, 12–13
> Stew, 208–9

Tsoureki, 110–11, *111, 119*

Tuna:
> Fried Bread, 144–45, *145*
> "Submarine," Tunisian, 126

Tunisian fare:
> bibliography for, 259–60
> Bread, Fried, 144–45, *145*
> Chickpea Soup, 8–9
> Chili Paste, Hot, 67
> Flat Bread, Omelet in, 127–28, *129*
> Kairouan Pastries, 228–29, *229*
> Pepper, Grilled, and Tomato Salad, 41
> "Submarine," 126, *126*
> Tagine with Parsley, 23–24
> Vegetables, Fried, à la Tunisienne, 60–61

Turkish fare, xvii, 48
> bibliography for, 260
> Bulgur Drink, *252,* 253
> Cannellini Bean Salad (sandwiches), 154
> Feta Cheese Salad, 33
> Hazelnut Dip, 70

Kebabs, 158–59

"Kibbé," 142–43

Meat Bread, 90–91

Mussels, Fried (sandwiches), 139–40, *140–41*

Mussels, Stuffed, 64–66, *65*

Saj Borek with Spinach and Cheese, *92,* 92–93

Sesame Galettes, 116–17, *117*

Tripe Soup, 12–13

Yogurt Dip, 73

Turnips, in Couscous with Seven Vegetables, 202–3

Tuscan fare:
> Anise Cookies, 237
> Chestnut Pudding, 215
> Lemon and Olive Oil Focaccia, 77–78

Tyropitta, 101

Tzatziki, 73

Veal gristle, boiled, 47

Vegetable(s):
> Baked, 185
> Fried, à la Tunisienne, 60–61
> Fritters, 52–53, *53*
> Grilled, and Cheese (sandwiches), 155
> Loaf, 21–22
> Seven, Couscous with, 202–3
> Stuffed, Italian, 27–32
> *see also specific vegetables*

Vermicelli, Rice, and Lentils with Hot Tomato Sauce, 188–89

Walnut Pancakes, 221–22, *223*

Watermelon Pudding, 216–17

Wheat:
    bulgur, in Turkish "Kibbé," 142–43
    Bulgur Drink, 252, 253
    Lamb Shanks with Chickpeas and, 200
White Rice Croquettes, 58

Yemeni fare:
    Bread, Fried, 83–84
    Cilantro Chutney, 69
Yiouvetsi, 173–74
Yogurt:
    Dip, 73
    Drink, 255

Za'lüq, 40
Za'tar, 89
    Manaqish bil-, 88–89
Z'houg, 69
Zucchini:
    Baked Vegetables, 185
    Couscous with Seven Vegetables, 202–3
    Fried Vegetables à la Tunisienne, 60–61
    Grilled Vegetables and Cheese (sandwiches),
      155
    Stuffed, 29
    Vegetable Fritters, 52–53, 53
Zucchini Ripieni, 29